George Clinch

Bloomsbury and St. Giles's

Past and Present

George Clinch

Bloomsbury and St. Giles's
Past and Present

ISBN/EAN: 9783337208738

Printed in Europe, USA, Canada, Australia, Japan

Cover: Foto ©ninafisch / pixelio.de

More available books at **www.hansebooks.com**

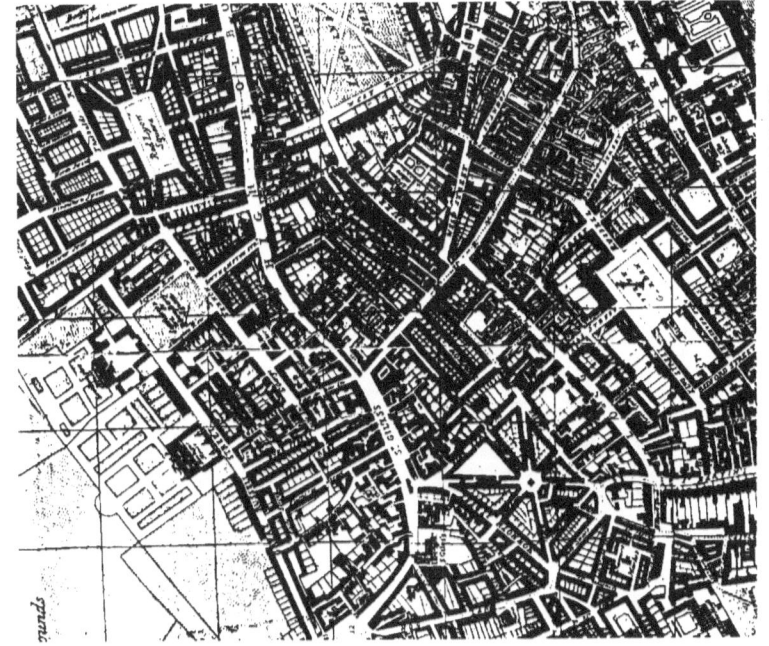

MAP OF St. GILES'S AND ITS VICINITY.

From R. Morden and Lea's Plan of the City of London, 1732

Bloomsbury

and St. Giles's:

PAST AND PRESENT;

*WITH HISTORICAL AND ANTIQUARIAN NOTICES
OF THE VICINITY.*

BY

GEORGE CLINCH,

OF THE DEPARTMENT OF PRINTED BOOKS, BRITISH MUSEUM, AUTHOR OF "ANTIQUARIAN JOTTINGS," ETC.

𝖂ith 𝕴llustrations,

INCLUDING NUMEROUS REPRODUCTIONS OF RARE ENGRAVINGS
AND MAPS IN THE BRITISH MUSEUM.

LONDON
TRUSLOVE AND SHIRLEY, 7, ST. PAUL'S CHURCHYARD.
1890.

PRINTED BY
HAZELL, WATSON, AND VINEY, LIMITED,
LONDON AND AYLESBURY.

PREFACE.

ICH as are the immediate environs of London in historical memories and associations, perhaps the ancient village which in the Middle Ages clustered around the Hospital and Church of St. Giles, and the aristocratic quarter which grew up in Bloomsbury in the eighteenth century, contain more features of antiquarian interest, were the scenes of more remarkable incidents in the history of England, and were the homes of more eminent men and women in the various walks of life than any other place of equal size, and equal distance from the heart of London.

In compiling the following account of the two parishes the author has found no lack of material; he has suffered rather from the richness of it. The work of selecting, with a due regard to the palates of his readers and the just demands of the subject he has undertaken to illustrate, has been no easy task. His sincere thanks are due, and are hereby offered, to Richard Garnett, Esq., LL.D., for kind assistance in that part of the volume which deals with the British Museum; to John R. Bourne, Esq., late Steward of the Bedford Estate; to J. Robinson, Esq., Vestry Clerk; to James Appleton, Esq.,

Secretary of the Almshouse Charities; to Fitzroy Gardner, Esq., Secretary of the British Lying-in Hospital; to W. S. Wintle, Esq., Secretary of the Foundling Hospital; and to the secretaries of the other hospitals and institutions mentioned in the book; and also to many private friends, too numerous for individual mention, for information, hints, and suggestions, which have proved of great service to the author in his pleasant task.

The illustrations have been produced by The London Stereoscopic Company in their Photomezzotype process.

CONTENTS.

ST. GILES-IN-THE-FIELDS.

CHAPTER I.

CHAPTER II.

CHAPTER III.

CONTENTS.

BLOOMSBURY.

CONTENTS.

LIST OF ILLUSTRATIONS AND MAPS.

ST. GILES-IN-THE-FIELDS.

CHAPTER I.

Early history.—Condition in Roman times.—Defences of London.—Blemund's Ditch.—Condition of St. Giles's in the Middle Ages.—The paving of High Oldburn.—Fox-hunting at St. Giles's. —St. Giles's in the time of Queen Elizabeth, and King James the First.—Rural condition.— St. Giles's at the Restoration.—Population.—The Lepers' Hospital; foundation, charters, abuse of the charity.—The Lepers' Chapel.—Parish Church.—Wealth of the hospital.— Dissolution of the hospital, and spoliation of its possessions.—Ancient custom connected with the hospital.—Jack Sheppard.—The manor of St. Giles.

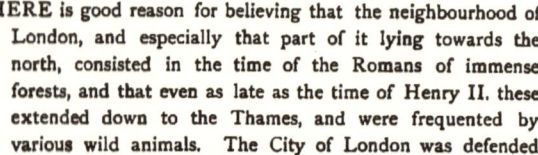HERE is good reason for believing that the neighbourhood of London, and especially that part of it lying towards the north, consisted in the time of the Romans of immense forests, and that even as late as the time of Henry II. these extended down to the Thames, and were frequented by various wild animals. The City of London was defended by fosses on every side, except those boundaries of it where the river Thames formed a natural barrier of defence. Between the manors of St. Giles and Bloomsbury there was an important foss or ditch, known as Blemund's Ditch, which it is probable was part of this system of ditches, constructed originally for the purposes of defence, probably, and becoming later on useful and patent boundary-marks of manorial areas and parishes. Blemund's Ditch ran nearly parallel with the north side of Holborn, and in an easterly direction connected itself with the creek which ran along Fleet Ditch.

The soil in this district appears to have been of a wet and marshy nature, from the number of ditches with which it abounded. The effect of draining, and the construction of sewers upon the extensive scale which modern increase of buildings and population have necessitated, have entirely altered this condition of things, but indications of a soil naturally inclined to dampness may still be observed in the heavy fogs of winter which often hover around Bloomsbury and St. Giles's, when Charing Cross and Westminster are comparatively free from them.

St. Giles-in-the-Fields in the Middle Ages was merely a suburban village, literally surrounded by fields, as its name suggests. In the time of King John, 1213, it was laid out in garden plots, cottages, and other buildings to a certain limited extent. In the time of King Henry III. it assumed the appearance of a scattered country village, having shops and an ancient stone cross, standing where High Street now is. About the year 1225 a little black-smith's shop stood at the north-west end of Drury Lane, which existed until the year 1595, when progressive buildings rendered its demolition necessary. The lower part of Holborn was paved in 1417 and in 1542. Stowe says that " High Oldburn Street, leading from the bars towards St. Giles was very full of pits and sloughs, and perilous and noisome to all that repaired and passed that way, as well on foot as on horseback or with carriage, and so were other lanes and places that led out of or into High Oldbourne, as Shoe Lane, Fetter Lane, New Street, or Chancery Lane. Upon complaint whereof an Act was made, in the thirty-second of Henry (8th), to pave all those parts with paving-stones from the farther part of Oldbourne unto St. Giles-in-the-Fields, as also on the east side of the city, the way from Aldgate to Whitechapel Church, which had the same ill passage, all to be paved and made by the Feast of St. John the Baptist, 1542, in manner and form as the cawsey or highway leading from Strand Bridge to Charing Crosse had been made and paved." Holborn had been partially paved and mended in the reign of Edward III., but this was the first complete paving.

The famous hospital for lepers, which formerly stood where St. Giles's Church now stands, was of course the most important feature in the earlier history of the parish, but it will be better to treat of that institution in another part of this volume.

Mention is made, in the reign of Queen Elizabeth, of the immense line of thick forests extending from the village of St. Giles westward towards Tyburn, and reaching for a very long distance to the north. This was the great black forest of Marylebone.

Stowe gives an interesting account of a visitation to the conduits at Tyburn in 1562, by the Lord Mayor Harper, and aldermen, and many other citizens, masters and wardens of the twelve companies, accompanied by their ladies in waggons, it being usual, after examining the state of them, to give a grand entertainment at the banqueting-house. On this occasion, says Stowe, " afore dinner they hunted the hare, and killed her, and thence to dinner at the head of the conduit. There was a good number, entertained with good cheer by the chamberlain. And after dinner they went to hunting the fox. There was a great cry for a mile, and at length the hounds killed him at the end of St. Giles's ; great hallowing at his death and blowing of hornes," etc. This account is sufficient to show the rural character of the neighbourhood all around St. Giles's at that time.

It would appear that the first signs of important increase in the number of dwelling-houses made themselves visible upon the north side of the main road which ran by the parish church eastward toward the city, and which answered very much to what are now High Street and Broad Street. In the reign of Queen Elizabeth the inhabitants and houses of St. Giles-in-the-Fields increased greatly, as was also the case with the city itself and its vicinity generally. The hospital had been suppressed in 1539, but the population nestled chiefly around its site, where the church still remained. In 1595 Holborn had extended west so as to nearly join St. Giles's Street (High Street). The old plans about this date show cattle grazing in fields crossed by footpaths where Great Queen Street now is. The accompanying reproduction of Ralph Agas's map of London, the date of which is said to be about the year 1591, will render many of these points clear to the reader. Drury Lane is shown as a simple lane without a single house in it, save one, Drury House, at the south end, and the whole stretch of land between it and St. Giles's Church is represented as being open meadow land, untouched by the builder. Very much the same condition of things is shown by the map to have existed all over the area which modern Bloomsbury now occupies. Southampton House, situated very near what is now Bloomsbury Square, is represented as an outlying mansion, standing in its own grounds, and environed by large stretches of pasture land. Holborn, too, had no houses except round about where the entrance to Red Lion Street is, and also near the north end of Drury Lane.

Early in the reign of James the First the meadows and lanes began to be built upon. In 1606 Great Queen Street was begun, and Drury Lane had some houses built upon its east side. Shortly after the year 1623, one hundred houses were built upon the north side of St. Giles's Street (High Street) ; seventy-one were built on the south side of Holborn ; fifty-six were built on the west side of Drury Lane ; in Great Queen Street there were fifteen houses, and in Bloomsbury there were built one hundred and thirty-six houses.

With the Restoration a second grand era of building commenced in the parish of St. Giles. Lincoln's Inn Fields, which had been laid out and partly built by Inigo Jones, was further improved, and the houses finished on the south side of Queen Street, besides many individual mansions of importance erected. This spirit of building continued during the remainder of the reign of Charles II., and during those of James II., William and Mary, and Anne, so that at length the whole parish, excepting some parts of Bloomsbury, became entirely covered with houses. The writer of "A New View of London," a curious work, published in the year 1708, mentions that the parish of St. Giles then contained about three thousand houses.

The enumerated population of the united parishes of St. Giles's and St. George, Bloomsbury, according to the census returns of 1881, was 45,382.

THE LEPERS' HOSPITAL.

It is recorded by Leland, the antiquary, that Matilda or Maud, daughter of Malcolm, King of Scotland, and the Queen of Henry I., in the year 1101 " founded, overagainst the west suburb of London, a house for the maintenance of lepers, with an oratory and offices, called the Hospital of St. Giles." By the charter of Queen Matilda, provision was made for forty lepers, one chaplain, one clerk, and one servant. To meet the expenses of this establishment the hospital was originally endowed with the sum of £3 per annum, a sum which was doubtless augmented by voluntary contributions. Henry II. granted, by royal charter, substantial aid towards increasing the annual revenue of the hospital. During the reigns of Richard I. and John the benevolence of private individuals endowed the hospital with many gifts of land and houses, rent-charges, etc., most of them lying in the City of London and surrounding parishes. The same liberality on the part of private persons continued during the reigns of Henry III., Edward I., Edward II., and Edward III., and there are extant several charters from these kings, confirming previous grants, and augmenting them in various ways.

It would appear that abuses of this excellent charity were soon prac- tised, for during the time of Edward II. persons were introduced into the hospital as residents who had no claim on the score of disease or otherwise, but were merely placed there through influence. St. Giles's Hospital, although intended for the maintenance of poor lepers, was made a sort of asylum for decayed domestics of the Court. Not only was this an injustice towards those whom the foundress of the hospital intended to benefit, but great danger to those who enjoyed sound health arose from mixing with the poor diseased inmates. Edward II., for these reasons, issued a charter which forbade the quartering of old Court servants upon the hospital, without licence first obtained from the master and brethren.

The ground upon which the hospital stood was originally Crown land, and was given, together with the manor of St. Giles, by the royal foundress, Queen Matilda. It consisted, according to the bull of Pope Alexander, of eight acres of land. As time went on it is probable that more land was added, and the whole area, as is shown by old maps, was enclosed by a high wall.

Upon this ground were built the hospital, with all necessary offices, and an oratory or small chapel. From the charter of King Henry II. it is evident that an earlier parochial church had stood upon this spot before the hospital was established.

From certain extant documents relating to this hospital, it is evident that considerable additions were made to the fabric from time to time. Mention is made of a great gate and chapter-house, and there is no doubt that as valuable gifts of property and money were made, so this excellent institution increased in importance, and added to its buildings and the number of its inmates.

The Parish Church of St. Giles was built by the side of the hospital church, probably upon its north side, and therefore was nearer the public road and more easily accessible to the parishioners than that which was designed for the use of the lepers. The high altar was situated at the east end, and the entrance-door at the west end of the church. The Lepers' Church was probably similar in form and size, but had at its east end an altar dedicated to St. Giles, the patron saint of lepers and of this church. Probably an image of the saint was placed upon the altar, and before this burnt a great taper, called St. Giles's Light, towards the expense of maintaining which, about the year 1200, William Christmas, a parishioner, bequeathed the annual sum of 12*d.*

There was a Chapel of St. Michael against the south wall of the church, and towards its eastern end. This no doubt formed a prominent feature in the church, and was probably provided with its own priest or chaplain.

From rude delineations of the Church of St. Giles, made about 1560, it appears that at the west end of the south or lepers' division of the building there was a circular tower, capped by an odd-looking dome, semi-globular, or rather, perhaps, semi-ovate in shape.

The wealth of St. Giles's Hospital had become so great in the time of Henry VIII. as to form a desirable prize for the cupidity of that monarch. His first recorded act in reference to this hospital was to institute an inquest to inquire into the hospital's right to certain houses in Holborn. His next was to effect an exchange with the hospital, he taking the greater part of the hospital and its lands in St. Giles's parish, together with the manors of Feltham and Heston, and giving in return the manor of Burton St. Lazar, in Leicestershire. Although by this exchange St. Giles's Hospital lost its best estates, and in return received others more distantly situated, and probably therefore of much less value, Henry seems to have been much too powerful to be resisted, and the master and brethren were compelled humbly to submit to an arrangement by which the best interests of the hospital were sacrificed.

But this arbitrary assertion of the royal will was merely a prelude to what was soon to follow. In 1536-9 the general dissolution of the monasteries took place, and in the last-named year, 1539, the Hospital of Burton St. Lazar, together with its appendant cell of St. Giles's Hospital, was also dissolved.

At this distance of time it is not very easy for one to appreciate clearly all the causes which led up to this wholesale spoliation, and which made it possible for a sovereign, by the weight of his own despotic power, to commit an act of such grave injustice to the inmates, and so much opposed to the spirit and intention of the pious founders and benefactors. Doubtless the glaring abuses of monastic life, which the printing-press was then holding up to ridicule, had to some extent unfavourably prejudiced the public mind upon the question; but it does not appear very fair or logical that the punishment for irregularities of monastic and conventual establishments should have been visited upon an institution such as St. Giles's Hospital, whose object was one of the highest and noblest to which it is possible for wealth and skill to be applied—the relief of the suffering and infirm or diseased poor.

Henry's stern measure aimed a carefully directed blow which was calculated not only to punish and reform abuses, but also to scatter riches and possessions which had been accumulated and bestowed in many cases by a pious and well-meaning ancestry. The blow was struck by a hand which was not slow to grasp any object which fancy desired or avarice coveted.

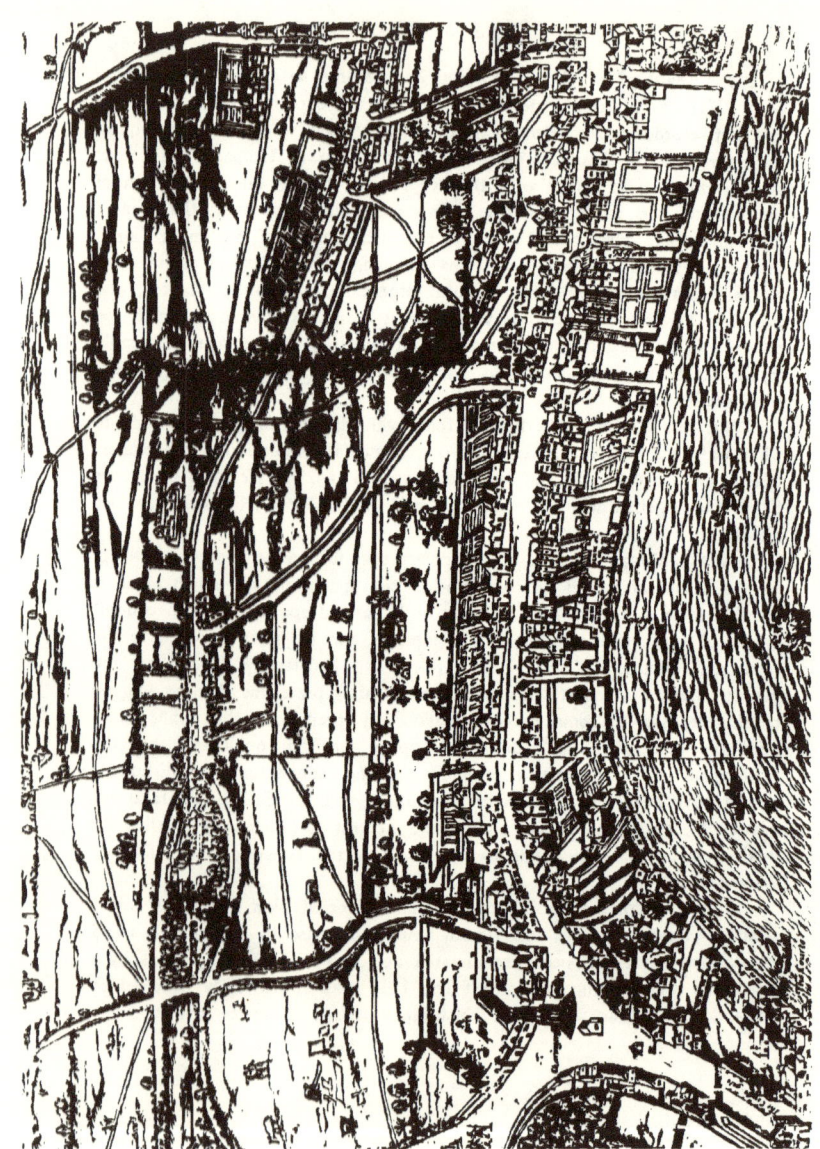

MAP OF St. GILES'S AND ITS VICINITY. 1591. *From Agas's Map of London.*

For six years the royal spoiler retained in his own possession the hospital and lands of St. Giles's, and then he bestowed it, together with Burton St. Lazar, upon "our beloved counsellor John Dudley, Knight of the Most Noble Order of the Garter, Viscount Lisle, and our great Admiral of England."

Lord Lisle, on receiving this grant of the hospital, fitted up the principal part of the building as a residence for himself, and leased various subordinate parts of the structure to different tenants, as well as portions of the adjoining ground, gardens, etc.; and having dwelt there two years, obtained the King's licence to convey the whole of the premises to John Wymonde Carewe, Esq.

An extraordinary custom was formerly connected with the Hospital of St. Giles, when the gallows stood at the north-west end of High Street. Criminals condemned to death, in journeying from the City or from Holborn, would necessarily have to pass the hospital wall. Here, at the great gate, they were presented with a bowl of ale, as their last refreshment in life. From long-continued usage, this became a confirmed custom, and was looked upon as a regular item in the melancholy programme when criminals were conveyed to their execution. In later days, when the gallows was erected at Tyburn, the custom of "Saint Giles's Bowl" was still observed. Even after the custom was dropped at the hospital gate, the dole was given at an inn close by, known as the "Bow," and afterwards the "Angel."

The notorious Jack Sheppard is said to have conformed to this custom when on his last journey to Tyburn, and after having taken a draught, he said, "Give the remainder to Jonathan Wild."

A custom of a somewhat similar nature formerly existed at York, in connection with which Pennant says that it gave rise to the saying that the Saddler of Bawtry was hanged for leaving his liquor. Had he stopped, as usual, his reprieve, which was actually on the road, would have arrived in time to have saved him from the gallows.

Alice, Duchess Dudley, who died in 1669, allowed an annual stipend to the sexton of St. Giles's Church to toll the great bell when the prisoners condemned to die were passing by, and to ring out after they were executed.

THE MANOR OF ST. GILES.

Upon the suppression of the old Lepers' Hospital, the estates and manor of St. Giles were conferred upon Lord Lisle. This possessor, although he only retained the buildings and land for about two years, when he conveyed them to Wymond Carewe, probably kept the manor itself, and he was probably the lord of the manor until his attainder and execution in the reign of Queen Mary, when it reverted to the Crown.

The manor and estates were bestowed upon Ambrose Dudley, son and heir of the Duke of Northumberland (formerly Lord Lisle), but it is pretty clear that he did not long enjoy them, as in the year 1565 the manor was held by Lord Mountjoy, in right of his wife, Katherine. After that, it is recorded that the estates were lost by mortgage to one Master Cope. Members of this family ranked for several years afterwards among the most distinguished inhabitants of the parish.

The manor was next held by Sir Walter Cope, who, dying, left it with his other estates to his sole daughter and heiress, Isabella Cope.

This lady married Sir Henry Riche, Knight (second son of Lord Riche, of Kensington), and thus the manor in her right became the property of her husband.

The manor was sold, in the 14th of James I., to Philip Gifford and Thomas Risley, Esqs., trustees for Henry, Earl of Southampton, for the sum of £600.

From Henry Earl of Southampton the manor of St. Giles, together with that of Bloomsbury, which was before in the same family, descended to his son and heir, Thomas Wriothesley, fourth Earl of Southampton, and Lord Treasurer to Charles II., who held it till his death in 1668, when it became the property of his daughter and co-heiress Lady Rachel Russell, the wife of the celebrated William Lord Russell, who by her marriage brought it into the Bedford family, the present holders of the manor of St. Giles with Bloomsbury.

CHAPTER II.

HE old Church of St. Giles, which had once belonged to the
Lepers' Hospital, was demolished in the year 1623. In 1617
the quaint old tower, to which reference has already been
made, was replaced by a larger and more ornamental steeple,
furnished with additional bells, but the fabric of the church
was in too unstable a condition to admit of repairs and
additions, and in 1623 an order of vestry was made for pulling down "divers
parts of the said church, the same being ruinous and decayed ; as also for the
rebuilding and re-edifying of the same." This rebuilding was undertaken none
too soon, for "the walls of the north and south aisles, together with the main
roof of the middle aisle and walls thereof, as well as all the pillars in church
and chancel, were found so rotten and decayed as to be in great danger of
falling down."

The foregoing quotation is from the Vestry minutes, which contain some
important information which is worthy of note. It appears that various
additions had been made to the church since it first did double duty as a
chapel to the Lepers' Hospital, and Parish Church of St. Giles. It had a nave,
chancel, and north and south aisles. The nave was divided from the aisles
by pillars and arches, above which rose walls, probably lighted by clerestory
windows, called in the minutes "the mayn wall over the arches." The nave

was divided from the chancel by a screen erected at the expense of Lady, afterwards Duchess Dudley.

In setting about the rebuilding of St. Giles's Church, in 1624, the first difficulty that arose was the obtaining of the necessary funds. A petition was addressed to the King, stating the necessity of wholly rebuilding the church ; that the expense would, according to estimate, amount to at least fifteen hundred pounds more than the parish could raise ; and praying his Majesty to recommend the Bishop of London to write to the clergy of his diocese to raise contributions in their respective parishes for the finishing thereof. The King granted the request, and as a result of the collections both in St. Giles's parish and in the London churches, a sum of £2,016 12s. 6d. was raised. The cost of the rebuilding was £2,068 7s. 2d.

The new church was finished, and consecrated by the Bishop of London on January 26th, 1630, upon which occasion a sumptuous entertainment was provided at the parish charge, at Mr. Speckart's house, which stood close by the church. Great preparations had been made for the Bishop's visit. A fence of deal boards was hired for making up the breach in the church wall ; and the three constables, with their head-boroughs, were directed to bring with them every one eight substantial wardens, with bills or halberds, to keep the church gates, walls, and fences. A rail was set up at the great west door to keep off the press of people. The inside of the church was thoroughly cleaned, and the communion-table was adorned with the best damask table-cloth, the green velvet cushion, and all the communion plate.

There is a particular account of this church in the "New View of London," published in 1708, from which it appears that the building of the church was commenced in 1624, some of the windows were put up in 1625, others and the lead pipes in the year 1628. The walls and tower were of brick, built with battlements and coped with stone, and the pillars and arches within are described as of an order "composed of the modern, Gothic, and Tuscan." The large windows were "of the Gothic order."

The whole structure was roofed with timber, and as time went on several internal ornaments and fittings were added. Externally the church appears (from a view of it taken in 1718) to have been spacious and handsome. The tower was in three stages, and was surmounted by a turret. The nave had clerestory windows, and was of lofty dimensions, but the chancel was insignificant. The following were the measurements of the church : Length, 123 ft. ; breadth, 57 ft. ; height of the chancel (flat roof), 26 ft. ; height of nave, 42 ft. ; height of tower, 60 ft. ; height of turret, 15 ft. ; total height of tower and turret, 75 ft.

There were galleries on three sides of the church, viz., north, west, and south. That on the south side was erected at the expense of William Bainbridge, Esq., in 1672 ; the north gallery was built in 1677. The church was well pewed with oak, and in the chancel there was a handsome door-case, with pilasters and entablature of the Corinthian order. There was also a very ornamental pulpit, with enrichments of cherubim, festoons, etc. ; both the pulpit and door-case were executed in Norway oak. A writer, contemporary with the old church, laments the want of an altar-piece and wainscot suitable to the church.

The chief ornamental feature of the old church was the painted glass with which its windows were adorned. The east window of the chancel, consisting of four compartments, was filled with four subjects taken from sacred history, the figures being life-size.

1. That on the north side of the east window had the figures of Abraham offering Isaac, the angel restraining him, and underneath were arms and inscription, with the date 1628, in which year the glass was given by Abraham Speckart, Esq.

2. Portrait of Moses with two tables in his hands. Underneath were arms, inscription, and the date 1628. Given by Hamo Claxton, Esq.

3. Portrait of King David playing upon the harp. Arms and date 1627. Given by Sir John Fenner, Kt.

4. King Solomon in a praying posture. Arms and inscription. Given by Fran. Lord Mount Norris. In the upper part of the window were three glories, finely painted.

About the middle of the north side of the church there was a finely painted window wherein were representations of Faith, Hope, and Charity, and below were written the following lines :—

> " Faith Root, Hope Stock, the Branch is Charity.
> Faith sees, Hope looks ; for Charity is free.
> Faith knits to God, to Heaven Hope, love to Men.
> Faith gets, Hope keeps, and Love pours out agen."

Another window on the north side was filled with glass on which were painted the arms of London and of the Fishmongers' Company, which

Company gave this window, and also the window at the west end of the south aisle, which had in it an effigy of our Saviour, with the words, "Come unto Me, all ye that labour and are heavy laden, and I will give you rest."

In the window over the entrance to the chancel were the royal arms, painted upon the glass.

As one might easily imagine, the ornaments of St. Giles's Church were offensive to the simple ideas of the Puritan party, and an attempt was made to despoil the church of every decent ornament, under the pretence of its being superstitious.

A petition was in 1640 exhibited to Parliament, against the then Rector, Dr. Heywood, "in whose parish church," it stated, "were set up crucifixes, and divers images of saints ; and likewise organs, with other confused musicke, hindering devotion, which were maintained to the great and needlesse charge of the parish." In one of the articles, entitled "Dr. Heywood's Superstitious and Idolatrous Manner of Administration of the Sacrament of the Lord's Supper, in the Parish Church of St. Gyles aforesaid," these "Popish reliques," as they are termed, are enumerated, and appear to have consisted principally of the gifts of Lady Dudley. The beautiful screen given by her seems to have become at this time particularly obnoxious. The whole article affords a good idea of the then state and appearance of the church (which it thus describes), with its ornaments :—

"1. The said church is divided into three parts : the *Sanctum Sanctorum*, being one of them, is separated from the chancell by a large skreene, in the figure of a beautifull gate, in which is carved two large pillars, and three large statues : on the one side is Paul, with his sword ; on the other, Barnabas, with his book ; and over them, Peter, with his keyes. They are all set above with winged cherubims, and beneath supported by lions. . . . Seven or eight foot within this holy place is a raising by three steps ; and from thence a long raile from one wall to the other, into which none must enter but the priests and sub-deacons. This place is covered before the altar with a faire wrought carpet ; the altar doth stand close up to the wall on the east side, and a deske raised upon that with degrees of advancement. This deske is overlaid with a covering of purple velvet, which has a great gold and silk fringe round about ; and on this deske is placed two great bookes, wrought with needle-worke, in which are made the pictures of Christ, and the Virgin Mary with Christ in her armes; and these are placed on each side the deske: and on this altar is a double covering, one of tapestry, and upon that a fine long lawn cloth, with a very rich bone lace. The walls are hanged round within the rayle, with blue silke taffita curtaines."

In consequence of the objection to these supposed "Popish relics," upon which the good people of St. Giles's felt so strongly as to petition Parliament, it appears that a sale of many of the ornaments of the church took place. In 1643 a painter was paid four shillings and sixpence "for washing the twelve Apostles off the organ-loft," and a glazier, for removing the ancient painted-glass windows, which had been the chief ornamental feature of the church, and for "fitting up new glass in its place," was paid £1 9s. 6d.

The screen, given by Lady Dudley, was taken down and sold for forty shillings, which money, together with other moneys, was given to the poor on Christmas Eve, 1644.

The money raised by the sale of the various church goods which were deemed unnecessary or superstitious amounted to £17 7s. 1d., and out of that sum payments were made to "the bricklayer, for mending the walls on both sides the chancell, where the screen stood," and "for the covenant, and a frame to putt it in to hang upp in yᵉ church," also five shillings "to Thomas Howard, pewterer, for a new bason, cut square on one side, to baptize in, more than the old bason came to."

In the year 1650 the royal arms were removed from the window in the church, and a payment is entered to the glazier, "for taking down the Kinge's arms and new glazing the window."

Soon after the Restoration of the monarchy in the person of Charles II. the royal arms appear to have been again set up in the vestry, probably painted upon a wooden panel, as there is an entry recording the payment of eight shillings "for varnishing the King's arms in the vestry."

In 1661 the sum of sixteen shillings was paid "to Mr. Sutton, the glasse painter, for new painting the window wherein is the King's arms, over the great arch in the quire, which was formerly the gift of Sʳ William Segar."

In the year 1670 the vestry ordered that a brass branch be provided for the church, containing sixteen candlesticks, and also that an hour-glass be bought for the pulpit, and an iron frame be made for the same to stand in.

Two hundred ₁pounds was paid to Mr. Christian Smith, in 1699, for making and setting up the organ in the church.

A gold communion cup of the total cost of £199 was purchased for the parish in the year 1716. The purchase was made pursuant to the will of Thomas Woodville, a parishioner, who dying the preceding year on shipboard, bequeathed £500 to the parish of his birth (found on search to be St. Giles's), £200 of which was to be expended in a communion cup, and £300 to be given to the poor.

Judging from the amount of money expended at various times, during the seventeenth century, upon the fabric and fittings of the Church of St. Giles-in-the-Fields, one would imagine that the building was of a substantial and enduring character, and that little further outlay would have been necessary to keep it in thorough repair for some time to come. Such, however, was not the case. Early in the eighteenth century the church was found to be in a state of decay, and so low, from the accumulation of earth around it, as to be damp and unwholesome. The parishioners, seeing how useless mere repairing and patching-up would be, set to work to get an entirely new church. By a resolution of the vestry in 1715, it was decided to "take the opinions of the Members of Parliament inhabiting the parish, concerning the petitioning Parliament to have the church entirely rebuilt at the public charge." In 1717 a paper was issued and circulated, entitled "Reasons Humbly Offered for a Bill *to Rebuild the Parish Church of St. Giles-in-the-*Fields, *at the Publick Charge, as one of the Fifty New Churches.*" The paper set forth that "the Church (which is Built with Bricks, and Coin'd and Cop'd only with Stone) is very Old and Ruinous, and upon a moderate Computation will Cost Three Thousand Pounds to put it into Repair and Order." The floor of the church was at least eight feet below the level of the street, and the churchyard had become unduly crowded with graves. The general plan and acoustic arrangements of the building were considered to be unsatisfactory, and it was shown that there were many defects which could only be successfully cured by replacing the old church by an entirely new one. The fifth reason advanced in favour of a new church was that "the Church Stands at the farthest end of that part of the Town, and Fronts *St. Giles's* High Street, which is the great Thorough-fair for all Persons who Travail the *Oxford* or *Hampstead* Roads, and a good Church there will be as great an Ornament, and be as much exposed to View, as any Church which can be Built in Town." Another reason was that "this being one of the Out Parishes and very Large, is so over Burthen'd with Poor, that the Expence of Main-

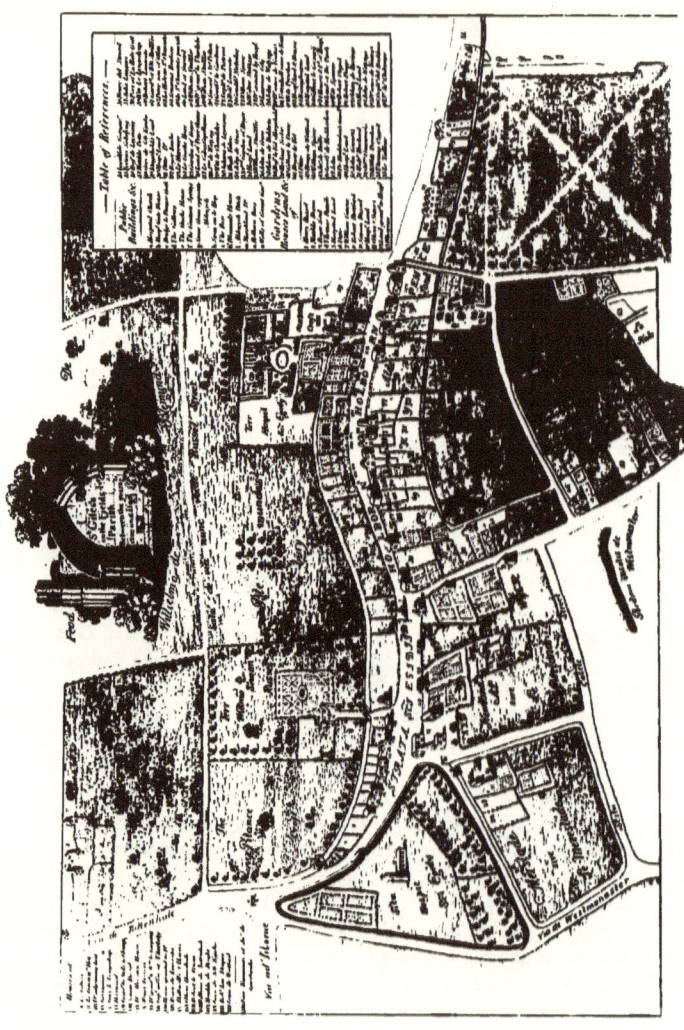

CONJECTURAL PLAN OF St. GILES'S AND THE VICINITY IN THE 13TH CENTURY.

From Parton's "History of St. Giles's Hospital."

taining and Relieving them Amounts *Communibus Annis* to Three Thousand Three Hundred Pounds at least, though their Allowance is very Small in Proportion to other Parishes, and the Poor's Rate is constantly fifteen Pence in the Pound ; besides six Pence to the Scavenger, and the Rates to the Highways, Windows, and Lamps."

An Act of Parliament was passed in 1711 which ordered that several new churches should be built in London in consequence of the destruction caused by the great fire. The object of the Act was to remedy the insufficiency of the accommodation afforded by the churches of London and its vicinity, and also to redress the inconvenience and " growing mischief which resulted from the increase of Dissent and Popery." The Act provided for the building of fifty new churches in the suburbs of the metropolis, a duty on coals being imposed to raise the necessary funds. That duty was to continue till £350,000 had been raised.

The parishioners of St. Giles's proposed to take advantage of this Act, and build their parish church as one of the fifty new churches. It was urged, in the " Reasons," from which we have just quoted, that " by making this One of the Fifty Churches, the Charge of Purchasing a Scite for the Church and Church-yard, and also the Maintainance for the Minister, will be sav'd to the Publick."

In December, 1717, a petition was presented to Parliament upon the subject, and in the following February a Bill was passed empowering the Commissioners to rebuild the church in pursuance of the Acts of Parliament which provided for the fifty new churches. No immediate action followed upon the passing of the Act, and it was not until the year 1730 that the sum of £8,000, appropriated out of the general funds, was paid into the hands of a treasurer, to meet the expenses of the proposed rebuilding of the church.

In the following year (9th June, 1731) the work of designing the new church was entrusted to Henry Flitcroft, who undertook, " at his own costs and charges, by or before the 31st of August then next ensuing, to pull and take down the east and west ends, and the steeple of the said church, to the bottom of the foundation thereof, and as low as a foot below the plinth or water-table on the north and south sides thereof, or lower, as shall be directed ; and also at his own like charges, in a substantiall, and workman like manner, to erect and build, on the ground where the said church then stood, one substantiall new

2

church and steeple of brick and stone, in such manner and form, and of such height, width, length, thickness of walls, etc., as were expressed of and concerning same, in such draughts or plans thereof, and the proposals thereof respectively annexed, as also the model thereof made and delivered by the same Henry Flitcroft; and that the said church and steeple respectively should be erected and built of and with such stone, brick, timber, and other materials, to be used and applied in such manner and with such workmanship as was more particularly mentioned and expressed in and by such draughts, proposals, and models as aforesaid. And that he would in like manner build contiguous to the church a good and substantial vestry-roome, with a waiting-room and passage agreeably to model. That he would, at his own charge, clear and remove from the church and churchyard all the old stuff and rubbish, carry away and drain off all superfluous water necessary to lay the foundations; and that the said new church and steeple, vestry-room, etc., should be in all respects completely built and finished, and the church-yard, streets, and avenues leading to the same entirely cleared, on or before the 25th day of December, 1733."

The sum to be paid to the architect for this work was £7,030, and it was agreed that all the material of the old church, except monuments, should also be his property. This sum did not include the cost of taking down and refitting the organ and church bells.

The proposals referred to contained very minute and particular specifications of all the various descriptions of work to be done in the church. In the plinth or base of the building Portland stone only was to be used, and no stones were to be less than eight inches in thickness; the steps were to be made of the best Purbeck stone; the rustic basement, with the rustic doorways and quoins above them, the large rustic windows, and the Venetian window, with their ornaments, etc., were to be of solid Portland stone, as were also the steeple and bell-tower, except part of the inside of them, which was to be of Bath or Oxfordshire stone. The inside of the church was generally to be paved with Purbeck stone, and the eight columns and fourteen pilasters were to be composed of solid Bath or Oxfordshire stone. The walls were to be built of suitable new stones, but it was particularly stated that no old stones, taken from the former church, were to be employed. The bricks used in the building were to be hard and well burnt.

The carpenter's work, it was decided, should be executed in the best maiden English oak, and yellow Christiana whole deals. New work was to be used for the pews and altar, but the old pulpit was to be set up in the church again.

The actual cost of the new church exceeded the sum of the original estimate by upwards of one thousand pounds, Flitcroft receiving altogether £8,436 19*s.* 6*d.*

Flitcroft's work was a decided success, and his fame was well and safely secured by the handsome and, at the same time, elegant church which he erected at St. Giles's.

Henry Flitcroft was the son of Jeffery Flitcroft, gardener to William III. at Hampton Court, and was born in 1697. In 1711 he was apprenticed to Thomas Morris, citizen and joiner of London. It is said that he was employed as a carpenter in the house of the third Earl of Burlington, and broke his leg by falling from a scaffold ; hence he attracted the notice of the Earl, who, noticing his talents, employed him as draughtsman on the edition of Inigo Jones's designs published by Kent in 1727, at the Earl of Burlington's expense.

After holding several offices, Flitcroft designed, in 1729, a mansion for John Baynes near Havering, in Essex, and in 1733 he made certain altera- tions in Carlton House. His fame was chiefly made, however, by the Church of St. Giles-in-the-Fields, upon which he bestowed great care and thought. The spire is justly considered an elegant and stately work, and in true harmony with the body of the church, which is very finely proportioned and admirably suited for its purpose.

Ralph, writing in 1736, says, " The new Church of St. Giles is one of the most simple and elegant of the modern structures. It is raised at a very little expense, has very few ornaments, and little besides the propriety of its parts, and the harmony of the whole to excite attention and to challenge applause, yet still it pleases, and justly too. The east end is both pleasing and majestic, and there is nothing. in the west to object to, but the smallness of the doors, and the poverty of appearance which must necessarily follow. The steeple is light, airy, and genteel, argues a good deal of genius in the architect, and looks very well, both in comparison with the body of the church and when it is considered as a building by itself in a distant prospect."

The area of the church within the walls is said to be 70 feet in length by 60 feet in width, exclusive of the recess for the altar. The roof is supported by Ionic pillars of Portland stone, and there are vaults under the building. The steeple is 160 feet high, and consists of a rustic pedestal supporting Doric pilasters. Above the clock there is an octagonal tower with three-quarter Ionic columns, supporting a balustrade with vases. Above this is the spire, which is also octangular and belted.

It is probable that the present churchyard of St. Giles's Church was in former times the place of interment of the hospital as well as of the parish, but it is not clear what were the limits of the ground at that early period. The churchyard is mentioned in the parish books in 1628, and it is there stated that there were formerly, standing in the churchyard glebe, certain cottages, for which the rent of £6 10s. was annually paid to the parson.

Before 1628, however, the space was needed for the churchyard, and the cottages were demolished. The mortality still continued to increase as the inhabitants of the parish grew larger, and in 1666, just after the Great Plague, the limits of the churchyard were extended by the purchase of some neighbouring ground.

Pennant, writing in 1790, speaks of a great square pit in the churchyard, in which interments were made in a very injudicious manner, little care apparently being taken of the health of the living.

At the entrance to the churchyard there is a very curious piece of carving in oak, which, from the subject depicted, has acquired the name of the "Resurrection Gate." This carving, which was executed in the year 1687, has been supposed to be to some extent a copy, with various alterations and additions, of Michael Angelo's "Last Judgment." The carving, and the gate in which it was placed, cost the parish £185 14s. 6d., £27 of which was paid to "Love, the carver." Although the carving is well known, and much admired as a work of art, nothing seems to be known of the man who carved it.

RECTORS OF ST. GILES-IN-THE-FIELDS.

			Instituted
Sir William Rowlandson	...	...	April 20th, 1547.
Geoffery Evans	...	...	November 8th, 1571.
William Steward	...	...	August 3rd, 1579.
Nathaniel Baxter	...	...	August 19th, 1590.
Thomas Salisbury	...	...	December 24th, 1591.
Joseph Clerke, M.A.	...	...	September 16th, 1592.

(Probably an interval.)

	Instituted
Roger Manwayring, D.D.	1604 ?
Gilbert Dillingham	?
Brian Walton, M.A.	January 15th, 1635.
William Heywood	1636.
Henry Cornish	1641.
Arthur Molyne	1648.
Thomas Case, M.A.	1651.
Robert Boreman	November 18th, 1663.
John Sharpe, M.A.	January 3rd, 1675.
John Scott, S.T.P.	August 7th, 1691.
William Haley	April 4th, 1695.
William Baker	October 7th, 1715.
Henry Galley, D.D. ..: ...	December, 1732.
John Smyth, D.D.	August, 1769.
John Buckner, LL.D.	1797.
Christopher Benson, M.A. ...	May 29th, 1824.
James Endell Tyler, S.T.P. ...	October 28th, 1826.
Robert Bickersteth, M.A. ...	November 29th, 1851.
Anthony Wilson Thorold, M.A.	February 20th, 1857.
John Marjoribanks Nisbet, M.A.	March 28th, 1867.

CURIOUS EPITAPHS AT ST. GILES'S CHURCH.

In addition to the monumental inscriptions which have yet to be quoted in connection with the accounts of celebrated men who have been buried at the church and churchyard of St. Giles-in-the-Fields, the following appear to be worthy of transcribing, on account of their quaint originality :—

"To the living memory of CHRISTOPHER DUDLEY, of Yeanwith, in Westmerland, Esq., was this Monument by his sorrowful Wife AGNES, for her dear Husband here erected.

A DUDLEY lodgeth here, peace idle Fame,
It's Epitaph enough to have that Name:
A DUDLEY too, who in the basest time
When to be just and loyal was a Crime,
Was both ; and 'gainst the Rebels bravely stood,
Unshaken and undaunted with a Flood

Of Tyranny. Now his Tomb's sole Intent
Shews he deserv'd, but needs not Monument.
When Rebels die, a Tomb some Life may give
He actuates the Marble, makes it live.
Shrines may pourtray our Features on a Wall
But Goodness crowns them, that is all in all.
Statutes present Lives, Families and Days;
But th' inward Structure only merits Praise.
This Shrine was rear'd by her whose Love was such,
Her Charge in his Concern was ne'er too much:
So dear is Nuptial Zeal, tho' th' inward part
Turn Dust, it holds Impression in the Heart.

Obiit Sept. 9, 1660."

" Near to this Marble JUDITH BAYLEY lies,
Who was both modest, sober, chast, and wise.
Religion was her Study, Zeal her Care,
A fervent Lover of the House of Prayer.
Her Parents had her Duty and her Love,
Who now are pleas'd in hope she's blest above.
Virtue was still her Guide, her End and Aim,
Her Zeal was constant to her as her Name.
Near 18 years of Age, who can forbear
To read her Character without a Tear ?

She departed this life the 18th of October, 1683.

Her Brother JOHN 14 days after dy'd,
Aged 7 years, lyes by his Sister's side.

She was the eldest Daughter, and he the only Son of JOHN and
JUDITH BAYLEY, of this Parish.

SARAH another Daughter sleeps in Mould,
She left this Life when almost 6 years old:
She that was fill'd with Duty, Wit and Love,
Is surely happy with the Saints above.
November 24, in Eighty-five,
She dy'd to us to be with Christ alive.

The said Mr. JOHN BAYLEY their Father died, January the 7th, 1696,
in the 63rd year of his age."

" Interr'd the Corps of BARON BYRCH lyes here,
Of Grays Inn sometime, by degree Esquire :
In Chequer 18 years a Judge he was,
Till Soul from aged Body his did pass.

Alive his wife ELIZA doth remain,
Of Stydfolk Stock, one Son and Daughters twain
She bare by him; the eldest in his Life
He gave to THOMAS BOWYER for his Wife.
His Body sleeps till Angel trump shall sound;
God grant we all may ready then be found.

JOHANNES BYRCH, Obiit Anno D. 1581, Maii 30, Ætat. suæ 66."

———

"Under this sad Marble, sleeps
She for whom even Marble weeps;
Her Praise lives still, tho' here she lyes,
Seeming dead that never dies.
Religion, Love in suffering Breast,
Her Charity, Mildness, and the rest,
Have crown'd her Soul; all mourn with Fame
Her Husband's loss, and Midwife's blame.
She dy'd in Child-bed 70 times blest and seven,
Her Child and she deliver'd both in Heaven.

Ob. 8 die Jan., 1611."

Around the margin of the stone which bore the above lines were the following words :—

"Full South this Stone four Foot doth lye,
His Father JOHN and Grandsire HENRY
THORNTON, of Thornton in Yorkshire bred,
Where lives the Fame of Thornton's being dead."

———

"Here lyes the best of Men, whose Life is at an end,
The best of Husbands, and the truest Friend;
Who rests, I hope, as I do hope to be
Happy with him to all Eternity."

JOHN HENSHAW, who died Dec. 17, 1695."

———

"Reader, it grieves me that I cannot bring
A Sea of Tears to drown my Sorrows in,
For the lamented Death of my dear Father,
Whose Soul God lately to himself did gather.
His Life was ever holy, and last Breath
Was full of Goodness, pious at his Death;
Which confidently makes me hope and trust
His Fame takes Wing from his so hopeful Dust.
Oh! Grief stops my Eye-streams; pray, Reader, then
Lend me some Tears till I can weep agen.

Memoria Pii Æterna."

The following inscription commemorates MARY HOPE, who died in 1670, aged twenty-seven years :—

> "All the rare Qualities the Poets fam'd
> On those they most ador'd, she justly claim'd ;
> Wit, Virtue, Wisdom, all in Hope are gone,
> To meet a glorious Resurrection.
> Mourn wisely then, Hope does not truly die,
> But change her Being for Eternity."

———

"Here lyes, expecting the coming of our Lord and Saviour, the Body of JAMES HEARNDEN, PRUDENCE his Wife, and WILLIAM their Son, all of this Parish. JAMES died, August 1653. PRUDENCE, Octob. 1656, and WILLIAM, Octob. 1662.

> Reader, let thy Reason know
> We were once as thou art now ;
> Whilst we liv'd, we wrought in Stone, ·
> And now attend the Corner one ;
> And in Health did this prepare
> For us, our Wives, and Children here.
> Death's only by the Wicked fear'd,
> The Righteous 'gainst his sting's prepar'd.
> Then, Reader, let thy Care in Life be such,
> Earth may thy Body, not thy Spirit touch."

———

"Here lyes the Bodies of JOHN, ANN and OBEDIAH, Children of JOHN and ANN EASTON, of this Parish.

> The ravenous Eagle Death, greedy of Prey,
> Whose piercing Eye found where these Infants lay,
> He crush'd them with his Tallons, and convey'd
> Their Souls to Heaven, and here's their Ashes laid ;
> Where now they rest in Providence's Store
> Till Time, and Death, and Tears shall be no more.

Also ANN the Wife of the said JOHN EASTON died, August 1679.

> Earth hath possess'd their Ashes, Clay, and Dust,
> And Heaven contains their Souls among the Just."

———

"Here under resteth the Body of JOHN, the Son of ROBERT and CONSTANCE WIGHT, who died the 10th of July, Anno Dom. 1678, aged 4 years and 10 months.

> My Time is short, the longer is my Rest,
> God called me hence because he thought it best."

ST. GILES'S CHURCH AND THE "RESURRECTION GATE."

CHAPTER III.

LORD HERBERT OF CHERBURY.

THIS eminent English writer was one of the parishioners of St. Giles's parish. He was born in Wales in 1581, and married at the age of fifteen. He came to London in 1600, and in 1625 he was advanced to the dignity of a Baron of the Kingdom of Ireland.

Lord Herbert was one of the first inhabitants of Great Queen Street, residing at the south side, near the east corner of Wild Street. He died at this house, on the 20th August, 1648. The house is still standing, and is one of fifteen houses built in the third year of the reign of James I. He was buried at St. Giles's Church, "under the south wall" according to one account, and "in the chancel" according to another. A flat marble stone was placed over his grave, and a Latin inscription was engraved upon it. The churchwardens' accounts of St. Giles's parish contain the following entry : "1648. The lord Herbert's brother sent £10, to be presently given to the poore, and sent one with the money to see it distributed."

A like gift, noticed in a subsequent entry, was from Henry, fourth and last Lord Herbert, and took place at his Lordship's funeral, April, 1691 ; viz., "1691, (April) Recd. the lord Herbert's gift of £10."

Lord Herbert of Cherbury wrote a "History of the Life and Reign of Henry VIII.," "De Religione Gentilium," and "De Veritate." He also wrote an account of his own life, which still enjoys considerable popularity.

ALICE DUCHESS DUDLEY.

One of the most generous benefactors to the church and parish of St. Giles was Alice, or Alicia, Duchess Dudley. This lady was the second wife of Sir Robert Dudley, who, being denied legitimacy, deserted his home for ever, and leaving his wife behind, fled to Tuscany with his mistress, Elizabeth Southwell.

Alice Dudley was created in her own right Duchess Dudley, in 1645, and the title was confirmed by Charles II. in 1660. She lived at Dudley House, St. Giles-in-the-Fields, once the residence of her husband's grandfather, the Duke of Northumberland, and she enjoyed the rents of some of her husband's landed property. She gave many articles of silk, velvet, plate, etc., for the furnishing of St. Giles's Church, and also an organ for providing music for the same. The latter gift, however harmonious it may have been from an artistic point of view, excited discord among the congregation, and was particularly mentioned as being obnoxious to the Puritan section of the parishioners.

At her death, in 1669, she was buried at Stoneleigh, and she gave considerable sums of money to be spent in that and other parishes in her memory. She ordered, too, that sixpence should be given to every poor body that should meet her corpse upon the road in its last sad journey from London to the place of its sepulture in Warwickshire.

The Duchess Dudley was remarkable for eminent mental faculties and a long life of virtuous and charitable actions. She lived until she was ninety years of age, and in her funeral sermon, preached by Rev. Dr. Boreman, at St. Giles's Church, on March 14th, 1669, it was said of her " that she made her own eyes her own overseers, and her own hands her own executors."

GEORGE CHAPMAN.

Against the south wall of the church is the tomb of this eminent poet and translator. He was also a dramatist, but is chiefly known for his spirited translation of Homer, which has justly been pronounced "one of the great achievements of the Elizabethan age, a monument of skill and devotion." Chapman died in the parish of St. Giles-in-the-Fields on May 12th, 1634 and was buried in the churchyard there.

The monument, which was designed by Inigo Jones, in the form of a Roman altar, is still standing ; but the inscription, which has been recut, does not tally with the inscription given by Wood in "Athenæ Oxoniensis." Habington, in his "Castara" (second edition, 1635), alludes to Chapman's grave being outside the church, and expresses a hope that some person might be found "so seriously devote to Poesie" as to remove his relics, and "in the warme church to build him up a tombe."

ANDREW MARVELL.

This witty and ingenious writer, the son of a minister and schoolmaster, was born at Kingston-upon-Hull in 1620. In process of time he became the assistant of John Milton, who at that time was Latin secretary to Oliver Cromwell. From 1660 until the time of his death (1678), Marvell represented his native town of Kingston in Parliament, and in that station he acquitted himself so much to the satisfaction of his constituents that they allowed him a handsome pension. Although he seldom took a prominent part in the Parliamentary debates, he exercised great influence in the political world, and numbered among his intimate friends the brave and chivalrous Prince Rupert. He was a man of singular purity of motive and integrity of character. His writings are now little read, but there are many beautiful passages in his poems, and in his controversial works he was undoubtedly the greatest master of ridicule of his time.

Marvell died in 1678, and was buried in the church of St. Giles-in-the-Fields. Ten years later the town of Kingston, in recognition of his merits and honest service, collected a sum of money to erect a monument over him, and procured an epitaph to be written by an able hand, but the minister of the parish forbade both the inscription and monument to be placed in that church.

JAMES SHIRLEY.

Another eminent man whose last days were closely associated with St. Giles's was James Shirley, the dramatist. Early in life he entered the Church, and took charge of a cure at or near St. Albans, but becoming unsettled in his principles, he joined the Church of Rome, and adopted the profession of schoolmaster at St. Albans. His first comedy is dated 1629, and it was followed at short intervals by nine or ten others. He was a Royalist, and during the Commonwealth, when stage-plays were prohibited, he was reduced to the necessity of returning to his old means of procuring a livelihood, by teaching. After the Restoration his plays were again acted, and he found himself surrounded by more cheerful circumstances. His death, which happened near the time of that of his second wife, was very sad. In 1666 the Great Fire of London forced him and his wife to fly from their house, in Fleet Street, to the parish of St. Giles-in-the-Fields, where being deeply affected by the loss and terror which the fire occasioned, they both died within twenty-four hours, and were buried in the same grave, October 29th, 1666.

SIR ROGER L'ESTRANGE.

Another noteworthy man whose remains were buried at St. Giles's Church was Sir Roger L'Estrange. He was a man who took a very active part in political and literary matters during the troublous times of Charles I., Cromwell, Charles II., and James II.

He was born in 1616, of an ancient and reputable family, and by birth and inclination was a staunch Royalist. In the year 1644 he made, in behalf of the King's cause, an unsuccessful attempt to capture the town of Lynn, in Norfolk, but he was seized, condemned to death, and imprisoned at Newgate. The execution of his sentence, however, was delayed for some years, during which time he was in hourly expectation of a summons to the scaffold. In 1648, about the time of the Kentish insurrection, he escaped from prison and went into Kent, and from thence he was enabled to escape to the Continent.

Upon the dissolution of the Long Parliament he returned to England, and sent a message to the Council at Whitehall to the effect that, finding himself within the Act of Indemnity, he thought it convenient to give them notice of his return. On his being summoned to that board, he was told by one of the Commissioners that his case was not comprehended in the Act of Indemnity, and he therefore formed the bold resolution of applying in person to Cromwell himself, which he effected in the Cockpit, and shortly after he received his discharge.

After the Restoration he was made Licenser of the Press, a profitable post, which he enjoyed till the eve of the Revolution. He established a news-paper entitled the *Public Intelligencer*, the first number of which was pro-duced on August 1st, 1663. The paper was a strong supporter of the Government. In 1679 he set up another paper, called the *Observator*, the design of which was to vindicate the measures of the Court, and the character of the King, from the charge of being Popishly affected.

L'Estrange was the author of many political tracts, and translator of several works from the Greek, Latin, and Spanish. A critic has justly re-marked that L'Estrange was one of the great corrupters of the English language, and one of the worst models of political controversy.

Sir Roger, in 1676, made a gift of £5 to the poor of the parish of St. Giles's. His death occurred on December 11th, 1704, in the eighty-eighth year of his age, and his body was buried in the Church of St. Giles-in-the-Fields, where an inscription was placed to his memory.

His tomb was described in the "New View of London" (1708) as "a very neat polished white Marble Monument, adorned with Cartouches, Leaves, Fruit, &c., and this Inscription thereon :—

"'In the middle Ile, near this place, lyeth the Body of Sir Roger L'Estrange, Knight. Born 17th of Decemb. 1616. Died 11th of Decemb. 1704.

"'His Arms ; *Gules 2 Lions Passant Argent.*'"

OLIVER PLUNKET, ARCHBISHOP OF ARMAGH.

This Roman Catholic prelate, who was also the Roman Catholic Primate of Ireland, being charged with overt deeds of high treason committed in Ireland, was tried before an English jury at Westminster, on June 8th, 1681. He was pronounced guilty of the grave charges brought against him, and on June 14th he was brought to the bar to receive judgment in accordance with the verdict. On the 11th of July in the same year Dr. Plunket was conducted from prison to the scaffold at Tyburn.

The Primate, before death, asked and obtained permission to be buried with the fathers of the Society of Jesus who had been executed at Tyburn. He was therefore interred with them close to the north wall of the Church of St. Giles-in-the-Fields. With the body of the Archbishop was deposited a copper plate bearing an inscription to this effect :—

"In this tomb resteth the body of the Most Rev. Oliver Plunket, late

Archbishop of Armagh and Primate of all Ireland, who, when accused of high treason, through hatred of the faith, by false brethren, and condemned to death, being hanged at Tyburn, and his bowels being taken out and cast into the fire, suffered martyrdom with constancy, in the reign of Charles the Second, King of Great Britain, on the 1st day of July, 1681 " (*i.e.* old style).

The head was separated from his body, which was divided into four quarters and buried in the churchyard, where they rested for more than two years ; and in 1684, when the body was disinterred, it was found to have been miraculously made entire ! Father Corker, an intimate friend of the Archbishop during life, and the person to whom his body was entrusted after the execution at Tyburn, undertook the exhumation of the Archbishop's remains, and the translation of them to Lambspring, in Germany, where he erected a handsome monument in the church of his order. The right hand of the prelate was placed in a rich case, and is said to be still preserved in the church at Lambspring. The head also he cased in a silver shrine, and in the course of time it was brought to Ireland, and placed in a little ebony temple in the Convent of St. Catherine of Sienna, at Drogheda.

RICHARD PENDRELL.

In the churchyard attached to St. Giles's Church there are a great many monuments and headstones of historical and antiquarian interest. Without attempting anything like a complete account of all of them, or transcripts of all of the inscriptions which are engraved upon them, it will be our aim to give some of the most important monumental inscriptions, and a few facts about the persons whom they were designed to commemorate.

Among the chief to be noticed is the monument to Richard Pendrell, a man closely associated with the escape of Charles II. after the battle of Worcester. The tomb is a little south-east of the church, and has been erected upon the top of the original tomb, that having become buried by the raising of the level of the churchyard. The black marble slab of the old tomb now forms the base of the more modern one. The inscription is worth quoting on account of its quaint, rhyming character.

"Here lies Richard Pendrell,

Preserver and conductor to his sacred Majesty King Charles the Second of Great Britain, after his escape from Worcester fight, 1651 who died Feb. 8, 1671.

Hold, Passenger, here's shrouded in this Hearse
Unparelell'd PENDRELL through the Universe
Like when the Eastern Star from Heav'n gave Light
To three lost Kings: So he in such dark Night
To Britain's Monarch, toss'd by adverse War,
On Earth appear'd a second Eastern Star.
A Pole astern in her Rebellious Main,
A Pilot to her Royal Sovereign.
Now to triumph in Heav'n's eternal Sphere,
He's hence advanc'd for his just Steeridge here ;
Whilst Albion's Chronicles, with matchless Fame,
Embalm the Story of Great PENDRELL's Name."

It is to be regretted that "Albion's Chronicles" have not embalmed the story of this man in a due and befitting manner. Few of the standard histories of England notice him, and none of the biographical dictionaries, to which we have had access, mention so much as his name. Under these circumstances we have gleaned what few particulars we could from various sources, including that great storehouse of historical material the "Calendars of State Papers."

Richard Pendrell appears to have occupied a humble station in life, being employed, together with his four brothers, and probably some other members of the family, in woodcutting at a secluded place on the borders of Staffordshire, called Boscobel.

The battle of Worcester (September 3rd, 1651) having resulted in the total defeat of the Royalist party, Charles II. fled immediately, and severing himself secretly from his friends, he went under the Earl of Derby's direction to Boscobel, entrusting his life to the Pendrell family, who made use of every means in their power to ensure the secrecy of his hiding-place. Death was denounced against any one who concealed the King, and a large reward offered to any one who would betray him, but these poor peasants maintained unshaken fidelity. Having clothed the King in a garb like their own, they led him into the neighbouring wood, put a bill into his hand, and pretended to employ themselves in cutting faggots. Some nights the King lay upon straw in the house, and fed upon such homely fare as it afforded. For better concealment he climbed into an oak-tree, where he hid himself amongst the branches for twenty-four hours ; and while there he saw several soldiers pass by, all diligently searching for him. The tree was afterwards called "the Royal Oak," and for many years was regarded by the neighbourhood with great veneration.

One Joan Pendrell gathered sticks in the wood, in order to divert the attention of the horsemen from the tree in which the King had hidden.

After the Restoration, the Pendrell family came up to London in order to pay their respects to the King. Humphrey Pendrell (probably an uncle of Richard) fell sick and died at " Hen. Arundel's house, Lincoln's Inn Fields, and in 1662 (Feb. 10th) a petition was presented to the King from Humphrey Pendrell for the money with which to pay for his funeral." It may be remarked that the Earl of Arundel had a hand in the plotting out of Lincoln's Inn Fields in 1618.

Charles II., when Fortune smiled upon him, did not forget to reward these lowly peasants, who had remained faithful to him at the peril of their lives, in the days when she frowned most ominously.

Numerous warrants for the payment of money to the Pendrells were issued at various times, viz., April 12th, 1662, £200 to Richard Pendrell, " whose services in a time of the greatest trial of his fidelity are known ; " June 10th, 1662, £100 each to William, John, Humphrey, and George Pendrell, " they being the brothers who assisted in the King's escape ; " July 10th, 1663, £100 to Joan Pendrell, " the person who gathered sticks, and diverted the horsemen from the oak his Majesty was in ; " July 18th, 1663, £300, to be divided equally among William, John, Richard, Humphrey, and George Pendrell ; July 14th, 1664, an annuity to William and Joan Pendrell of £100, £100 to Richard and Mary Pendrell, and 100 marks each to John, Humphrey, and George Pendrell, " for their services in saving the King's life."

It is probable that the Pendrell family settled in St. Giles's parish, as some persons bearing their name were living here for several years after the dates just mentioned, and one William Pendrell was overseer of the poor in 1702-3.

Some very interesting objects were some time ago in the possession of a descendant of the Pendrell family.   These were a curious heart-shaped watch-key and a pair of snuffers, and they were given by Charles II. as a mark of his gratitude to the Pendrells, who had been very instrumental in his Majesty's preservation.   The snuffers were somewhat larger than the size now in common use ; the stand and extinguisher were in the same proportion. The angular and circular parts, which formed a sort of framework, were made of brass, and the interstices were filled up with plates of coloured porcelain.   The watch-key also was of a rather large size, and was made of the heart of oak.

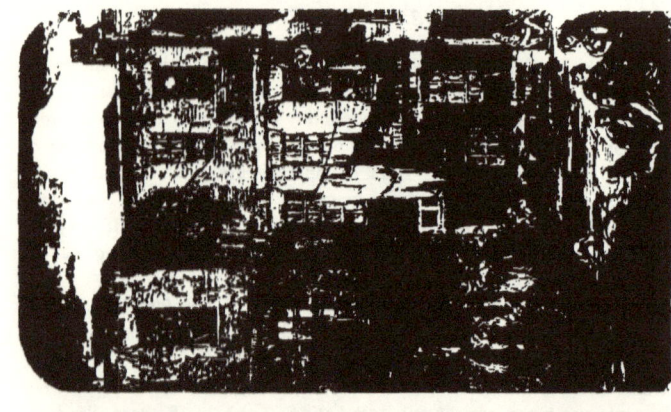

SKETCHES OF OLD HOUSES IN St. GILES'S.

It was about three-eighths of an inch thick, and was faced on each side by a plate of silver, and surmounted by an acorn of the same metal. On one side was engraved the branching oak, with the head of Charles II., and on the other side was the following inscription : " Quercus Car. 2$\underset{.}{\text{d}}$ Conservatrix. 1651." The pipe of the key was of brass.

These relics, some years back, were in the possession of Mrs. Cope, of No. 3, Regent Street, Westminster, who was a descendant of the Pendrell family, and was said to be the rightful heir to the pension granted by King Charles to her ancestors ; but the registers which would have proved this were burnt with the Catholic Chapel, Moorfields, many years ago, by the mob excited to desperation by the cry " No Popery."

From the " Report of the House of Commons Committee on Perpetual Pensions," 1887, p. 92, it appears that the pension to the Pendrell family was at that date still in existence.

ISAAC RAGG, BELL-MAN.

A curious broadside, bearing the following title, was issued in the year 1683 :—

"A COPY OF VERSES,

PRESENTED BY

Isaac Ragg, Bell-man,

To his Masters and Mistresses of *Holbourn* Division,
In the Parish of *St. Giles's* in the Fields.

PROLOGUE.

> Time (Master) calls your Bell man to his Task,
> To see your Doors and Windows are all Fast,
> And that no Villany or Foul Crime be done
> To you nor yours in absence of the Sun:
> If any base Lurker I do meet
> In private Alley, or in open Street,
> You shall have warning by my timely Call,
> And so God Bless you, and give Rest to all."

A number of short verses of rhyme upon various subjects follow, but they are not worth quoting. In the middle of the sheet is a very curious and roughly executed woodcut, representing the bell-man with a bell in one hand and a pointed staff in the other, and accompanied by a fierce-looking dog.

3

At the bottom of the sheet is the following imprint : "LONDON, Printed by William Downing in Bartholomew Close, 168¾."

A copy of this curious print is preserved among the "Luttrell Ballads," at the British Museum (Lutt. ii. 50), and a manuscript note in a contemporary handwriting gives the date of " 27 Dec. 1683," so we may assume that the sheets were intended to be given away in return for gratuities, or sold about Christmas-time, when the bell-man was doubtless, in accordance with the old English custom, " remembered."

WILLIAM WRENCH, STEEPLE-KEEPER.

In the year 1774 a man named William Wrench, steeple-keeper and bell-ringer of St. Giles's Church, issued a sort of broadside, whereon were printed an engraved view of St. Giles's Church enclosed in an engraved orna-mental border, and the following doggerel lines :—

> " Willm Wrench, Steeple-keeper to St. Giles's in ye Field's.
>
> Richd Chapell ⎫
> Robt. Landall ⎰ Church Wardens, 1774.

> " A Copy of Verses, Humbly presented to all my Worthy Masters and Mistresses, of the Parish of St. Giles's in the Fields. By WILLIAM WRENCH, Steeple-keeper and Bell-ringer, of the Five and Nine o'Clock Bell.

> "My constant Task I ev'ry Day pursue,
> And annually, kind Sirs, I wait on you;
> Hoping, kind Masters, I shall always find,
> That you to your Bell-ringer will prove kind.
> To you, this merry Season of the Year,
> I come to taste the comfort of your cheer!
> May you be blest and happy in your Wives,
> And Children be the Comfort of your Lives,
> I then with Care will strive to make Amends,
> And with my Diligence to please my Friends.
>   At Five o'clock I ring the Morning Bell,
> As ev'ry honest lab'ring hand can tell;
> The Porters, Joiners, Bricklayers, Market folks
> Are all in arms, and crack their harmless jokes.
> The Jolly Dyers, now, whose gaudy Trade
> Decks both the Duchess and the Chamber-maid ;
> Wak'd by my Bell, they then begin to Rise,
> Jump up in bed, and rub their sleepy Eyes,
> Slip on their Cloaths, and then to work they hie,
> Nor think it Time to lay their Labour by,

'Till Nine at Night, I give them my dismission,
And then tow'rd home they go by my permission.
God bless my Mistresses and Masters kind,
Who never fail their Bell-ringer to mind ;
May Health and Wealth, Prosperity and Peace,
Always attend you with each Year's encrease."

These verses were evidently intended for distribution at Christmas among the
principal inhabitants, in return for money or "the comfort of" their "cheer,"
as the bell-ringer delicately expresses it.

SIMON EDY.

Simon Edy, or "Old Simon" as he was generally called, was born at
Woodford, near Thrapston, Northamptonshire, in 1709. He was a remarkable
beggar, who, with his dog, generally took his station against one of the gate
piers of St. Giles's Churchyard. He had a discoloured, yellow-white beard
and wore several waistcoats and coats, increasing in sizes, so that he was able,
by the extent of the uppermost garment, to cover part of the bundles of rags
and parcels with which he was girded about. They consisted of books,
canisters containing bread and cheese, matches, tinder-box, and meat for his
dog, cuttings of curious events from newspapers, scraps from Fox's "Book of
Martyrs," and three or four old greasy numbers of the *Gentleman's Magazine.*
From these books and papers he obtained information, and sometimes entertained persons who paused to look at him. He and his dog lodged under
a staircase in an old shattered building in Dyot Street, called "Rats' Castle."
His walks extended to the entrances only of the adjacent streets, whither he
went to make a purchase either at the bakers' or the cooks' shops. Rowlandson
drew and etched him several times ; in one instance Simon had a female
placed before him, which the artist called "Simon and Iphigenia." A large
whole-length print of him was published by John Seago.

A curious story is told of Old Simon's dog. A Smithfield drover, whose
dog's left eye had been much injured by a bullock, solicited Simon to take
him under his care till he got well. The mendicant cheerfully consented, and
forthwith with a piece of string confined him to his arm ; and when by being
more quiet he had regained his health sufficiently to resume his services to
his master, Simon with the most affectionate reluctance gave him up, and was
obliged to content himself with the pleasure of patting his sides on a market-

day, when he followed his master's drove to the slaughter-house in Union Street. These tender and stolen caresses from the hand which had bathed his wound Rover would regularly stop to receive at St. Giles's porch, and then hastily run to get up with the bullocks. Poor Simon, after missing the dog as well as his master for some weeks, was one morning most agreeably surprised to see the faithful animal couch behind his feet, and with an uplifted and sorrowful eye—for he had entirely lost the blemished one—implore his protection by licking his beard, as a successor to his departed and lamented keeper. Rover was ugly and deficient in sight and tail, but he proved a most useful and pleasant companion to Simon Edy until the old man's death, which happened on May 18th, 1783.

BENJAMIN FRANKLIN.

Franklin, when working as a journeyman printer in London, was employed in the printing-office of Mr. Watts, which was on the south side of Wild Court, a turning out of Great Wild Street, near the western end of Great Queen Street. The date of Franklin's working there was from 1723 to 1726, and the press at which he had formerly worked he afterwards recognized at Messrs. Wyman's office, to which place it had been removed. Messrs. Harrild and Sons afterwards became possessed of the press, and in 1840 it was parted with to Mr. J. V. Murray, of New York, on condition that he would secure for them in return a donation to the Printers' Pension Society of London.

A plate on the front of the press bears the following inscription :—

" Dr. Franklin's Remarks relative to this Press made when he came to England as Agent of the Massachusetts, in the year 1768. The Doctor at this time visited the Printing-office of Mr. Watts, of Wild Street, Lincoln's Inn Fields, and, going up to this particular Press (afterwards in the possession of Messrs. Cox and Son, of Great Queen Street, of whom it was purchased), thus addressed the men who were working at it : ' Come, my friends, we will drink together. It is now forty years since I worked like you, at this Press, as a journeyman Printer.' The Doctor then sent out for a gallon of Porter, and he drank with them—

' SUCCESS TO PRINTING.'

" From the above it will appear that it is 108 years since Dr. Franklin worked at this identical Press.

" June, 1833."

"OLD JACK NORRIS, THE MUSICAL SHRIMP MAN."

An old account says, " A short time ago Old Jack Norris died suddenly, and an inquest was held on the body, before Mr. Stirling, Coroner, at the Black Horse, George Street, St. Giles's. It was reported the deceased was starved to death. The evidence proved that latterly the deceased, who was nearly seventy years of age, was unable to pursue his occupation of a dealer in shrimps, which, from his peculiar cry, gained him the appellation of the 'Musical Shrimp Man;' he shortly since applied for parochial relief, and received a trifling sum from the overseers of St. Giles's, and a pass to his own parish, St. Margaret's, Westminster ; but of this he did not avail himself, as he retired to his lodgings in George Street, where in a few days he was found dead. Norris was considered the father or veteran chief of low life in St. Giles's. He was, it is said, down to everything, and his advice on the subject of 'cadging' was considered of the first order. No man could in finer style than he evade the clauses of the Vagrant Act, and none in his day, when he could work, could make a more profitable harvest of a cadging ramble, in his profession of shrimp-dealer. He had by fighting, and mere dint of beating, driven out of a certain walk all the dealers in that way, and monopolized to himself the business. In this monopoly he always could command a party to defend him and substantiate his pretensions. He was known for the last fifty years at the markets. In fact, the whole of his life was a busy round of eccentric trickery and begging. The Black Horse is the house where Holloway and Haggerty, the murderers of Mr. Steele on Hounslow Heath, were secured. 'Old Jack Norris' was present, and was instrumental in the capture of the murderers. The jury found a verdict of ' Died by the visitation of God.' "

ANNE HENLEY.

On May 7th, 1820, died in Smart's Buildings, in her 105th year, Anne Henley. This extraordinary woman was born at West Chester, in 1716, and completed her 104th year on March 4th, 1820. She had enjoyed an uninterrupted state of health till within six days of her death, and retained her faculties in full vigour till within a few hours of her end. Her beverage in her fortieth year was whey, which she discontinued upon coming to London. The latter part of her life she received something weekly from the parish, but supported herself chiefly by making pincushions, which were neatly executed, and without the aid of glasses. She had borne thirteen children, four of whom survived her, the youngest being upwards of sixty years old. She used to sit at various doors in Holborn to sell her pincushions. She was short in stature, mild and modest in her deportment, cleanly in her person, and generally wore a grey cloak.

JOHN MITFORD.

This eccentric and dissipated character was nearly related to Lord Redesdale, and to Mitford the historian of Greece. He was originally in the Navy, and fought under Hood and Nelson, but he was expelled in consequence of some disgraceful forgery of letters professing to be connected with Queen Caroline. For many years his means of subsistence were of a very precarious nature, and he often slept three nights in the week in the open air, when his finances did not admit of his paying threepence for a den in St. Giles's. Though formerly a nautical fop, for the last fourteen years he was ragged and loathsome. He was of a most improvident disposition, and never thought but of the necessities of the moment. Having had a handsome pair of Wellington boots given to him, he sold them for one shilling. The fellow who bought them pawned them for fifteen shillings, and came back in triumph with the money. "Ah!" said Jack, "but you went out in the cold for it." He was a tolerable classical scholar, and a man of varied attainments, and he maintained his miserable existence by literary efforts, the memory of which is not worth preserving. Among them was a libellous life of the late Recorder Sir John Sylvester. His largest work was "The Adventures of Johnny Newcombe in the Navy," the publisher of which gave him a shilling a day until he finished it. Incredible as it may appear, he lived the whole of this time in Bayswater Fields, making a bed at night of grass and nettles. Two pennyworth of bread and cheese and an onion were his daily food ; the rest of the shilling he expended in gin. He thus passed forty-three days, washing his shirt and stockings himself in a pond when he required clean linen. He edited the *Scourge* and *Bon Ton Magazine*.

A hundred efforts were made to reclaim Mitford, but they were without avail. A printer and publisher took him into his house, and endeavoured to render him decent. For a few days he was sober, and a relative having sent

him some clothes, he made a respectable appearance. But he soon degenerated into his former habits, and whilst editing a periodical called the *Bon
Ton Gazette* the printer was obliged to keep him in a place, half kitchen,
half cellar, where, with a loose grate tolerably filled, a candle, and a bottle of
gin, he passed his days, and, with the covering of an old carpet, his nights,
never issuing from his lair but when his bottle was empty. Sometimes he
got furious with drink, and his shoes having been taken from him to prevent
his migrating, he would then run out without them. In winter he was known
to have taken off his coat and sold it for half a pint of gin. At the time of
his death he was editing a penny publication called the *Quizzical Gazette
and Merry Companion.* He wrote the popular song "The King is a true
British sailor," and sold it to seven different publishers.

Notwithstanding his habits, he was employed by some religious publishers.
This miserable man died in December, 1831, in St. Giles's Workhouse, and
was buried by Mr. Green, of Will's Coffee House, Lincoln's Inn Fields, who
had formerly been his shipmate.

CHAPTER IV.

THE GALLOWS.

HE space where Tottenham Court Road, New Oxford Street, High Street, Charing Cross Road, and Oxford Street now meet is the spot upon which the City gallows formerly stood. It appears that a new gallows was set up for the occasion of the execution of Sir John Oldcastle, Lord Cobham, the first execution at St. Giles's of which we have any account, although it is probable that an older gallows had existed there and had been made use of previously.

Lord Cobham's crime was that he made himself obnoxious as leader of the Lollards, who, it was pretended, were treasonable plotters. As is well known, however, their offence was their exposition of the vices and ignorance of the clergy, and their discovery of a purer theology. Lord Cobham, a man of great weight and importance, was a great supporter of the Lollards' cause, and was, for that reason, the first who was singled out for destruction ; but as he ranked high in the favour of his sovereign, it was thought necessary that he should be charged with some crime of greater gravity than that of mere complicity with the followers of Wickliffe. To avoid persecution, the Lollards were in the habit of holding their religious meetings in fields and secluded places, and St. Giles's Fields were selected and used by them for that purpose. The secrecy of their meetings, and the large numbers of their members who attended them, afforded some colour to the accusation of treasonable proceedings which their enemies made against them, and steps were taken for suppressing the supposed rebellion. Lord Cobham was arrested and brought before the Primate, Bishops, and Doctors in 1414. As he declined to subscribe to certain tests which were submitted to him, the Archbishop " modestly, mildly, and sweetly " (as he himself said) pronounced a sentence of condemnation against him as an obstinate heretic, and handed him over to the secular arm to be dealt with accordingly. The night before his intended execution he found means to escape from the Tower of London, wherein he was confined, and he was able so far to evade his persecutors as to live in concealment in Wales for a period of four years. At length, however, he was captured by Lord Powis, having been disabled by a stool which an old woman threw at him, and which is said to have broken his legs. He was brought up to London, and made to appear before the Parliament then sitting at Westminster, by which he was condemned to be strangled and burnt, " and upon the daye appoynted was he (sir Johan Oldcastle the lord Cobham) broughte out of the Tower with his armes bounde behynde him, havynge a verye cheereful countenance. Than was he layd upon an hurdle, as though he had bene a most heynouse traytour to the crowne, and so drawne forth into Saynct Giles's Felde, where as they had set up a newe payre of gallowes. Then was he hanged up there by the myddle in cheanes of yron, and so consumed alyve in the fyre."

Cobham has been charged with fanaticism, but the mind which could fearlessly face torments so frightful, and go to so shameful a death with a " verye cheereful countenance " surely belonged to a true hero, and a man with the genuine spirit of a martyr.

But even if Cobham were only a wild fanatic, that was no justification for a punishment so grossly inhuman.

It is difficult to picture the scene of Cobham's revolting execution in the busy streets and crossings close by the modern " Horseshoe," but it is pretty certain that that was the identical spot upon which stood the gallows whereon this brave man endured the pain and agony of a most excruciating death rather than forfeit liberty of faith and freedom of opinion.

In the time of Queen Elizabeth, Babington, the conspirator, met with his death in Lincoln's Inn Fields. The Roman Catholic party appears to have conspired to dethrone and murder Elizabeth. Babington was at the head of the conspirators, who met at St. Giles's Fields. One of their number betrayed the plot, and steps were taken at once to stamp it out. After hiding for ten days in St. John's Wood, described as "neare to the citie," Babington and some of his accomplices were captured, tried, found guilty, and condemned to death.

Several of the conspirators, including the leader, were hanged and quartered in Lincoln's Inn Fields on September 20th, 1586. It may be added, as an interesting item in relation to an old mansion upon which we shall have occasion to touch later on, that Babington's Plot is supposed to have been concocted in Southampton House, in this parish.

THE POUND AND THE CAGE.

The Pound and Cage originally adjoined each other, and stood in the middle of the High Street, from whence they were removed in the year 1656, to make way for the Almshouses which were afterwards built there. The Pound, it is probable, existed from a very early period, as a necessary append-age to the parish while a village and abounding in pasture-lands and open spaces, although it is unnoticed in the parish books till Lord Southampton's grant of the ground on which it stood for the Almshouses, where it is described as occupying a space of 30 feet square, which was to be the dimensions of the new Pound, therein directed to be removed to the end of Tottenham Court Road. The charge for removing and re-erecting the Pound and Cage, including some repairs done to the Almshouses, on this occasion, amounted to £118 16s. 5d. In 1690 Mr. Tucker was ordered by the Vestry to be paid his bill for paving work done at the Pound. The spot appears previously to that period to have been unpaved. Ten years later a second order occurs, "that the roads from the Pound be paved, from the paving belonging to the corner house, the Crown, to the boundary posts." Miles were measured from St. Giles's Pound in the same way as from the Standard at Cornhill.

The Cage appears to have been used as a prison, and the following entries relating to it, extracted from the churchwardens' accounts, seem to show that its use was not confined to prisoners who underwent short periods of punishment only :—

		s.	d.
" 1641.	Pd. to a poor woman that was brought to bed in the cage ...	2	o
„	For a shroud for a poor woman that died in the cage ...	2	6
1648, (July 9.)	To Ann Wyatt in the cage, to relieve her and buy her a truss of straw	1 .	6
„ (July 12.)	Paid for a shroud for Ann Wyatt	2	6 "

It has been suggested that the Cage was probably done away with when the second Watch-house was erected in the parish, in the year 1716.

The Pound, which was mentioned in the following couplet of an old song—

> " At Newgate steps Jack Chance was found,
> And bred up near St. Giles's Pound,"

was finally swept away in the year 1765, after which many improvements were made in the neighbourhood, particularly by the erection of the great brewery of Messrs. Meux and Co.

THE ROUND HOUSE.

The Round House was situated near the west end of the church, close by the churchyard. It was built in a cylindrical form, like a modern martello tower, though, from bulging, it resembled an enormous cask set on its end : it was two storeys high, and had a flat roof, surmounted by a gilded vane, in the shape of a key. In 1686 a gate was ordered " to be made out of the wall of the church-yard, near the round house." The same year it was further ordered "that care be taken to have a wall erected at the west part of the round house for the security thereof, in regard the old buildings adjoining are taken away."

It is extremely probable that the "old buildings" referred to were remains of the hospital, or they may have been part of the buildings connected with Dudley House. A Vestry minute dated 1690 advises "to consider of the disposal of the round house of this parish." The Round House was soon afterwards destroyed, probably on account of the insecurity of its walls.

THE WATCH-HOUSE.

The Watch-house was built in 1694, by Mr. Rathbone (from whom Rathbone Place is named), and the sum of £8 was paid to him by the parish, "due in part for building the watch-house." This first Watch-house stood in the middle of Holborn, a little to the west of Southampton Street, leading to Bloomsbury Square. The ground on which it was situated was given to the parish for the purpose by the Duke of Bedford. The Watch-house was probably either enlarged or rebuilt in 1716, when the Vestry ordered " that the watch-house in Holborn be viewed, and an estimate made of the expense to make a watch-house, and other conveniences for the keeping of prisoners." In the early part of the present century the Watch-house was situated in Smart's Buildings, near Drury Lane.

THE STOCKS AND THE WHIPPING-POST.

There were Stocks and Whipping-post in St. Giles's parish, as appears from the following entries in the parish records :—

		£	s.	d.
" 1683.	Paid the workman's bills for the whipping-post ...	7	17	6
1703.	Paid Mr. Pollett for painting the stocks, whipping-post and shed	2	0	0 ".

It is not known at what part of the parish they were situated, but from the latter entry it is evident that they were placed near together, and protected by some kind of shed or covering.

FIRE-ENGINE.

In the year 1639 a Vestry minute ordered the churchwardens of St. Giles's to provide for the parish an engine, buckets, and hooks, to help the inhabitants when any danger from fire should arise. An entry in the parish records, made in the year 1671, shows that care was taken to have everything in proper order when a fire should break out ; an allowance of ten shillings a year was made to John Pollard, one of the beadles, for looking after the engine.

Ten years later (1681) the standing watchmen were ordered to assist with the fire-engine at fires. By some means, probably by fire, the engine sustained such injury at a fire at Whitehall that in 1697 it was found to be of no use, and it was accordingly ordered by the Vestry that it should be sold to the best advantage. It was also ordered that a new fire-engine should be provided in its place.

INNS AND ALE-HOUSES.

There were, in the good old times, many inns and houses of refreshment or the St. Giles's people. Some of them date back to a very early period.

These will be duly noticed in their proper order, but as the list is rather a long one, perhaps it will be best and most convenient to arrange them in an alphabetical rather than a chronological order.

THE BLACK BEAR.

This was a house of considerable antiquity, and was several times referred to in entries in the parish books. It stood in " Black Bear Yard," to which it probably gave its name. In the year 1623 Black Bear Yard was assessed, and is said to have contained twenty-nine householders. In 1629 the church-wardens were ordered by the Vestry " to repair to the landlord of the Black Bear, in Black Bear-yard, and to deal with him concerning the opening and cleansing of a well in the street at the Black Bear-yard, according to an order from the Privy Council."

Although it is not definitely known when the Black Bear ceased to exist as a public-house, it is probable, from its name being nowhere mentioned after the end of the reign of Charles II. that it was discontinued as such, or pulled down, at about that date.

THE BLACK JACK.

This and the two houses next to be mentioned were situated near St. Giles's Church. The Black Jack is described in a deed, dated 1654, as being situated opposite a messuage called " the Alley-gate," meaning the gate leading to Sharper's Alley.

THE BLACK LAMB.

In 1654 this house was described as "a messuage known by the signe of the Black Lamb, late in the occupation of Thomas Gunston," and is afterwards similarly noticed in a subsequent deed, dated 1680, as " all that messuage containing nine roomes, a yard or backside, and an house of office," called as before, and then occupied by Judith Gunston, widow, " situate on the south side of the old town of St. Giles's in the Fields, leading towards the church." It was leased to the said Judith Gunston for forty-one years, from 1672, at £8 per annum.

THE BOWL.

The name of this public-house was preserved for many years in that of Bowl Yard, in or close to which spot it formerly stood. It appears to have been built upon a spot which, in 1623, was called Canter's Alley. Before 1654 it was held by one John Merritt. It seems to have been destroyed in 1661, when other premises were built. Its name, the Bowl, and the name of a public-house which was situated near it, the Black Jack, are both curiously suggestive of the ancient dole of a cup or bowl of ale which was given to condemned criminals on their last journey to the gallows, first in High Street, St. Giles's, and later on at Tyburn.

THE COCK AND PYE.

The Cock and Pye public-house stood, according to tradition, at the south-west corner of the Marsh-land, and gave the name of the Cock and Pye Fields to the open space of land upon which the Seven Dials were afterwards built. The original sign of the house was that of the Cock only, and the additional sign of the Pye was adopted at a subsequent date.

It may be remembered that this phrase, "cock and pie," is used by Shakespeare, who puts it into the mouth of Justice Shallow when addressing Sir John Falstaff, thus :—

"By cock and pie, sir, you shall not away to-night" (2 Hen. IV., v. i.).

It is probable that the phrase had an allusion to the peacock or pheasant pie, a highly esteemed dish with our ancestors. It is said to date its origin from the days of chivalry, when it was usual for the knights to take their vows of enterprise at a solemn feast, on the presentation to each knight in turn of a roasted peacock in a golden dish. For this was afterwards substituted, as the most magnificent dish which could be brought to table, a peacock in a pie, preserving as much as possible the form of the bird, with the head elevated above the crust, the beak richly gilt, and the beautiful tail spread out to its full extent.

The fields around were, to some extent, a popular resort in the summer, as long as they retained any rural attractions, but when the Seven Dials were built, and the rustic character of the neighbourhood was lost, visitors fell off, and the business of the Cock and Pye was so much injured that the place fell into obscurity.

The exact spot where this old inn formerly stood was afterwards marked by a more modern public-house, and known as the Two Angels and Crown. It was situated where now meet three streets, called Little St. Andrew Street, West Street, and Castle Street.

THE CROCHE HOSE.

This was one of the earliest inns in the parish, and was probably situated near the north-east corner of the Marsh-land, opposite the entrance to Monmouth Street, afterwards called Dudley Street, and now forming part of Shaftesbury Avenue. In the reign of Edward I. this house belonged to Herbert de Redemere, the cook attached to the Lepers' Hospital. That possessor gave the place to the hospital. It was probably demolished before the dissolution of the monasteries in the reign of Henry VIII.

The Croche Hose, or Crossed Stockings, was adopted as the sign of the hosiers, and was represented as a red and white stocking crossed in the manner of a St. Andrew's cross.

THE CROOKED BILLET.

The Crooked Billet was situated at the corner of Hog Lane, facing the Pound. An entry in the parish books reads thus :—

" 1662. Paid for the ditch at the Town's-end, by the Crooked Billet."

This ditch was afterwards called the Cock and Pye Ditch. At the date just mentioned it is probable that it extended along part of Hog Lane.

It has been supposed that the Crooked Billet was subsequently known as the Crown, but there is some uncertainty about the matter, and it is quite possible that the Crown was a public-house situated very near the Crooked Billet.

THE CROWN.

There appear to have been two public-houses in this parish bearing the sign of the Crown. One, to which we have just referred, stood at the corner of Hog Lane ; and the other was situated in Greyhound Court, and its site is now occupied by the Workhouse.

THE FORTUNE TAVERN.

This public-house is mentioned among those the proprietors of which were fined for permitting tippling on Sundays. The following is an extract from the parish accounts :—

" 1655. Rec^d of two men, for drinking at Mr. Walter Leigh's, at the Fortune Tavern, 10s.—Received of Mr. Leigh, for that offence, 5s."

THE GEORGE AND BLUE BOAR.

For more than two hundred years this was one of the famous coaching houses, whence stages went to, and where they arrived from, the north and midland counties. It was situated in Holborn, upon the site which is now occupied by the Inns of Court Hotel.

One of the most important events in its history is recorded in the following extract from a letter from Cromwell to Lord Broghill, wherein he relates circumstantially how he and Ireton intercept at this inn a letter from Charles I. to his Queen, which was sewed up in the skirt of a saddle:—

" The reason," says Cromwell, " why we would once have closed with the king was this : We found that the Scots and the Presbyterians began to be more powerful than we ; and if they made up matters with the king, we should be left in the lurch : therefore, we thought it best to prevent them, by offering first to come in, upon any reasonable conditions. But while we were busied in these thoughts, there came a letter from one of our spies, who was of the king's bedchamber, which acquainted us that on that day our final doom was decreed ; that he could not possibly tell what it was, but we might find it out, if we could intercept a letter, sent from the king to his queen, wherein he declared what he would do. The letter, he said, was sewed up in the skirt of a saddle, and the bearer of it would come with the saddle upon his head, about ten of the clock that night, to the Blue Boar Inn in Holborn. This messenger knew nothing of the letter in the saddle, but some persons at Dover did.

" We were at Windsor when we received this letter ; and immediately upon the receipt of it, Ireton and I resolved to take one trusty fellow with us, and with troopers' habits to go to the Inn in Holborn ; which accordingly we did, and set our man at the gate of the Inn, where the wicket only was open

BROAD STREET, St. GILES'S, about 1830.

to let people in and out. Our man was to give us notice, when any one came with a saddle, whilst we, in the disguise of common troopers, called for canns of beer, and continued drinking until about ten o'clock : the centinel at the gate then gave notice that the man with the saddle was come in. Upon this we immediately arose, and, as the man was leading out his horse saddled, come up to him with drawn swords, and told him that we were to search all that went in and out there ; but as he looked like an honest man, we would only search his saddle and so dismiss him. Upon that we ungirt the saddle and carried it into the stall, where we had been drinking, and left the horse-man with our centinel : then ripping up one of the skirts of the saddle, we there found the letter of which we had·been informed ; and having got it into our own hands, we delivered the saddle again to the man, telling him he was an honest man, and bid him go about his business. The man, not knowing what had been done, went away to Dover.

"As soon as we had the letter, we opened it, in which we found the king had acquainted the queen, that he was now courted by both the factions, the Scotch Presbyterians and the Army ; and which bid fairest for him should have him ; but he thought he should close with the Scots sooner than the other. Upon this," adds Cromwell, "we took horse, and went to Windsor ; and finding we were not likely to have any tolerable terms from the king, we immediately from that time forward resolved his ruin."

THE HAMPSHIRE HOG.

This inn was situated opposite St. Giles's Church, and gave the name to Hampshire Hog Yard close by. A sum of £3 a year, issuing from the ground-rent of this house, was, in 1677, given to the poor by Mr. William Wooden, a vestryman of the time.

THE HORSESHOE.

This house, which has now become one of the widest known and most commodious hotels in the metropolis, has a long history. As early as the year 1623 we find it named in the assessment as standing on the north side of the town, or somewhere in Bloomsbury.

4

The Maid in the Moon.

Very little seems to be known about the public-house which bore this singular sign, but it is known that it stood near Prince's Street, Drury Lane, in 1708.

The Maidenhead Inn.

This inn, situated in Dyot Street, was established as early as the reign of Queen Elizabeth. At that early part of its history it formed part of the estate of Lord Mountjoy.

Dyot Street derived its origin, although not its name, from the Maidenhead Inn, which stood near the south end of the street, and was originally called "Maidenhead Close" and "Maidenhead Row." Its name of Dyot Street it derived from Richard Dyot, Esq., a parishioner and vestryman in the reign of Charles II., who then owned the estate and resided on the spot.

The Maidenhead Inn seems to have been one of the leading inns of the parish, as for many years the parish meetings were held there. In the reign of Charles II. it was a very flourishing house, but by the commencement of the eighteenth century it had become a "house of great resort for mealmen and countrymen." A writer in the earlier part of the present century describes it as a "public-house and liquor-shop of the very lowest description, and the haunt of beggars and desperate characters."

It was a roomy and somewhat handsome building, three storeys high, exclusive of attics. The porch over the main entrance, too, was massive and shapely.

Before the year 1834 it was demolished, together with a great part of the east side of Dyot Street, and the ground upon which they stood was converted into a stone-yard, under the direction of the Paving Board.

The Rose.

This inn was situated in Lewknor's Lane, and is mentioned in deeds as early as the reign of Edward III. It was part of the possessions of the Hospital of St. Giles, and is mentioned in the exchange with Henry VIII. In the year 1667 it was conveyed by Edward Tooke to Luke Miller. It seems to have been demolished or discontinued as an inn after the year 1675. It had some pasture-land attached to it, which with the site of the house has, of course, long ago been covered with buildings.

LE SWAN ON LE HOP.

In the reign of Edward III. this inn is mentioned in a deed, and from that and other notices it is probable that it stood on the south side of Holborn and east of Drury Lane. It had probably been destroyed or changed its name before the reign of Henry VIII.

TOTEN, OR TOTTEN, HALL.

Although the site of this old inn is not now within the boundary of Bloomsbury or St. Giles's, there is reason to believe that at one time it was.

As early as the time of Henry III. the house, the property of William de Tottenhall, was a mansion of eminence, and was probably the court-house of the manor of the same name.

It was of course much later when the old mansion was turned into an inn. Its situation, a little way out in the pleasant fields, doubtless attracted many visitors and customers, especially on Sundays, when freedom from work gave a little leisure for pleasure and wholesome recreation. There is a very curious entry in the parish books to the following effect :—

> "1645. Rec^d of Mr. Bringhurst, constable, wh^{ch} he had of
> Mrs. Stacye's maid and others, for drinking at Tottenhall court on
> the Sabbath daie xij^d apiece ...   . 3^s."

Part of this old house was afterwards made into an inn, and called the Adam and Eve.

THE TURNSTILE TAVERN.

The situation of this inn was at the corner of the turnstile or footpath leading into Lincoln's Inn Fields. It does not appear to have been established as an inn at a very early date, and it had ceased to exist before the year 1693.

THE VINE.

The Vine public-house stood on the north side of Holborn, a little below the end of Kingsgate Street. It appears to have been known at one time as the Kingsgate Tavern. It is not known when it was established, but it was taken, and two other houses built upon its site, in 1817.

THE WHITE HART.

In the reign of Henry VIII. the White Hart was mentioned as having eighteen acres of pasture land belonging to it. It stood at the Holborn end of Drury Lane. From certain old plans, it appears that this pasture-land was bounded on the west by Drury Lane, on the east by the way now called Little Queen Street, and on the north by Holborn. An embankment separated it from the thoroughfare of Holborn. The inn appears to have been demolished early in the eighteenth century, but its name was retained by a court, called White Hart Yard, until the beginning of the nineteenth century, when that also was swept away by the encroaching builders.

CHAPTER V.

CHARITIES.

OME of the charities appertaining to the parishes of St. Giles-
in-the-Fields and St. George, Bloomsbury, are curious and of
considerable antiquity. The following are some of the chief
facts in connection with them, arranged according to the
chronological order of their foundation. It may be explained,
however, that the chief facts in relation to them having been
taken from the " Second Report from Commissioners " " appointed to Enquire
concerning Charities in England for the Education of the Poor," printed by
order of the House of Commons in 1819, and from a " Further Report " of
the same Commissioners, printed by order in 1826, certain details as to the
application of them have become modified subsequently.

SKYDMORE, OR SCUDAMORE'S, GIFT.

An annual sum of twenty shillings is received from the Vintners'
Company, being the gift of Stephen Skydmore, in 1584, for fuel to the poor
of the parish, charged, with other similar gifts to other parishes, on some houses
in the parish of St. Anne, Blackfriars, given by him to the Company. This
money is not now given away in fuel, but is accounted for by the church-

wardens, together with certain other charities, in a weekly distribution of bread. This is now incorporated with the Almshouse charities.

HOLFORD'S CHARITY.

By deed of feoffment, dated December 5th, 1659, Richard Holford, in consideration that several messuages, situated in the parish of St. Giles-in-the-Fields, being the inheritance of the said Richard Holford, were erected upon a parcel of ground, containing by estimation eight acres, parcel of the lands of the old Lepers' Hospital, although the said hospital was long since dissolved, and the lands and revenues thereof were for valuable considerations sold and conveyed to divers persons, whereby the said acres of land were lawfully come to the said Richard Holford and his heirs ; and in respect that it was the desire and will of Henry Holford, father of the said Richard Holford, that a yearly rent of twenty shillings should be paid to the poor of the said parish, towards their relief and maintenance, and also out of the pious intention and desire which the said Richard Holford had to revive so much of the charitable relief for the poor of the said parish as the eight acres of ground were really worth before the same were built upon, and for other good causes, etc., granted and enfeoffed to Thomas Case and nine other inhabitants of the parish of St. Giles, and their heirs, two messuages or tenements, each containing in the front, from east to west, forty-eight feet of assize, or thereabouts, situated on the north side of Princes Street, in the said parish ; and another messuage or tenement, and little yard thereto belonging, situated on the north side of the said street, containing in width on the front thereof, from east to west, fourteen feet ; upon trust to pay the rents and profits of the said premises to the churchwardens and overseers of the poor of the said parish for the time being, to the intent that the yearly sum of twenty shillings thereof might be by them paid every Christmas Day to twenty poor men and twenty poor women of the said parish, according to the desire and will of the said Henry Holford, deceased ; and that the residue of the said rents and profits should be, by the said churchwardens and overseers, yearly paid and disposed to such of the most aged, poor, diseased, and leprous people of the said parish as they in their discretion should think fit.

Several subsequent conveyances of the trust property have been made, the last of which (up to the year 1826) was by lease and release, dated

July 19th and 20th, 1798, whereby the premises were conveyed to John Lord Bishop of Chichester and twelve others, trustees chosen by the vestrymen of the said parish. The property was sold in 1880 to the Metropolitan Board of Works, for street improvements, and the money was reinvested in 1889 in the freehold ground-rents of Nos. 1-8, Crescent Road, Tunbridge Wells. They amount to £96 per annum.

In the year 1826 the property consisted of two adjoining messuages in Princes Street, Drury Lane.

The whole of the rent of the property is carried to the account of the fund for the support of the Almshouse ; but the sum of one pound is yearly distributed at the church on Christmas Day, in compliance with the provisions of the trust deed, in sixpences, to twenty poor men and twenty women of the parish. This custom is continued to the present time.

SHELTON'S CHARITY SCHOOL.

Mr. William Shelton, by his will dated July 5th, 1672, devised all his messuages, lands, and tenements whatsoever, in Parker's Lane, to the minister and churchwardens of the parish of St. Giles-in-the-Fields, upon trust that out of the rents and profits they should lay out fifteen pounds yearly, for buying twenty gowns for twenty poor old men and women of the said parish, together with other similar gifts elsewhere ; and also that they should hire and provide a fit-schoolmaster, to teach school and instruct in learning, in the school and room he had appointed in Parker's Lane, fifty children of the poorest sort, thirty-five whereof were to be of St. Giles's parish, ten of the parish of St. Martin, and five of the parish of St. Paul, Covent Garden, and to pay the said schoolmaster twenty pounds yearly, and to buy him a gown yearly of twenty shillings' value, and also a coat yearly for every one of the said fifty scholars, of the value of six shillings, and to provide yearly two chaldrons of coals, for a fire for the said scholars in winter. All these coats and gowns were to be of a green colour.

And he directed that the schoolmaster and children should be nominated, and the different articles provided, and the rents received by his wife during her life, and after her decease by the minister and churchwardens and the testator's heir-at-law ; and he declared his will to be that his heir-at-law should for ever thereafter receive out of the rents and profits yearly ten pounds ; and he further directed that the schoolmaster should not teach any other scholars besides the fifty scholars, and that the surplus of the rents and profits should be employed for the binding forth some of the said scholars apprentices.

The premises which passed under this will were a piece of ground, with the buildings thereon, on the south side of Parker's Lane, which the testator had purchased in 1661, and which ground was then described as containing in front next the said lane and in rear 105 feet, and in depth 50 feet, little more or less; which are within a few inches the dimensions of the premises belonging to the trust in 1819.

When the parish of St. George's, Bloomsbury, was formed and united to the mother-parish of St. Giles-in-the-Fields the fifty boys educated in the Shelton Charity School were selected from the united parishes.

Out of this fund thirty-five poor men or women were furnished annually with a coat or gown of green kersey, twenty of whom were selected from St. Giles's and St. George's, ten from St. Martin's, and five from St. Paul's, Covent Garden, and they were recommended by the respective rectors and churchwardens of those parishes. The proportion of men and women varied according to the discretion of the parties recommending. This charity is now applied for educational purposes and for providing clothing for the poor. It is in the management of the Rector and Churchwardens of St. Giles's.

Gifts of Sir William Coney and the Hon. Robert Bertie.

It is stated upon a tablet in St. Giles's Church, and also in an old Churchwardens' account-book, that Sir William Coney, in the year 1672, gave fifty pounds for bread to the poor.

Also that the Hon. Robert Bertie, in 1679, gave fifty pounds, which is further said in the Vestry minutes to have been for a distribution of sixty dozens of bread, to be distributed by the Churchwardens at their discretion, on certain appointed days.

The Hon. Robert Bertie was son and fifth child of the great Robert Bertie, the first Earl of Lindsey, who was slain at the battle of Edgehill, in 1642. His elder brother, Montague, succeeded to the title, and was afterwards Lord Great Chamberlain of England. This family, afterwards the ducal family of Ancaster, resided for many years at the mansion called Lindsey, and subsequently Ancaster House, Lincoln's Inn Fields.

These two sums, together with the fifty pounds given by Carter, were carried into the joint stock of the parish, and it is considered that the interest thereof is accounted for in the following distribution of bread :—

Twenty-four twopenny loaves are given by the churchwardens twice a week, viz., on Wednesdays and Saturdays ; twenty of these are given to the almswomen, the other four to the other distressed inhabitants whom the churchwardens select.

MARGARET BOSWELL'S GIFT.

Margaret Boswell, by will, dated September 22nd, 1720, gave to the parish of St. Giles-in-the-Fields one hundred pounds capital stock of the South Sea Company, in trust that the income thereof should be yearly given to ten poor sick and distressed families, such as should become necessitous by misfortune and not by extravagance or looseness.

ELIZABETH CUMMING'S GIFT.

It appears, from an entry in the Vestry-book, that Elizabeth Cumming, widow, gave by will, in 1735, the sum of two hundred pounds, the interest whereof was to be distributed by the direction of the minister and church-wardens, in bread monthly for ever, to the industrious poor of St. Giles-in-the-Fields not taking alms of the parish. In the year 1826 this charity produced the annual sum of £6 2s.

FRANCES BATT'S GIFT.

Frances Batt, by will, dated October 21st, 1736, gave to the minister and churchwardens of the parish of which she should be an inhabitant at the time of her death the sum of one hundred pounds, which was to be put out on good security, and the interest of which was to be annually divided amongst the poor of the parish, under the superintendence of the Rector and churchwardens. Mrs. Batt died in the parish of St. Giles, and in the year 1826 the charity produced the annual sum of £3.

EDWARDS'S GIFT.

Mr. Thomas Edwards bequeathed to the gentlemen of the Vestry of the parish of St. Giles-in-the-Fields five hundred pounds, to be invested in

Government security, and the dividends of which were to be used for the purchase of bread, to be distributed every Sunday to such poor people as the
Vestrymen for the time being should deem proper objects of charity.

This legacy, which was received in the latter end of the year 1791, was
invested in Three per Cent. Consolidated Annuities, and the dividends, which
amount to upwards of sixteen pounds, are applied to a weekly distribution
every Sunday, at the Vestry-room, of twenty-five threepenny loaves, to a list of
twenty-five poor women of the parish, who are appointed by the Vestry to
receive them. The capital has since been transferred to the Charity Commissioners, and the dividends are distributed by the Rector amongst the poor
of the parish.

ATKINSON'S GIFT.

In the list of the charities contained in the Vestry-book there is mentioned
a rent-charge of one pound, the gift of William Atkinson, issuing out of the
Bull's Head, in Lewknor's Lane, and it is there stated that the house had
been in ruins many years, and that fourteen years' annuity were in arrear in
March, 1805.

A Report on the Charities in 1826 states—

" This house, situated in what is now Charles Street, is in a deplorable
state, though not absolutely in ruins. The lower part was a chandler's shop,
but is at present shut up ; the rest is occupied by lodgers of the lowest description. We have not hitherto been able to find out who is the owner of the
premises, and their condition is such that any attempt to obtain the arrears or
the annual rent-charge by distress would apparently be fruitless."

DONOR UNKNOWN.

From the Vestry minutes of the parish of St. Giles-in-the-Fields it appears
that at a Vestry held on February 14th, 1822, Mr. Charles Stable, one of the
Vestrymen, stated that a lady (whose name was unknown) had transferred
£90 Navy Five per Cents. into the names of the Right Rev. John Buckner,
Lord Bishop of Chichester, George Brettingham, Churchwarden, and Charles
Stable, as trustees, the interest thereof to be distributed annually by the
Churchwardens for the time being of the parish of St. Giles and the said
Charles Stable, to nine poor Irish women, during their confinement in child-bed,
living in the said parish.

In the year 1826 this stock was £94 10s. New Four per Cents., producing an annual dividend of £4 2s. 9d., which was applied in the manner directed by the donor.

LEVERTON'S CHARITY.

By his will dated February 21st, 1823, Thomas Leverton left a sum of money (£4,455 12s. 3d.) in the trust of the Rector, Churchwardens, and six senior Vestrymen of St. Giles-in-the-Fields, the interest of which was to be paid in sums of £25 annually to each of six widows and reduced gentle-women who have lived respectably in houses in the parish of St. Giles. It was essential that the houses should be of the annual rental of £40 ; that the recipients of the charity should be not under forty years of age, and have lived in the parish for not less than three years. It was also essential that they should not receive alms from the parish, and above all that they should be descendants or kindred of the testator.

The six annuities are now worth £22 5s. 6d. each per annum. Although the charity was intended chiefly for the parishioners of St. Giles's, it was pro-vided that one annuitant might be taken from the parish of St. George, Bloomsbury.

ALMSHOUSES.

The following charitable gifts being in connection with the Almshouses, they are here grouped together in chronological order :—

DANVERS'S CHARITY.

Wriothesley Danvers, by will bearing date March 24th, 1618, gave to the use of the poor of the parish of St. Giles-in-the-Fields, for ever, two messuages or tenements, situated at Rainham, Essex ; he also gave all the goods and chattels whereof he should die possessed, to be given and distri-buted at the discretion of the executors and overseers of his will.

The premises devised by this benefactor consisted, in the year 1826, of a public-house called the Bell, with a yard and garden, and were let by the Churchwardens, under the directions of the joint Vestry, by tender, to John Draper, for a term of thirty-one years from Michaelmas, 1795, at the clear yearly rent of £20, the lessee agreeing that he would lay out the sum of £120 in repairing the premises.

The rent is applied towards the support of the poor women in the Almshouse.

ANTHONY BAILEY'S CHARITY.

Anthony Bailey, by his will, bearing date October 8th, 1640, gave to the poor of St. Giles's parish an annuity of £4, payable out of his messuages and tenements at or near Turnstile, in Holborn. The sum of £3 12s. is annually received on account of this gift from the occupier of a house, No. 282 in High Holborn, at the western corner of Great Turnstile, and is devoted to the fund for the maintenance of the almswomen.

EARL OF SOUTHAMPTON'S GIFT.

Thomas Earl of Southampton, by deed dated June 10th, 1656, demised to Thomas Blythe and another, Churchwardens of the parish of St. Giles, and to two other inhabitants of the said parish, a piece of land near St. Giles's Church, where the Cage and Pound then stood, for the term of five hundred years, at the rent of one shilling, to the intent that the inhabitants of the said parish should, before Michaelmas, 1657, erect five several houses thereon for the residence of ten poor persons, to be placed therein from time to time by the said inhabitants, and the almshouses were erected accordingly.

These almshouses, which were situated in the middle of the street called Middle Row, St. Giles's, were pulled down in pursuance of an order of the joint Vestry in 1782, for the purpose of enlarging the street ; and the parish purchased other premises, on which the present Almshouses have been built, as will be mentioned hereafter.

DUCHESS DUDLEY'S GIFT.

Lady Alicia Duchess Dudley, by will bearing the date of November 2nd, 1669, gave £400 for the purchasing of £20 per annum for the use of the poor people who were or should be in the Almshouse of the parish of St. Giles, for ever, to be equally divided among them on Christmas Day and Whitsunday.

In the year 1826 the premises consisted of the following parcels :—

1. A messuage at the corner of College Hill and Elbow Lane, in the parish of St. Michael Royal, City, producing an annual rent of £15.

2. Another messuage in Elbow Lane, adjoining the above, producing an annual rent of £12.

3. A small messuage abutting north on Elbow Lane, together with three wine-cellars or vaults, producing a rent of £21 a year.

4. A messuage in Elbow Lane, abutting west on the last-mentioned house, producing a rent of £21 a year.

This property is now represented by 17, College Hill, and 24, 25, 26, College Street, City, which properties are let on lease to Messrs. S. Tudor and Sons, at £450 per annum.

CARTER'S GIFT.

It is stated, in a list of benefactions in the Vestry minute-book, that Henry Carter gave £50. The collections made by Parton for his history of the parish contain the further information that the gift was made in 1676, and was given to the Churchwardens, for them to distribute five shillings every monthly sacrament, and the like sum on every Christmas Day and Good Friday, among the poor of the Almshouses; the principal to be kept for ever in the Churchwardens' hands.

WOODEN'S GIFT.

William Wooden, by will dated 12th September, 29th Car. II., bequeathed to the poor widows in the Almshouses £3 per annum; it is witnessed that Richard Street and Abigail his wife had granted to James Partheritch and others, trustees of the said Almshouses, the yearly rent of £3, issuing out of a messuage called the Hampshire Hog, in trust for the said poor widows. The parish came into possession of this charity in the year 1681.

In the year 1817 it was ordered that the stock should be transferred from the general parish fund, and the dividends in future be carried to the Almshouse account, which was accordingly done. The money is now invested in Two-and-three-quarter per Cents.

HOUSES IN MACKLIN STREET, DRURY LANE.

By deed-poll bearing date October 3rd, 1783, reciting that by indenture bearing date September 26th preceding, William Cardale, by the direction of

Benjamin Cooper and John Edwards, in consideration of £560, had conveyed to Philip Dyot and nine others, their heirs and assigns, five freehold messuages or tenements, yards, and workshops, two of which messuages, it is stated, according to a late survey, fronted Lewknor's Lane, thirty feet or thereabouts on the south, and abutted on a dwelling-house and premises of David Walker seventy feet on the west, and fronted the coal-yard (now known as Goldsmith Street) and Sword-bearer's Alley forty-six feet on the north, and contained on the east, running south from Sword-bearer's Alley towards Lewknor's Lane, about twenty-four feet, then running west fourteen feet, and then south to Lewknor's Lane forty-six feet, as described in a plan in the margin of the said purchase deed, marked (A); and of the three other messuages, two are described as being situated in Lewknor's Lane, and the other as lying behind.

The said five messuages were conveyed to Philip Dyot and others upon the trusts thereafter mentioned, viz., to suffer the premises to be enjoyed, and the rents and profits received, by such persons as the joint Vestry should appoint.

In 1826 the trustees of the property were Peter Ludgate, Samuel Remnant, and John Abraham Goldwin.

Ten almshouses were erected in 1783, by the parish, upon the site of the premises marked (A) in the margin of this purchase deed, each house containing two dwellings, and they were occupied by twenty poor women, decayed housekeepers of the joint parishes.

In the year 1879 the trustees bought an adjacent piece of ground in Macklin Street, and in 1885 the Almshouses were rebuilt on the enlarged site, at a cost of £2,723, by Messrs. Colls and Sons, builders, of Moorgate Street, from designs by E. H. Burnell, Esq., of 32, Bedford Row.

The Mortuary and Coroner's Court were built in 1880, upon a portion of spare ground close by where the houses had stood which had been purchased from William Cardale in 1783.

The Almshouses provide accommodation for ten poor women of good character, and at least of sixty years of age. They must have been resident in either of the parishes not less than five years, and preference is given to those reduced, by misfortune, accident, or calamity, from better circumstances.

SHAKESPEARE'S GIFT.

Among the personal funds belonging to this charity is a sum of £1,500 Three per Cent. Consols, the gift of Messrs. William and Henry Shakespeare.

The money was to be devoted to the support of the poor almswomen. £1,000 was received by the parish in 1799, and a further sum in 1805, by the reversion of £500.

MRS. GREGORY'S GIFT.

In the year 1809 Mrs. Martha Gregory, formerly of this parish, caused the sum of £666 13s. 4d. Three per Cent. Consols to be transferred into the names of the two Rectors, in aid of the fund for the support of the almswomen.

LEVERTON'S GIFT.

A legacy of £100 was left in the year 1823 to the almswomen, by Mr. Thomas Leverton, of Bedford Square.

Miss Winter Ashfield gave £2,000 in 1851, and Charles Startridge gave £100 in 1855, to the Almshouses.

CHARITIES LOST OR EXPIRED.

It is said that Bartholomew Ivery, in 1647, gave three tenements in the Great Almonry, Westminster, to the poor of this parish, which were subsequently sold, and the proceeds carried to the Churchwardens' account. No trace is now to be found of it.

It is also said that one Sowerby, in 1690, gave £50 for 50s. per annum to be paid to Mr. Merydale for the use of the poor. There is no trace of this gift.

Also that Robert Hulcup, in 1686, gave to the poor a rent-charge of £40, issuing out of certain tenements in Drury Lane. It appears from the Vestry books that this was an annuity which expired shortly after the donor's death.

BLOOMSBURY PAROCHIAL SCHOOLS.

These schools, founded in the year 1705, were formerly situated in Museum Street, but in 1880 they were removed to No. 27, Little Russell Street, specially built for the purpose from designs of Mr. Peacock. By this charity twenty-five girls are boarded, clothed, educated, and trained to become useful servants, and eighty boys are clothed and educated.

The following useful facts are derived from one of the annual reports of

the institution : " It may be interesting to here revert to the circumstances
under which the institution became the recipient of Dr. Carter's beneficence.
The Rev. Dr. Benjamin Carter, formerly of St. Giles-in-the-Fields, by his will,
gave to certain Trustees 'all that old capital messuage, or tenement, wherein
one Elizabeth Lloyd formerly dwelt, in the parish of St. Giles-in-the-Fields, in
the county of Middlesex' (which was afterwards pulled down, and several
tenements erected, which were in the year 1727 of the annual value of £55),
upon trust *inter alia* ' to yearly pay the Governors and Trustees of the Charity
Girls' School of the parish of St. Giles-in-the-Fields, in the county of Middlesex,
the annual sum of £10, to be applied by them for the use of the said charity
girls, as they should think proper.'   In the year 1832 the payment of £10
had become augmented to the sum of £20, and then was and had for some
years past been paid to the Treasurer of the Charity School of St. Giles and
St. George, Bloomsbury.   By an order of the High Court of Chancery, made
in the second year of the reign of his late Majesty King William IV., it
was ordered that two eleventh parts of the estates given by Dr. Carter, after
making certain payments thereout, should be paid 'to the Treasurer of the
United Charity Girls' School of the parishes of St. Giles and St. George,
Bloomsbury, to be applied towards the purposes of the education of the
charity girls of the said parish of St. Giles,' and that if there should be any
residue of the income arising from the charity, after making the payments
directed by the said order, then at the discretion of the Trustees it should be
applied, as to part, in augmentation of the share provided for ' the said Charity
Girls' School of the said parish of St. Giles.'

" This arrangement continued from time to time, and the property
gradually increased in value, until within the last few years the income derived
varied from £50 to £70 per annum."

Candidates for admission to these schools must be the children of poor
but respectable parishioners of St. Giles's or St. George's parishes.   Girls are
admitted at seven years of age, and remain until they are fifteen.   Upon being
admitted they are supplied with the school clothing as soon as possible, the
patterns and articles of dress being determined from time to time by the
Ladies' Committee, subject to the approval of the Committee of Management.
Each girl is expected to rise at six o'clock in the morning, from Lady Day to
Michaelmas inclusive, and at seven o'clock during the other six months of the
year, and to retire to bed at eight o'clock at night, except in June, July, and

August, during which period they are expected to retire at nine o'clock. Every girl who has conducted herself to the satisfaction of the Committee of Management, and has not been withdrawn before she has attained fifteen years of age, is presented with a Bible and Prayer Book.

Boys between the ages of seven and twelve, whose parents have resided two consecutive years previous to the election in either of the parishes, are allowed to be candidates. Their education is freely given them at the National Schools of the united parishes. Each boy receives a complete suit of clothing in the month of March annually, and a second shirt, pair of stockings and boots, at the Christmas following ; he also receives a Bible and Prayer Book upon attaining the age of fourteen, if his conduct has been satisfactory, and if opportunity offers he is apprenticed to a trade.

Lying-in Hospital, Endell Street.

The British Lying-in Hospital is one of the oldest institutions in Bloomsbury, and the oldest lying-in charity in England. We learn from the minute-book of the Board of Management that "a meeting of the Society of Gentlemen for Establishing a Lying-in Hospital was held at the Bear and Rummer Tavern, in Gerard Street, Soho, on the 6th of September, 1749," at the instigation of the Duke of Portland and several other Governors of the Middlesex Hospital who had severed their connection with that institution, in consequence of the refusal of a majority of its Governors to apply a certain sum every year to the maintenance of lying-in wards. At the meeting above alluded to a scheme was framed according to which a subscription-book was to be opened, and a weekly meeting held at the Bear and Rummer, to promote the establishing of the new hospital, and the circular stated, " The company of any gentlemen inclined to the same good work will be taken as a favour." The details of this scheme were advertised in the *Daily Advertiser*, the *General Advertiser*, and the *London Gazette*. It is curious to note that the original President of the charity in 1749 was the second Duke of Portland, and that in 1890 the sixth bearer of that title occupies the same position. Dr. Sandys was the first medical officer, and Mr. Thomas Yewd the first Secretary. Subsequently we find that "with a view to avoid an election for several years, because such elections generally disturb the peace of such institutions as are supported by voluntary contributions," a staff consisting

5

of seven "gentlemen of the faculty" was appointed. The following well-known names appear from time to time among the members of the medical staff: Drs. William Hunter, George Macaulay, Edward Borman, and Cæsar Hawkins. The charity originally occupied a house in Brownlow, now called Betterton, Street. Brownlow Street received its name from Sir John Brownlow, Bart., a parishioner in the reign of Charles II., whose house and gardens then stood on this spot. It is probable that he resided there in 1676, his house being called Brownlow House, but he seems to have removed before the year 1682. The central part of this house, which had evidently been robbed of its wings, was used as the British Lying-in Hospital until that institution removed into the new premises in Endell Street. The parish accounts contain frequent mention of certain portions of the house having been removed to make way for improvements. An engraving of it, with allegorical figures, is preserved in the King's Library, British Museum (xxv. 28).

Michael Mohun, the actor, died in a house in Brownlow Street in the year 1684.

In 1849 the present premises were erected in Endell Street. The first patient admitted in the original hospital was "Sarah, wife of William Saunders," on November 23rd, 1749. The plan of diet at that time included "water-gruel, beer caudle, and occasionally trotters." On February 5th, 1750, we are told that the Committee ordered "that half a dozen of wine in pint bottles and half a pound of green tea be purchased for the hospital." In 1757 the dietary was as follows: "For the first nine days after delivery the women are allowed brown caudle, boiled veal, boiled fish, and light pudding, as is most agreeable to them; and if weakly, white caudle, sago or panado, with a little wine." The meat then was purchased at $3\frac{1}{2}d.$ per lb. When the first matron was appointed, "Captain Hebden, of the 4th Troop of Horse Guards, commanded by the Earl of Crawford, attended the Committee, and informed them that the husband of Elizabeth Blunt, who offered herself as a candidate for the office of Matron, had been in his troop, and that he was abroad in Flanders with him about four years, and always behaved particularly well."

In August, 1851, the Committee sat in solemn judgment on one "Mary Pitts, the cook-maid, who went out on Sunday before she had done the necessary business of the house, and behaved very pertly to the Matron," and in 1799 "the temporary porter had pledged a bed," and was prosecuted and imprisoned. From the first until about twenty years since the hospital has been in an almost constant state of financial depression. Of late it has never figured among those charities which swell their funds by means of balls and other entertainments, but in May, 1759, there was a special performance on its behalf, given at the Opera House, when tickets were sold at half a guinea. In 1761 the Society of Arts gave "a grand benefit performance" in the Strand, and in 1762 and 1768 Mr. George Garrick arranged performances at Drury Lane, and in 1765 a grand ball was given at "Almack's," all on behalf of "the Lying-in Hospital," as the institute was then known. In 1752 the system of training midwives for which this hospital has been and is still noted was instituted, "so that the Hospital would not only be what it is now, a most comfortable receptacle for distressed poor, in the perilous season of child-bearing, but would also extend its benefits to all parts of the Kingdom, by supplying them with well-instructed and experienced Midwives, whereby many lives both of Mothers and Infants might be hereafter saved to the Publick."

In 1793 a special appeal to the public was made for funds as follows : " The Governors having from the beginning made the relief of pregnant wives of seamen and soldiers an object of their attention and care, are now sensible of a greatly increasing demand on their assistance by the calling out of those brave men to the defence of their country, and the support of the allies, and the Governors in appealing to the Publick express their loyal sentiments for the preservation of our most Gracious Sovereign and all the Royal Family and the British Constitution as by Law Established." In January, 1792, the Duchess of York, through her surgeon, presented fifty guineas to the hospital, and in May of the same year became Patroness, and was succeeded in 1820 by the Duchess of Clarence. In 1850 the Duchess of Kent consented to become Patroness. Among some of the earliest Vice-Presidents appear the Duke of Ancaster and Lord Eardley. Lord Chief Baron Parker was a liberal supporter, and among deceased Governors are the names of Sir John Fielding, the celebrated blind magistrate at Bow Street, and his brother Henry, whom he succeeded. Mr. Woodfall, whose descendant is now a partner in a gigantic printing business in Long Acre, used to print the appeal circular for the Lying-in Hospital during the last century. Probably few of those who pass by the dingy red brick building in Endell Street have any idea of the antiquity of the institution that it represents.*

* Our best thanks are due, and hereby offered, to F. Gardner, Esq., Secretary to the Lying-in Hospital, for the chief part of the foregoing account of that institution.

CHAPTER VI.

COCK AND PYE FIELDS.

HAT are now the Seven Dials, Long Acre, and Soho were formerly, before the enormous increase of buildings and population, open fields, known first as "Marsh-land," and after the year 1666 as the "Cock and Pye Fields," so-called from the Cock and Pye public-house, which, according to tradition, was situated at the junction of Little St. Andrew Street, West Street, and Castle Street. The public-house was first called the Cock; afterwards the word Pye or Magpie was added to its name. In the time of the Commonwealth it was in the occupation of Peter How, and worth £6 per annum.

When the new buildings in the neighbourhood deprived the spot of its former rural attractions, the Cock and Pye declined in popularity, and its later history is lost in obscurity.

In the year 1647 the great ditch by which these fields were enclosed was called simply the ditch, but after 1666 the name of "Cock and Pye Ditch" was applied to it. In 1671 the ditch, having become a public nuisance, was cleaned out and partially arched over. Its course is said to be traceable in the site of the present sewer. The arching over of the ditch was followed by the commencement of the building of the Seven Dials. Thomas Neale, in whom the fee of the property was then vested, granted leases of the ground to

STONE COLUMN WHICH FORMERLY STOOD IN THE SEVEN DIALS,
Now the Monument to the Duchess of York at Weybridge.

certain builders, who soon transformed the locality, and the open fields became, in process of time, a busy centre of life, remarkable for its closely built houses and overcrowded population.

Evelyn, writing in his celebrated " Diary " under the date of October 5th, 1694, says, " I went to see the building beginning neere St. Giles's where 7 streets make a star from a Doric pillar plac'd in the middle of a circular area, said to be built by Mr. Neale." It appears that this Mr. Neale was a speculator. He took a large piece of ground on the north side of Piccadilly, of Sir Walter Clarges. He was to lay out £15,000 upon it in building, but he did not, and Sir Walter got the lease back and built Clarges Street.

The entry in Evelyn's " Diary " fixes with considerable exactness the date of the construction of the Seven Dials. That neighbourhood, when the grand new houses were erected, was considered by our forefathers to be quite an aristocratic quarter, and there is no doubt that, in contrast to the poor and meaner houses which then existed in High Street and some neighbouring localities, the Seven Dials presented an imposing appearance.

The following extract from Gay's poem entitled " Trivia " gives some interesting details about the column at the Seven Dials :—

> " Where fam'd Saint Giles's ancient Limits spread,
> An inrail'd Column rears its lofty Head,
> Here to sev'n Streets, sev'n Dials count the Day,
> And from each other catch the circling Ray.
> Here oft the Peasant, with enquiring Face,
> Bewilder'd, trudges on from Place to Place ;
> He dwells on ev'ry Sign, with stupid Gaze,
> Enters the narrow Alley's doubtful Maze,
> Tries ev'ry winding Court and Street in vain,
> And doubles o'er his weary Steps again.
> Thus hardy Theseus, with intrepid Feet,
> Travel'd the dang'rous Labyrinth of Crete ;
> But still the wand'ring Passes forc'd his Stay,
> Till Ariadne's Clue unwinds the Way."

The stone column, the capital of which had only six faces, was removed in 1773, to facilitate a search which was made for a treasure which, it was imagined, was concealed beneath its base. The stones are said never to have been replaced, but they were purchased of a stonemason, and removed, for some forgotten purpose, to a place in the neighbourhood of Chertsey, called Sayes Court. In the year 1822 the column was surmounted with a ducal coronet, and set up on Weybridge Green as a memorial to the Duchess of York, who died at Oatlands in 1820. The dial was used as a stepping-stone at the Ship Inn, at Weybridge. The marks were plainly discernible where the indices of the various dials were placed, and portions of the metal with which they were secured remained for a long time.

The column looks handsome and imposing in its present position at Weybridge. Blocks of white marble have been inserted in two of the panels of its pedestal, and the following inscriptions have been cut upon them :—

THIS COLUMN

WAS ERECTED BY THE INHABITANTS

OF WEYBRIDGE AND ITS VICINITY,

ON THE 6TH DAY OF AUGUST, 1822,

IN TOKEN

OF THEIR SINCERE ESTEEM AND REGARD

FOR HER LATE ROYAL HIGHNESS

THE MOST EXCELLENT AND ILLUSTRIOUS

FREDERICA CHARLOTTE ULRICA CATHERINA,

DUCHESS OF YORK,

WHO RESIDED FOR UPWARDS

OF THIRTY YEARS

AT OATLANDS IN THIS PARISH,

EXERCISING EVERY CHRISTIAN VIRTUE,

AND DIED UNIVERSALLY REGRETTED

ON THE 6TH DAY OF AUGUST, 1820.

————

YE POOR, SUPPRESS THE MOURNFUL SIGH ;

HER SPIRIT IS WITH CHRIST ON HIGH,

IN WHOSE BRIGHT REALMS OF HEAV'NLY PEACE,

WHERE CHARITY SHALL NEVER CEASE,

HER DEEDS OF MERCY AND OF LOVE

ARE REGISTER'D IN COURTS ABOVE.

The monument is enclosed within a substantial iron railing.

An evil reputation seems to have clung to the Seven Dials throughout all its past history. The Cock and Pye Fields were notorious as the rendez-vous of the idle and vicious, even before the ground was occupied with buildings.

The subsequent overcrowding of the poorest and lower classes of society did not improve matters, but made them very much worse. The place at one time bore a very unenviable character for drunkenness, profanity, Sunday trading, and cheap and ill-ventilated lodging-houses, and its death-rate was very high. Hogarth has chosen the locality for some of his paintings which picture vice and cruelty in their most hideous and revolting aspects, and many writers of fiction have chosen it as a scene for villainous and unwholesome incidents.

It is pleasant to turn from the darker side of the Seven Dials to one of more cheerful character, viz., its literature, for which it has attained considerable fame, although it is fame of a not very exalted order.

James Catnach, the well-known printer of cheap literature, established himself, in 1813-14, as a printer at Nos. 2 and 3, Monmouth Court, a small thoroughfare connecting Monmouth Street with Little Earl Street.

Having set up his father's old wooden printing-press, and provided himself with some scraps of type and old woodcuts, he chose for himself a particular line of printing, viz., children's books, which he sold for a farthing each. He also printed ballads upon all popular topics, and was open to purchase the original manuscripts of them from the poor authors who wrote them, for sums ranging from one shilling to half a crown each. Among the woodcuts with which he illustrated his miscellaneous publications were some old ones of seventeenth-century date, and also some of Bewick's, much worn down by excessive use. When these were not forthcoming he cut blocks for himself, which, although roughly executed, were considered sufficiently striking for his purpose.

Catnach was quick to discern subjects which were likely to become popular with the purchasers of street literature, and in 1838 he retired from his business, having made enough money upon which to settle down comfortably for the remainder of his life. He died in 1841, aged forty-nine. During his life he must have printed an immense number of broadsides, ballads, and booklets, and as most of his customers paid him with coppers, he used to take them to the Bank of England, in large bags, in a hackney coach, because most of his neighbours, knowing from whom he received them, dreaded to take them from him in exchange for silver, for fear of infection.

Song and ballad printing became an important profession in the neighbourhood after Catnach had once set the fashion, and proved how much money could be made by it. The following printers' names and addresses are frequently to be seen on old ballads :—

"J. Pitts' Wholesale Toy and Marble Warehouse, 6, Great St. Andrew Street, Seven Dials."

"E. Hodges, from Pitts', printer, Wholesale Toy and Marble Warehouse, 31, Dudley Street, Seven Dials." E. Hodges afterwards removed to "26, Grafton Street, Soho."

"C. Paul, Printer, 18, Great St. Andrew Street."

"T. Birt, Printer, 39, Great St. Andrew Street, Seven Dials ;" also "10, Great St. Andrew Street."

"Ryle and Co., Printers, 2 and 3, Monmouth Court, Seven Dials."

Two very curious broadsides relating to cruelties practised in the St. Giles's Workhouse were printed about the middle of the last century. One is entitled "The Workhouse Cruelty, Workhouses turn'd Goals, and Goalers Executioners. . . . Printed for Charity Love-poor, near St. Giles's Church." The other is a ballad of sixteen four-lined verses, entitled "The Workhouse Cruelty ; being a full and true Account of one Mrs. Mary Whistle, etc. . . . Printed for Christian Love-poor, near St. Giles's Church." The upper part of the sheet is adorned with six very quaint woodcuts, and both the ballad and prose accounts are disfigured by wretched orthography, composition, type, and ink. The ballad is mere doggerel, but the circumstances related have in a certain sense a local interest, and it is worthy of note that an establishment for the printing and sale of this kind of street literature existed at St. Giles's at a period so early. Doubtless there were important reasons why the real name of the printer should be kept a secret, and sarcastic pseudonyms used in its place.

THE GREAT PLAGUE.

St. Giles's has the unenviable reputation of being the scene of the first appearance of the Great Plague. In December, 1664, three men died of the plague in Long Acre, or rather at the upper end of Drury Lane. Early in the following year the bills of mortality showed an ominous increase in the parish of St. Giles's, and although great care was taken to keep the matter quiet, it soon came to be known that this increase arose from the prevalence of the

BIRD FAIR, SEVEN DIALS.

plague in that quarter. The result proved that the pestilence had taken a firm hold of the district of St. Giles's, and many hundreds of victims fell a prey to its ravages during the plague year. The crowded houses and imperfect drainage which at that period characterized the district around the Seven Dials doubtless contributed in no small degree to this lamentable result.

As early as the year 1625 a pest-house had been built in St. Giles's, upon the occasion of one of the earlier visitations of the plague. The site upon which it was built was some ground which was the property of William Shelton, Esq. When the place was pulled down the materials of which it was constructed were sold, and from the small sum which they produced it is probable that the building was only of a temporary character.

FRENCH REFUGEES.

Among the large numbers of French Protestants who were exiled by the revocation of the famous Edict of Nantes in 1685, many fled to London, and some settled in the neighbourhood of St. Giles's. In this way was founded the French colony which still exists in that quarter and in Soho.

THE ROOKERY OF ST. GILES'S.

Attention has already been invited to the over-built and over-crowded condition of the Seven Dials and the immediate vicinity. Henry Fielding, writing in 1751, gives some interesting details about the deplorable condition of things which arose from over-population at that comparatively early date. He wrote a curious tract in 1751, entitled "An Enquiry into the Causes of the late Increase of Robbers," etc. (8vo, London), and, in an account of the poor and low class of lodging-houses of Bloomsbury he gives some facts, which he mentions he obtained from Mr. Welch, then the High Constable of Holborn. He says that in the parish of St. Giles there were great numbers of houses set apart for the reception of idle persons and vagabonds, who were accommodated with lodgings for twopence a night. One woman alone rented seven of these lodging-houses, all properly accommodated with miserable beds from the cellar to the garret. In these arrangements lodgers were placed indiscriminately together, without regard to sex, and no attention was paid either to the sanitary or moral welfare of the inmates. The same writer says that gin was sold in all these low lodging-houses at a penny a quartern, so that a very small sum of money provided sufficient means for intoxication.

Henry Mayhew's "London Labour and London Poor" graphically describes the condition of St. Giles's about the middle of the present century. He writes—

"In Bainbridge Street, one side of which was nearly occupied by the immense brewery of Meux & Co., were found some of the most intricate and dangerous places in this low locality. The most notorious of these was Jones Court, inhabited by coiners, utterers of base coin, and thieves. In former years a bull terrier was kept here, which gave an alarm on the appearance of a stranger, when the coining was suspended until the coast was clear. This dog was at last taken away by Duke and Clement, two police officers, and destroyed by order of a magistrate.

"The houses in Jones Court were connected by roof, yard, and cellar with those in Bainbridge and Buckeridge Streets, and with each other, in such a manner that the apprehension of an inmate or refugee in one of them was almost a task of impossibility to a stranger, and difficult to those well acquainted with the interior of the dwellings. In one of the cellars was a large cesspool, covered in such a way that a stranger would likely step into it. In the same cellar was a hole, about two feet square, leading to the next cellar, and thence by a similar hole into the cellar of a house in Scott's Court, Buckeridge Street. These afforded a ready means of escape to a thief, but effectually stopped the pursuer, who would be put to the risk of creeping on his hands and knees through a hole, two feet square, in a dark cellar in St. Giles's Rookery, entirely in the power of dangerous characters."

Many of the houses in this quarter were lodging-houses. In some of the better class houses the beds, furnished with a warm bed-cover and flock bed, with sufficient warm and clean clothing, were let for the low charge of two shillings a week, or fourpence a night. But some of the houses were of the most disreputable character, and frequented by the most abandoned members of society. A large proportion of the inhabitance was of Irish origin, as many who inhabit the Seven Dials now are.

In some of the very lowest houses it is known that as many as sixteen adult persons, male and female, were housed in one single room, 12 feet by 10 feet. At night they lay on loose straw littered on the floor, their heads to the wall and their feet to the centre, and decency was entirely unknown among them.

The Seven Dials, and several low places around, including the famous "Rookery," were well-known haunts of base coiners. Spurious money so made was sold at the rate of tenpence for five shillings' worth of spurious coins.

The difficulty of passing off this base money as genuine gave rise to many cunning and, it must be confessed, ingenious tricks. Detection, of course, always followed sooner or later after the fraud, and considerable variety of trick was necessary in order to pass off the bad money at all.

"Ringing the changes" was and still is a favourite method of passing off the base coin. The form in which this trick is worked varies from time to time, and according to the ingenuity of the swindler. The old way was for a person to offer a good sovereign to a shopkeeper to be changed. The gold piece is chinked on the counter or otherwise tested, and is proved to be good. The man hastily asks back and gets the sovereign, and pretends that he has some silver, so that he does not require to change it. On feeling his pocket he finds he does not have it, and returns a base piece of money resembling it, instead of the genuine gold piece.

The area which the famous "Rookery" formerly covered was enclosed by Great Russell Street, Charlotte Street (Bloomsbury Street), Broad Street, and High Street, all within the parish of St. Giles-in-the-Fields. Within this space were George Street (once Dyott Street), Carrier Street, Maynard Street, and Church Street, which ran from north to south, and were intersected by Church Lane, Ivy Lane, Buckeridge Street, Bainbridge Street, and New Street. These, with a great many almost endless courts and yards crossing each other, rendered the place nearly as intricate as a rabbit-warren.

In Buckeridge Street stood the Hare and Hounds public-house, formerly the Beggar in the Bush. In 1844 it was kept by a then well-known man, Joseph Banks (generally known as "Stunning Joe"), a civil, rough, good-hearted Boniface. His house was the resort of all classes, from the aristocratic marquis to the vagabond whose way of living was a puzzle to himself.

At the opposite corner of Carrier Street stood Mother Dowling's, a lodging-house and provision-shop, which was not closed nor the shutters put up for several years before it was pulled down to make way for the construction of New Oxford Street. The shop was frequented by vagrants of every class, including foreigners, who, with moustache, well-brushed hat, and seedy clothes—consisting usually of a frock-coat buttoned to the chin, light trousers, and boots gaping at each lofty step—might be seen making their way to Buckeridge Street to regale upon cabbage, which had been boiled with a ferocious pig's head or a fine piece of salt beef. From 12 to 1 o'clock at midnight was chosen by those ragged but proud gentlemen from abroad as the proper time for a visit to Mrs. Dowling's.

The construction of New Oxford Street upon the very site of the old " Rookery," and various improvements effected upon that and subsequent occasions, have effectually removed what was once a disgrace to the neighbourhood.

DUDLEY STREET.

A good view of Dudley Street, just off the Seven Dials, is contained in Blanchard Jerrold's " London : a Pilgrimage," page 158. It has been drawn by the masterly hand of Gustave Doré, and depicts very vividly the ancient condition of the neighbourhood—the roadway crowded with children and adults, and the cellar-tenements occupied by dealers. in second-hand clothes and shoes, whose stock-in-trade is represented as hanging from pegs attached to the walls of the houses, or ranged round the entrances to the wretched underground dwellings.

LEWKNOR'S LANE.

The situation of this lane was on the east side of Drury Lane, from which it struck out at right angles, nearly opposite Short's Gardens ; in fact, it is identical with the present Macklin Street. It acquired its name from Sir Lewis Lewknor, who had a house and grounds thereabout early in the seventeenth century. In process of time, probably in the early years of the reign of Charles I., the estate began to be built upon, and the street had become generally known as Lewknor's Lane before the end of the reign of that monarch. By that time Sir Lewis Lewknor had probably died or removed from the neighbourhood. He was the translator of Cardinal Contarini's " Commonwealth and Government of Venice," in 1599 ; and he wrote a curious little work entitled " The Estate of English Fugitives under the King of Spain and his Ministers," which was printed in 1595. Also he was the translator of " The Resolved Gentleman," from Olivier de la Marche's " Le Chevalier délibéré." Lewknor, whose translation is said to have been done from the Spanish, probably used the edition of Hernando de Acuña, who translated, or

THE ROOKERY, St. GILES'S, about 1800.

rather versified, La Marche's work from the original French into the Spanish language.

Lewknor's translation is a work of very great rarity, and no copy of it is to be found among the bibliographical treasures of the British Museum.

The social condition of this quarter does not appear ever to have been of a very exalted kind. From the time when the grounds of Sir Lewis Lewknor were covered with small houses the neighbourhood has borne a bad character. Jonathan Wild kept a house of ill-fame here, and Sir Roger L'Estrange speaks of the lane as a " rendezvous and nursery for lewd women, first resorted to by the Roundheads." Authors and play-writers have made frequent mention of Lewknor's Lane, and generally with some uncomplimentary allusion or circumstance. Lewknor's Lane appears to have been sometimes called Lutenor's Lane during the eighteenth century.

SHORT'S GARDENS.

The name "gardens" applied to any spot where buildings crowd so closely together as they do here seems paradoxical, or takes the mind back many years, to the date when the ground actually was open and cultivated as gardens.

Short's Gardens were actual gardens in 1623, and the ground between the street which now bears that name and that which is now Betterton Street (formerly Brownlow Street), and round about that part, was occupied by scarcely any houses. It is stated that at that date only four housekeepers resided there.

The place acquired the name of Short's Gardens at a somewhat later date than that just mentioned. There is every reason to believe that the name arose from the circumstance of the residence there of Dudley Short, Esq., an influential parishioner and Vestryman in the time of Charles II.

The house in which this man lived was afterwards inhabited by Thomas Short ; then it was the property, and probably the residence, of — Tomlinson, and afterwards of Ralph Bucknall, brewer. The house abutted on the Mulberry Garden, south ; on a garden of Robert Clifton, west ; on Greyhound Court, north ; and on a piece of garden ground, east. The situation of the mansion was in Greyhound Court, and there was also a fenced-in court in front of it, 18 feet long by 18 feet broad. These details are taken from a deed dated

1707. The same document gives the following particulars of the adjoining premises :—

"A parcel of ground, and three messuages built thereon, situate on the west side of Greyhound Court, occupied by — Toms, victualler, with a piece of ground where was formerly a faire brick house standing ; and a garden or piece of ground lying behind the same, extending 38 feet from east to west and 95 feet from north to south ; with an adjoining piece at the back of the same, 48 feet from east to west, and 54 feet from north to south ; and which last piece of ground was adjoined south by a piece of ground commonly called the Mulberry Garden, abutting east on Dudley Short's house, as aforesaid ; together with thirteen messuages built on the said parcels of ground, demised by Dudley Short, and then held by Thomas Watson. Two other messuages demised by same, one of them called the Crown ; a piece of ground demised to Ralph Bucknall, who had a stable thereon ; a messuage on the south side of St. Giles's High Street, of John Walter, farrier ; and a back yard to it, with stables and buildings in the same, extending from the said messuage southward to Greyhound Court ; and a piece of ground, part of Greyhound Court, adjoining the south side of one of the stables built as above," etc.

NELL GWYNNE.

Eleanor Gwynne began life in humble circumstances and among humble surroundings. She was born at the Coal Yard, a low alley, on the east (or City) side of Drury Lane, on February 2nd, 1650. Her father, it is said, was Captain Thomas Gwyn, or Gwynne, of an ancient family in Wales. But other accounts tend to show that he was a fruiterer in Covent Garden. Still another account speaks of her father as "a tradesman." Her mother, whose Christian name was also Eleanor, but whose maiden name is not known, lived to see Nell a favourite of the King, and a mother by him of at least two children.

The elder Eleanor Gwynne was accidentally drowned in a pond near the Neat Houses, at Chelsea.

It is pretty certain that Nell's parents belonged to the poorer class of society, and there appears to have been little money available for her education, as to the end of her life she was only able to sign her initials instead of writing her name. Her first means of earning a livelihood were obtained by taking the position of an upper servant in a respectable family. Upon leaving that situation, she ardently wished to try what she could do upon the theatrical stage, and is said to have had an interview with Betterton, who recommended her to further prepare herself by study and practice before entering upon the life of an actress. So great was her love of the theatre, however, and so great her anxiety to improve her knowledge of the player's art, that, when she was no longer able to afford to pay for admission, she adopted the dress and condition of one of the girls who sold oranges in the pit of Drury Lane Theatre, and went there to the performances. Her extraordinary beauty and sharp wit, as well as a certain refined delicacy which was one of the distinguishing features of her character, soon won attention and admiration from all who saw her. Means were soon found by which she gained admission to the stage, where, although her acting was never of the highest order, her talents and figure merited and obtained the most enthusiastic and popular applause.

Samuel Pepys, in his oft-quoted " Diary," gives, under the date of May 1st, 1667, an interesting peep into Nell Gwynne's life. He went to Westminster, "in the way meeting many milk-maids, with their garlands upon their pails, dancing with a fiddler before them ; and saw pretty Nell [Gwynne] standing at her lodgings' door in Drury Lane, in her smock sleeves and bodice, looking upon me : she seemed a mighty pretty creature."

The story of her subsequent life until she became the mistress of Charles II. need not be told here, but it is only fair to add that the smiles of fortune did not make her indifferent to the sorrows and needs of the poor, as is so often the case with those who rise from obscurity to positions of power and wealth. She was instrumental in the establishment of Chelsea Hospital, and numerous other benevolent acts show the natural kindness of her heart.

Nell Gwynne died of apoplexy in November, 1687, in her thirty-eighth year. She left many charitable bequests, and on the night of November 17th, 1687, she was buried, according to her own request, in the church of St. Martin-in-the-Fields. Dr. Tennison, afterwards Archbishop of Canterbury, preached her funeral sermon, in which he said much to her praise, but the sermon does not appear ever to have been printed, and unfortunately it gave an opportunity for bigots and some of Dr. Tennison's personal enemies to speak maliciously of the good Doctor's intentions. That an eminent ecclesiastical personage should presume to preach a funeral sermon upon a woman whose life was perhaps not quite what it ought to have been, was accounted a grave offence and later on it seemed to stand in the way of Tennison's preferment. But

wiser and more generous counsels prevailed, and, as we have just remarked,
Dr. Tennison in process of time was advanced to the archiepiscopal throne of
Canterbury.

THE COCKPIT THEATRE.

This theatre was situated in Drury Lane, about half-way down, on the
site of a small court which was known as "Cockpit Alley," and afterwards as
"Pitt Place." The spot is now occupied by model lodging-houses.

It is not known at what date the Cockpit Theatre was first built.
Indeed, if one may judge by the name it bore, it seems highly probable that
it was originally intended, not for theatrical representations, but for the cruel
sport of cock-fighting, then so much in fashion.

In the year 1617 it is described as having been lately erected, so we
should probably be right in ascribing its establishment either to the first or
second decade of the seventeenth century. Whatever may have been the
exact date of its building, it is certain that it was used for theatrical purposes
before the year 1617. In that year it was pulled down by the mob, for some
unknown offence, and the dresses of the actors were torn to pieces. The
Cockpit was a private and aristocratic theatre, and it has been suggested that
jealousy of its privileges as such may have had something to do with the
riot.

The house was soon rebuilt, and it is probable that in the name of the
Phœnix, which was then given to it, there was an allusion to the rapidity
with which it made its appearance out of the ruins of the old demolished
building. Success evidently attended the new theatre, for we find that in the
year 1623 the company acting there liberally gave twenty pounds towards
rebuilding the Parish Church of St. Giles. This sum is expressly stated to
have been the donation of "the plaiers of the Cockpitt Plaiehouse," and we
may from that fairly conclude that a theatre whose performers were rich enough
to spare so large a gift was in very comfortable and prosperous circumstances
as far as financial matters were concerned.

The Cockpit, or Phœnix (for the theatre appears to have been called by
both names), was one of the six theatres licensed by the Government in the
reign of Charles I., and its performances were continued until the year 1648,
when they were suppressed by ordinance of Parliament.

ELEANOR GWYNN.
From an Original Picture in the Possession of Mr. Thane

From an entry in the Churchwardens' accounts, under the date 1646, it appears probable that the theatre was made use of as a school for children, as it is there recorded that sixpence was paid to "the teacher at the Cockpitt of the children." Of course it is quite possible that the employment of the building for this purpose did not interfere with the regular theatrical performances for which the place was rebuilt, as the school might easily have been held at such times as the theatre was not engaged for performances.

In the year 1658 Sir William Davenant opened the Cockpit Theatre with an entertainment entitled "The Cruelty of the Spaniards in Peru," expressed, as the advertisement sets forth, " by vocal and instrumental musicke, and by art of perspective in scenes ; represented daily at the Cockpit in Drury lane, 1658."

This theatre is remarkable as the house in which Betterton made his first appearance as an actor before the public. This interesting event took place in 1659, Betterton being at that time not much more than twenty years of age ; but notwithstanding his youth, he immediately gave proof of genius and merit, and won great praise and applause for his share in the representation of "The Loyal Subject," "The Wild Goose Chase," "The Spanish Curate," and several other plays of Beaumont and Fletcher, which were then the pieces most in vogue.

In 1660 the theatre had to pay a fine of twopence a day to the parish poor, for every day when there was acting there.

Little, if anything, seems to be known about the size or form of the theatre, but its entertainments are described, about the year 1642, as being of an inferior kind, and its audiences of a lower degree, than those of some of the other contemporary playhouses.

The following is extracted from one of the newspapers, under the date of February 18th, 1814 : "At the Cock-Pit, St. Giles's, whilst preparations were making for the setting-to of the cocks, Mr. Thorpe, a well-known respectable character, had taken his seat in the front of the pit, and offered a bet of ten guineas. He was observed to lean his head forward, and appeared somewhat ill. He made a kind of moan, and instantly his colour changed, and he was a corpse. Surgical aid was ineffectual. Half-an-hour before his death he had said, ' The last time I was here I said, if ever I attended the pit again, I hoped I should die there.' The deceased was opulent, and between 50 and 60 years of age."

6

DRURY LANE.

Hoole, the translator of Tasso, was born in a hackney-coach, which was
conveying his mother to Drury Lane Theatre, whither she was going to witness
the performance of the tragedy of " Timanthes," which had been written by her
husband.   Hoole died in the year 1839, at a very advanced age.   In early
life he figured among the literary characters that adorned the last century,
and for some years before his death had outlived most of the persons who
frequented the *conversazioni* of Dr. Johnson.

The neighbourhood of Drury Lane will be long remembered by the
readers of Dickens's novels as the locality of Mr. Swiveller's apartments.
Although not the most aristocratic district in the world, there were doubtless
certain redeeming features which recommended it.   Unfortunately, however,
many of its delights were lost upon Mr. Swiveller, inasmuch as his pecuniary
embarrassments closed for him some of the streets while the shops were open.
" This dinner to-day," he says, " closes Long Acre.   I bought a pair of boots
in Great Queen Street last week, and made that no thoroughfare.   There's
only one avenue to the Strand left open now, and I shall have to stop up that
to-night with a pair of gloves.   The roads are closing so fast in every direction that in about a month's time, unless my aunt sends me a remittance, I
shall have to go three or four miles out of town to get over the way."

ANCIENT BATH, ENDELL STREET.

At the rear of Nos. 23 and 25, Endell Street, there are some considerable
remains of an ancient bath, probably dating from the seventeenth century.
Formerly a copious spring of pure water, remarkable for its coolness and
ferruginous qualities, kept up a constant supply sufficient for the bath.   Its
medicinal properties were commonly supposed to be of considerable benefit to
persons affected with rheumatic complaints, and it is probable that this bath
was constructed for the purpose of securing the use of those supposed benefits
more effectually.

At what date the virtues of the spring were first detected it is impossible
to say, but it seems pretty certain that at the latter part of the seventeenth, or
the beginning of the eighteenth century the earth was dug out round the

spring, and over it was built a lofty domed apartment, about 12 feet by
10 feet area, and about 24 feet in height from the floor to the crown of
the roof. The floor of the bath was paved with squares of marble, alter-.
nately black and white, and the sides were covered with Dutch tiles, some
white, and some with blue-and-white designs upon them. To secure the bath
from leakage more effectually, sheets of copper were inserted under the flooring
and wall-tiles.

There was a dressing-room near at hand, from whence was a descent of
several steps to the bath. Light was admitted to this room by narrow sky-
lights, and to the bath by means of a narrow window in the crown of the roof,
and four small circular windows around it. Upon one side of the bath there
was a platform from which bathers could plunge into the water, and altogether
the place seems to have been fitted up with a considerable amount of attention
to convenience and elegance. Close by the bath-room proper there have
been found traces of sweating-rooms, which were formerly heated by hot-air
flues.

The house which formerly stood where the present ironmonger's premises
now are was an ancient one, and in olden days was known as No. 3, Belton
Street. It is said to have been inhabited by a medical man whose patients
made use of the waters of the bath.

There is a tradition that this bath was a favourite resort of Queen Anne,
and indeed it is known among old inhabitants as Queen Anne's Bath; but
there does not appear to be any evidence, except such as is purely traditional,
that Her Majesty was ever in any way connected with the place.

A few years before 1846 the spring which fed the bath was cut off by
the construction of some sewers in the vicinity, and after that the supply of
water for the bath was derived from the New River Company.

In the year 1846 the house known as No. 3, Old Belton Street, together
with the bath in the rear, was taken on a lease by Mr. John King, ironmonger,
and upon that occasion the old bath first ceased to be used as such. The
space proved of greater value for storage than to keep as a mere curiosity, and
therefore Mr. King set about suiting it to the purpose which he had in view.
He constructed a wooden floor upon the same level as that of his shop, which
cut the bath into two useful-sized rooms. The upper part is used as a work-
shop, and the lower part as a store-room for iron bars and other goods. It is
much to be regretted that the floor of the old bath has in this way become

hidden beneath a deposit of rubbish.   But Mr. King deserves the thanks of all antiquarians for the care he has taken of this curious bath, and the courteous kindness with which he is ready to impart information respecting it or to show it to those who are interested in it.

It may be added that in ancient times Old Belton Street was reached by an entrance under a low archway, which effectually excluded all vehicles which were heavily laden with any bulky materials, such as hay and straw.

CHAPTER VII.

LINCOLN'S INN FIELDS.

" Where Lincoln's Inn, wide Space, is rail'd around,
Cross not with venturous Step; there oft is found
The lurking Thief, who, while the Daylight shone,
Made the Walls echo with his begging Tone:
That Crutch, which late Compassion mov'd shall wound
Thy bleeding Head, and fell thee to the Ground,
Though thou art tempted by the Linkman's Call,
Yet trust him not along the lonely Wall;
In the Mid-way he'll quench the flaming Brand,
And share the Booty with the pilfering Band.
Still keep the public Street where oily Rays,
Shot from the Crystal Lamp, o'erspread the Ways."

GAY's " *Trivia.*"

 CURIOUS hoard of Roman coins was discovered in Lincoln's Inn Fields about the year 1750. It consisted of several hundreds of copper pieces of the Lower Empire, the variety of which did not exceed three or four, and those varieties were of a very common type, of no sort of real value. The greater part of them were either of Victorinus or of Tetricus. The coins, though in bad preservation, seemed not to have been much injured by long currency, and were probably placed in the urn in which they were found, soon after they came from the mint. They were rudely formed, and a writer in the *Gentleman's Magazine* (February, 1788) was of the opinion that they were made in France.

The urn in which the coins were found appears to have been carved out of stone, and was thirteen inches high, and nine inches broad.   Its inside was cylindrical, and its outside had four sides, each of which was elaborately carved with various devices, including two human figures, and an altar, whereon was perched a bird (probably an eagle), and close by there was also a representation of a bow and arrow.   The four upper corners were decorated with a sort of scroll-work ornament.

In ancient times this spot was called Fikattesfeld, Ficetsfeld, Fiket's Field, and also the Templar's Field.   Mention of the place in hospital deeds shows it to have been actually a field at that time, but whether it was merely pasture-land or not is doubtful.   It is certain that some part of it was planted and laid out as a promenade, and from a petition respecting it which was presented to Parliament during the Commonwealth, we learn that about the year 1376 this field was a common walking and sporting place for the clerks of Chancery, apprentices, students of the law, and citizens of London.   The same document mentions that one Roger Leget was imprisoned for setting " iron engines called caltrappes" in this field with malicious intent.

Fikattesfeld continued to be a place of recreation and promenade, for the students of Lincoln's Inn and the public, until it was first built upon at the end of the reign of Queen Elizabeth.   Before that time it had become intersected by irregular paths.

In the year 1618 James I. granted a Commission to dispose of the whole, the ordering of which was entrusted to the Lord Chancellor Bacon, with the Earls of Pembroke, Worcester, Arundel, and others, assisted by the King's architect, Inigo Jones.   This eminent architect drew the plan of a magnificent square, and gave it the exact dimensions of the Great Pyramid of Egypt, but it is probable that only the west side of it was completed at that time, the remaining three sides being either unbuilt or occupied by cottages and mean buildings.

There were three fields or waste places, viz., Purse Field, Fiket's Field, and Cup Field, occupying the square, and a common horse-pool was constructed therein.   The whole place became in time much neglected ; rubbish was shot there in so great quantity as to deprive the inhabitants of their ancient rights of recreating themselves in the open spaces, and in wet weather the paths were miry and impassable.

It was resolved, in the year 1657, that two further sides should be built which, with Portugal Row, would complete the square. A water-house, not exceeding ten yards square, was to be built in the middle of the square.

Notwithstanding these improvements, the space of open ground itself was much neglected, and was the common resort of the vicious and outcast members of society.

In the year 1735 trustees were appointed by Parliament to superintend the railing-in and planting of the square. A pool or reservoir of water was constructed in the centre, and the whole place was made orderly and decent.

Lincoln's Inn Fields was in 1683 the scene of an ever-memorable event in the history of England. William Lord Russell, who, upon wholly insufficient evidence, had been found guilty of high treason, by reason of his supposed connection with the Rye House Plot, was brought here to be executed. His lordship's residence was Southampton House, a mansion occupying the north side of Bloomsbury Square.

As soon as the plot was discovered, and Lord Russell was alleged to have had some secret part in it, a messenger of the Council was sent to wait at his gate, in order to stop him if he attempted to go out. Lord Russell had walked for several hours about his grounds, and had he so chosen, might easily have escaped from the rear of his house, which was not watched.

The object of his enemies in stationing the messenger there was clearly to injure his character. Lady Rachel Russell, Lord Russell's excellent and devoted wife, went to visit some friends in order to have the benefit of their advice. Lord Russell made no attempt to escape, and as soon as the King arrived in London he was taken before him and the Council, imprisoned, and after a most unfair trial, sentenced to death.

It is said that some proposed that Lord Russell's execution should take place in Southampton (now Bloomsbury) Square, but the King opposed it as indecent ; so it was decided that he should be executed in Lincoln's Inn Fields, that being the most convenient place near Newgate, the place of his lordship's confinement.

It is unnecessary in this place to enter into any particulars as to the Rye House Plot, or of the part which Lord Russell is said to have taken in it. That belongs to the province of the historian, and has been frequently discussed. There are, however, certain details as to Lord Russell himself which deserve our attention, especially as they are closely associated with the locality of which it is our immediate business to treat.

Some very interesting particulars of the last few hours of Russell's life are contained in Bishop Burnet's " History of his own Time," an account of particular value and importance, as the work of one who had the advantage of contemporary observation and personal intercourse with the men of weight and action during a stirring period of the seventeenth and eighteenth centuries.

On the morning of July 21st, 1683, he went into his chamber six or seven times, and prayed by himself. He drank a little tea and some sherry. He wound up his watch, and said now he had done with time, and was going to eternity. He asked what he should give the executioner. Bishop Burnet told him ten guineas. He said, with a smile, it was a pretty thing to give a fee to have his head cut off.

Accompanied by Bishops Tillotson and Burnet, he went in the coach to the place of execution. Some of the crowd that filled the streets wept, while others insulted ; he was touched with a tenderness that the one gave him, but did not seem at all provoked by the other. He was singing psalms a great part of the way, and said he hoped to sing better very soon. As he observed the great crowds of people all the way, he said to his companions, " I hope I shall quickly see a much better assembly."

When he came to the scaffold he walked about it four or five times ; then turned to the sheriffs and delivered his paper. He protested he had always been far from any designs against the King's life or government. He prayed God would preserve both, and the Protestant religion. He wished all Protestants might love one another, and not make way for Popery by their animosities.

Lord Russell's execution gave rise to much dispute and contention, and there is no doubt that with the people generally it was an unpopular event. His speech was printed and sold in the streets within an hour after his execution. It was supposed that it was the work of Bishop Burnet, but that prelate, in the " History of his own Times," distinctly disclaims any such authorship.

Among those productions of the printing-press which originated in this sanguinary event was a curious broadside, in the form of a satirical dialogue, entitled " The Night-Walker of Bloomsbury ; being the Result of several late Consultations between a Vintner, Judge, Tallow-Chandler, a Brace of Fishmongers, and a Printer, &c. In a Dialogue between Ralph and Will. . . London : Printed by J. Grantham, MDCLXXXIII."

TRIAL OF LORD WILLIAM RUSSELL.

1. *Sheriff of London.* 5. *Sir F. Pemberton.* 9. *Baron Gower.*   13. *Serj't Jefferies.* 17. *Lord Howard.*   21. *Lord Rofroll.*   25. *Marquis of Halifax.*
2. *Judge Wingham.*   6. *Sir W. Montague.* 10. *Sir W. Leroy, Recorder.* *Lord.* 14. *Ward.* 18. *Col. Rumsey.*   22. *Lord R't Gentleman.* 26. *M'r Howard.*
3. *Wilkins;*   7. *Judge Adams;*   11. *Sir R. Sawyer, Att. Gen.l* *Rofroll.* 15. *Holt.* 19. *Doughurd.*   23. *Lord R't Cavendish.* 27. *Rev. M'r Villiams.*
4. *—— Levings*   8. *—— Jones;*   12. *Sir H. Finch, Sol.t Gen.l* 16. *Ditlesforu Goward.* 20. *Lady Rofroll.* 24. *Duke of Somerset.* 28. *Rev. M'r Burnet.*
                                                                                                                                                        29. *Serj't at the Tower.*

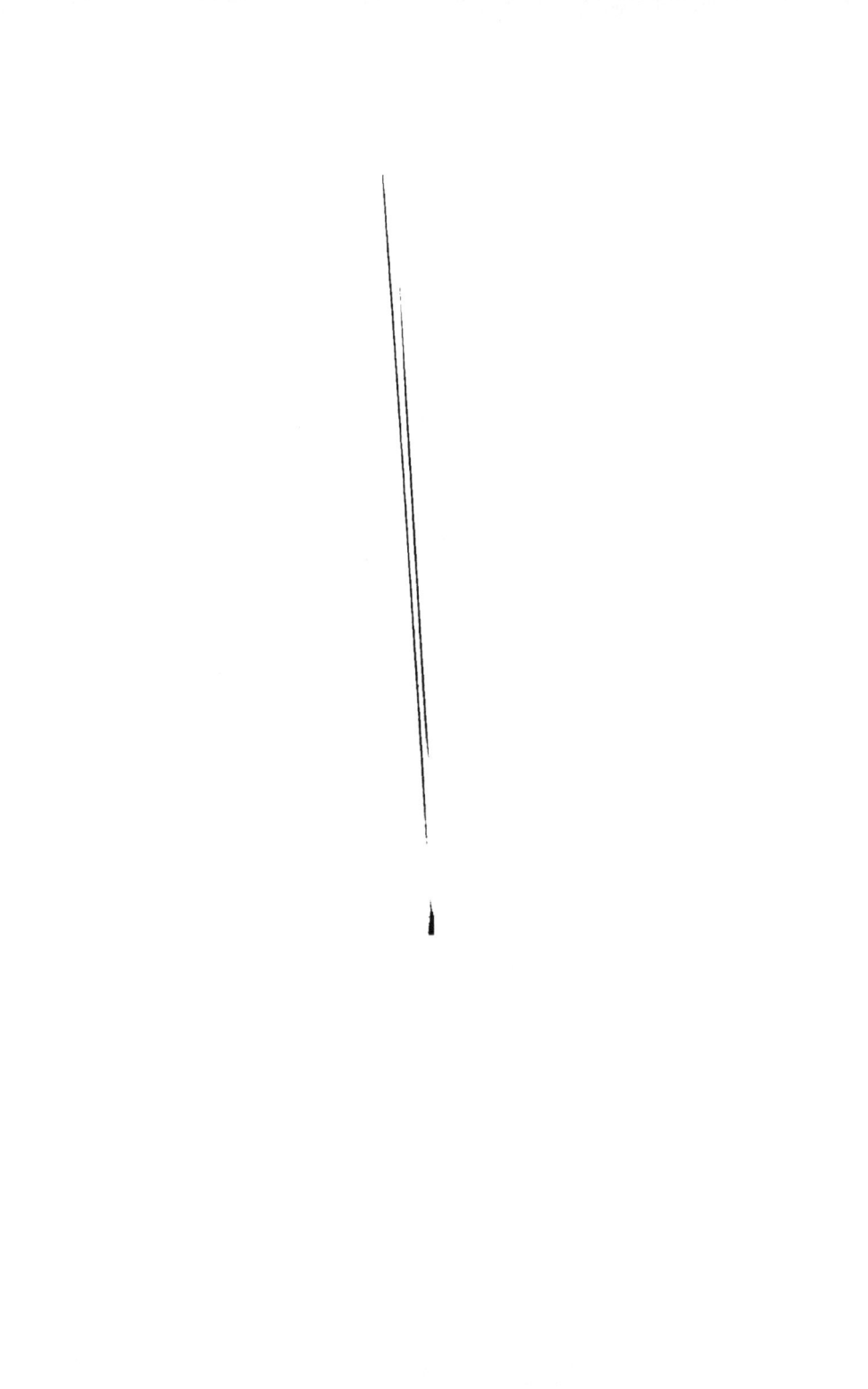

The authorship of this very curious broadside is ascribed to Langley Curtis, who is said to have been sentenced to pay £100, and to stand in the pillory.

In Lincoln's Inn Fields, Lilly, the astrologer, when a servant of Mr. Wright's, at the corner house over against Strand Bridge, spent his idle hours in bowling with "Wat the cobler, Dick the blacksmith, and such like companions;" and here Blount tells us, in his Law Dictionary (fol. 1670), that he had seen the game played by idle persons of "the Wheel of Fortune," "wherein they turn about a thing like the hand of a clock," which some had supposed, he says, to have been the same as the old game of "closh," forbidden by a statute in the reign of Edward IV.

The following were among the eminent inhabitants of Lincoln's Inn Fields in former times :—

The Earls of Bristol and Sandwich, in the time of Charles II.; Sir Richard and Lady Fanshawe, in a house on the north side ; Duke of Newcastle, in Newcastle House ; the great Lord Somers, in Powis House ; Lord Kenyon, at No. 35, in 1805 ; Lord Erskine, at No. 36, in 1805 ; and Spencer Perceval, at No. 57, in 1805.

It is related of Lord Chancellor Finch, afterwards Earl of Nottingham, an eminent public character in the reign of Charles II., that after he lost his wife he comforted himself by taking the Great Seal to bed with him, and that thus he saved it from the fate which then befell the mace, and afterwards the Great Seal itself, in the time of Lord Chancellor Thurlow. About one in the morning of November 7th, 1677, the Lord Chancellor's mace was stolen out of his house in Queen Street. The seal was under the Lord Chancellor's pillow.

This daring act was done by one named Thomas Sadler, who somehow got the knowledge where the Lord Chancellor's servants usually placed the mace and purse, the insignia of that illustrious office. Without weighing the danger or considering the consequences, he resolved to make himself master of them, and with that intention, he and two of his confederates, about 5 o'clock one Sunday morning, were observed by a person, who afterwards gave evidence at the trial, to be walking up and down that street, waiting about, as it was supposed, for an opportunity of putting their design into execution. But no good opportunity occurring, the scheme was put off until the following Tuesday night. It was thought that an entrance to his Lordship's balcony was effected by means of a rope. From thence the thieves managed to get upon a ledge jutting out of the wall, and along that to the window of the closet wherein the objects of their wish were kept. Then they broke a pane of glass, and so were able to open the casement, and take away the precious but fatal prize. The plunderers were extremely elated with the success of their scheme, and so full of insolence and vanity that while passing through Lincoln's Inn Fields one bore the mace openly on his shoulders, and another the purse before him, whilst, with hat cocked and arms akimbo, Sadler walked behind, strutting with grandeur.

Sadler and one of his associates repaired to a lodging in Knightrider Street, where they had formerly lived, and in taking off the fringe and jewels from the purse, scattered several small pieces of gold about the room, which led to the detection of the crime. The mace, which they hid in a cupboard, was discovered by the daughter of the hostess, who, seeing the coronet or upper part only, called out to her mother that the gentleman had got the King's crown in the closet. A watch was set, and the culprit was brought to justice, and soon after hanged on Tyburn tree.

The writer of a contemporary account of this singular affair suggested the following lines as an epitaph for this notorious man :—

> "Here Sadler lies! Reader! come not too near,
> The nimble Ghost may pilfer still, we fear;
> His presence fifteen times did Newgate grace;
> But died oppressed with a too ponderous Mace:
> So used to make all doors before him fly,
> His very coffin dreads a Burglary,
> And Pluto fears he'll jilt his treasury."

THE DUKE'S THEATRE.

We have already mentioned the existence of a row of buildings upon the south side of Lincoln's Inn Fields, previous to the year 1657, called Portugal Row, a name given in allusion to Catherine of Portugal, the Queen of Charles II.

This appears at one time to have been a somewhat grand quarter, several large houses being built there. In one part of Portugal Row there was a tennis-court, which later on served as the site for a theatre. This first theatre of the three which at various times have been built in Lincoln's Inn Fields was called the Duke's Theatre, from the Duke of York, who was its chief patron, and also the Opera, on account of its musical performances.

In the year 1662, a renewal of the patent having been obtained from Charles II., Sir William Davenant opened the theatre with his operatic piece "The Siege of Rhodes." In 1671-72 the actors removed to Dorset Gardens, and the King's company, burnt out of Drury Lane, took possession of it for a year, after which it reverted to its former use, and became again a tennis-court.

In or about the year 1668 the Earl of Rochester lived in a house next door to the Duke's Theatre.

Thomas Betterton, the famous actor, played at this theatre in 1661, and when it was reopened, in 1662, and for some time afterwards.

Pepys went to see Betterton act at the Duke's Theatre several times; for instance, under date of July 28th, 1664, he writes in his "Diary"—

"Home and then abroad, and seeing the Bondman upon the posts, I went to the Duke's House and saw it acted. It is true for want of practice, they have many of them forgot their parts a little; but Betterton and my poor Ianthe, outdo all the world."

Again, on August 13th in the same year, Pepys went to see a new play "at the Duke's House, of 'Henry the Fifth,' a most noble play, writ by my Lord Orrery," and he appears to have been particularly pleased with it. Several other visits are recorded in the "Diary," of this methodical and observant man.

It is said by Malone that scenery was first introduced upon the public stage, by Sir William Davenant, at this theatre in Lincoln's Inn Fields, and that it was afterwards much improved, with the addition of curious machines, by Betterton, at his new theatre in Dorset Gardens.

About the month of March or April, 1695, the tennis-court was once more turned into a theatre. It was opened with Congreve's "Love for Love," Betterton taking the character of Valentine. "This play," says Downes, "was superior in success to most of its precedent plays; it was extraordinarily well acted, and took 13 nights successively."

Early in the eighteenth century the theatre was taken down, and a new one, erected on its site for Christopher Rich, was opened in 1714, by John Rich. In 1732 Rich abandoned it for Covent Garden, and it was used for such purposes as the proprietors could find for it.

In 1735 Mr. Gifford took possession, keeping it open for about two years, after which it was closed. Tradition has handed down the following story in connection with the final shutting up of the theatre: "Upon a representation of the pantomime of ' Harlequin and Dr. Faustus,' when a tribe of demons, necessary for the piece, were assembled, a supernumerary devil was observed, who, not approving of going out in a complaisant manner at the door, to show a devil's trick, flew up to the ceiling, made his way through the tiling, and tore away one-fourth of the house, which circumstance so affrighted the manager that the proprietor had not courage to open the house ever afterwards."

The building then became a barracks, then an auction-room, and afterwards the chinaware repository of Messrs. Copeland and Spode, being finally taken down in 1848 for the enlargement of the Museum of the College of Surgeons, the front of which building is adorned with some columns which are said to have formed part of the theatre.

NEWCASTLE HOUSE.

This lofty and spacious brick building was erected in 1686, by the Marquis of Powis, from whom it received its original name of Powis House. The architect is said to have been Captain William Wynde. It has stone quoins and dressings and a grand double flight of stone steps. Upon the purchase of the house by the Duke of Newcastle, the well-known minister of George II., it was called Newcastle House.

When it was occupied by Sir Nathan Wright, the Lord Keeper, the Government had the intention, or at least the proposal was suggested, to purchase Newcastle House, and settle it officially on the Great Seal.

THE FIFTH OF NOVEMBER.

In former days the Fifth of November used to be kept in this district with considerable enthusiasm, and a bonfire on a large scale was annually made in the open space opposite Newcastle House. It is said that old people remember when upwards of two hundred cart-loads of fuel were brought to make and feed the bonfire, and more than fifty " guys " were burnt upon gibbets between 8 and 12 o'clock at night.

SOANE MUSEUM.

This useful institution is situated at No. 13, Lincoln's Inn Fields, the former residence of Sir John Soane, an architect of considerable eminence. He rose from humble circumstances, being the son of a bricklayer, and was born near Reading, in 1752. Having acquired a practical knowledge of the profession of architecture, he studied in the schools of the Royal Academy, where he obtained first a silver medal, and in 1776 the gold medal for his design for a triumphal bridge. After that he travelled for three years in Italy, and upon his return to England he obtained the appointment of architect to the Bank of England. Subsequently he was, in 1791, clerk of the works at St. James's Palace, the Houses of Parliament, and other public buildings, and in 1795 architect to the Department of Woods and Forests. In the same year he was elected an associate, and in 1802 a full member, of the Royal Academy, and in 1806 Professor of Architecture. In 1807 he was appointed clerk of the works at Chelsea Hospital, and erected the new infirmaries, and about the same time the new picture-galleries at Dulwich College. On a commission from the Treasury, he made designs' in 1820 for new law courts, which were afterwards carried out. In 1831 he was knighted, and in 1835 completed the State Paper Office.

Having made a considerable fortune, Sir John Soane built for himself a large house in Lincoln's Inn Fields, which he made a storehouse of art-treasures. He died at this house, at the age of eighty-four, on January 20th, 1837, and was buried in the ground belonging to St. Giles-in-the-Fields, adjoining the old church of St. Pancras.

He left his magnificent collection of art-treasures, with the sanction of a private Act of Parliament, to the nation. At his death 'this Act came into operation ; the trustees named therein entered on their trust, and immediately took the necessary steps for carrying into effect the enactments thereof to the fullest extent of which the funds placed at their disposal by the founder would admit.

The rooms of the house are small, and such a large number of objects are crowded together in three different stories that it is the work of some hours to gain even a superficial view of them. The contents consist of many different kinds of objects, such as architectural ornaments and sculpture of

various kinds and ages, from various parts of the world.   One object deserves
special mention.   It is an Egyptian sarcophagus, said to be the finest ever
found, 9 feet 4 inches in length, 3 feet 8 inches in width, and 2 feet 8
inches in depth, and it is composed of a single block of what is called
Oriental alabaster, or rather, from the examination of mineralogists, of what
is properly called aragonite.   The sides are about 2½ inches thick.   At the
bottom a full-length figure, in profile, representing Isis as guardian of the
dead, is very carefully engraved, the outlines of which, as well as the hiero-
glyphics with which it is entirely covered, have been filled with a black
substance.   The stone is so transparent that when a candle is put into the
sarcophagus it appears of a beautiful red.   This splendid relic, which was
discovered by Belzoni, in 1816, in a tomb in the valley of Beban el Malook,
near Gournou, was brought by him to Alexandria, and subsequently offered
by Mr. Salt to the British Museum for £2,000.   In 1824 it was purchased
by Sir John Soane.   Sir Gardner Wilkinson considered the name inscribed
to be that of Osiris, father of Rameses the Great.

This beautiful sarcophagus had a lid formed entirely out of one piece of
stone, but it was broken into several pieces before it was found by Belzoni.
This cover when placed upon the sarcophagus added 15 inches to its height.
Portions of it have been preserved in the Students' Room.

The cover was probably lifted on to the chest, and placed in position by
means of cords passing through holes, of which three remain ; and to guard
against any accident to the brittle stone, in placing the heavy lid upon the
chest, the edges of both chest and lid were shielded with a thin plate of copper,
some remains of which are still visible.   The date of this curious sarcophagus
has been supposed to be about 1350 B.C., and it is supposed that it was made
to receive the remains of Seti I., of the Nineteenth Dynasty, and father of
Rameses II.

Although it is quite impossible to allude to, or even to enumerate, the
many objects of artistic and architectural beauty which are collected in this
Museum, it would be unpardonable to overlook some of the paintings which
adorn the various apartments.

Among them the pictures by Hogarth deserve first mention.   In the
Picture Room the originals of his series of four pictures representing "An
Election " are exhibited.   The four subjects are " The Entertainment," " The
Canvassing for Votes," " The Polling," and " The Chairing of the Members."

These pictures were painted between the years 1753 and 1758, and purchased of Hogarth by David Garrick, under rather peculiar circumstances, for £200. They were purchased by Sir John Soane, at the sale of Mrs. Garrick's effects in 1823, for 1,650 guineas. In the same room is a very beautiful " View on the Grand Canal at Venice " by Canaletti, said to be the *chef-d'œuvre* of that artist.

Another very important set of pictures is exhibited in the South Drawing-room. This is the well-known series by Hogarth illustrating " The Rake's Progress." They are eight in number, and represent " The Heir," " The Levée," " The Orgies," " The Arrest," " The Marriage," " The Gaming House," " The Prison," and " The Mad House." They were painted about the year 1734, and in 1745 they were sold by auction, at Mr. Hogarth's, in Leicester Fields, and produced twenty-two guineas each ; total, £184 16s. They passed into the hands of Mr. Beckford, of Fonthill, in Wiltshire, and from him they were purchased by Sir John Soane, in the year 1802, for 570 guineas.

ROYAL COLLEGE OF SURGEONS.

The Royal College of Surgeons of England possesses a handsome building on the south side of Lincoln's Inn Fields. The origin of the College can be traced back to the year 1308, when, in the reign of Edward II., Richard was chosen supervisor of the Barbers, one of the City guilds. In 1375 some of the Barbers had come to be Barber-Surgeons, and the Company consisted of two branches, the Barbers who practised shaving, and the Barbers who practised surgery. The Barber-Surgeons were incorporated one of the livery companies of the City of London in the year 1460.

Side by side with the Barbers, the Guild of Surgeons existed, and although always as a small body, they numbered among their members some of the best surgeons of their time. The Surgeons amalgamated with the Barbers' Company in 1540, and after a union of more than two hundred years' standing, they severed themselves from the Barbers and established a new body, called the Surgeons' Company. A site in the Old Bailey was leased from the City authorities, at the comparatively low rental of £53 6s. 8d. per annum, and the Court of Assistants ordered " unanimously that a theatre be the first part of the new intended building, and that the same be erected with.

all possible dispatch." By a foolish blunder the Company forfeited its charter in 1796, and failing to obtain an Act of Parliament for the reconstruction of their Company, the Surgeons were incorporated by a charter of George III. in the year 1800. The premises at the Old Bailey were sold to the City authorities for the sum of £2,100. In the meantime they had purchased for £5,500 a freehold house in Lincoln's Inn Fields, belonging to a Mr. Baldwin. A supplementary charter was granted by George IV. in 1821, and in 1843, Queen Victoria conferred the title of "Royal" upon the College by charter.

THE MUSEUM.

The Hunterian Collection, which forms the basis, and still a large proportion, of the contents of the present Museum of the Royal College of Surgeons of England, was originally arranged in a building which its founder, John Hunter, erected for it in 1784, behind his house in Leicester Square.

John Hunter died on October 16th, 1793, aged sixty-five. By his will he directed that the Museum should be offered, in the first instance, to the British Government, on such terms as might be considered reasonable, and in case of refusal to be sold in one lot, either to some foreign state or as his executors might think proper.

In the year 1799 Parliament voted the sum of £15,000 for the Museum, and an offer of it being made to the Corporation of Surgeons, it was accepted upon the terms proposed by Government.

In 1806 the sum of £15,000 was voted by Parliament in aid of the erection of an edifice for the display and arrangement of the Hunterian Collection. A second grant, of £12,500, was subsequently voted, and upwards of £21,000 having been supplied from the funds of the College, the building was completed in Lincoln's Inn Fields, in which the Museum was opened for the inspection of visitors in the year 1813.

In consequence of the large number of additions, this building became too small for the adequate display and arrangement of its contents ; and more space being at the same time required for the rapidly increasing library, the greater portion of the present building was erected, wholly at the expense of the College, in 1835, at a cost of about £40,000, and the Hunterian and Collegiate Collections were rearranged in what are now called the Western and Middle Museums, which were opened for the inspection of visitors in 1836.

Further enlargement of the building having become necessary by the continued increase of the collection, the College, in 1847, purchased the extensive premises of Mr. Alderman Copeland, in Portugal Street, for the sum of £16,000, and in 1852 proceeded to the erection of the Eastern Museum, at the expense of £25,000, Parliament granting £15,000 in aid thereof. The rearrangement of the specimens was completed, and the additional portion of the building opened to visitors, in 1855.

Many of the additions to the collections of specimens have been presented by Fellows and Members of the College, and other persons interested in scientific pursuits. Among the largest contributions of this kind were the collection presented in 1811 by Sir William Blizard, and that presented in 1851 by Sir Stephen L. Hammick. Among the specimens purchased at various times were those belonging to the following: Sir Ashton Lever, in 1806; Mr. Joshua Brookes, in 1828; Mr. Heaviside, in 1829; Mr. Langstaff, in 1835; Mr. South, in 1835; Mr. Howship and Mr. Taunton, in 1841; Mr. Liston, in 1842; Mr. Walker, in 1843; and deserving of special mention on account of the great number and value of the specimens acquired, those of Sir Astley Cooper, in 1843, and Dr. Barnard Davis, in 1880.

The nucleus of the Histological Collection are several specimens given by Dr. Hunter, and considerable additions to it have been made by purchase from Dr. Tweedy, J. Todd, Mr. Nasmyth, and Professor Lenhossek.

THE LIBRARY.

The Library of the College dates from the year 1800, in July of which year the first grant of a sum, not exceeding £50, was made for Library purposes. It had been the intention of the old Corporation of Surgeons to form a Library, but they failed to carry their intention into effect. In its early years the Library was considerably increased by presentations and bequests of books, the principal donors being Dr. Baillie, Sir Everard Home, Sir Charles Blicke, the widow of Mr. Sharp, Sir Ludford Harvey, Dr. Fleming, Mr. Cotton, and Mr. Long. The Court of Assistants also directed from time to time the expenditure of small sums of money for the purchase of books. Sir Charles Blicke, in the year 1816, invested the sum of £300, the proceeds of which were to be devoted to the same object. By these means extensive purchases were from time to time made, from the libraries of Mr. Pitt, Mr. St. Andre, Sir Anthony Carlisle, and others. The progress of the Library, however, for the first twenty-six years of its existence, was very slow. In the year 1827 and the two following years a large sum of money was spent upon the purchase 'of books for the Library.

In 1835-36 the College was practically rebuilt by Sir Charles Barry, and during that period the Library was closed, and the books were packed in cases and stored in the Museum Gallery.

On February 15th, 1837, the Library was reopened, the rooms in the new building allotted to this department being the present Reading-room and the Librarian's room.   In the year 1888, owing to the munificent gift of Sir Erasmus Wilson, the Council were enabled to increase the Library accommodation, and to improve and redecorate the existing building.   The residence of the Conservator of the Museum, at the east end of the College, was pulled down, and the building erected on its site was devoted to Library purposes. Additional rooms were built, and the new building has room for shelving 26,000 volumes.   Improvements were also effected in the lighting, heating, and decoration of the building ; and owing to the increased room for the books, it was possible to rearrange them in such a way as to make them more accessible to readers.

The first catalogue of the books in the Library was issued in 1831.   A classed catalogue was prepared by Dr. Willis, and was in use in MS. for some years.   In 1838 a synopsis of it was printed, and the work itself was published in the year 1843.   In 1853 an index of subjects was issued, and four supplements to the author-catalogue were published between the years 1840 and 1860.   Since the last-named date no catalogue of the Library has been printed, but preparations are now being made for a catalogue of the books arranged under both the authors and subjects.   This catalogue is being compiled upon cards, which are useful for reference now, and will serve as copy for the printer later on.

This Library is particularly rich in the Transactions of societies, and in periodical publications relating to medicine, surgery, and accessory sciences. It also contains a fine series of illustrated works on zoology, anatomy, etc., and a good collection of portraits of members of the medical profession.   The total number of volumes in the Library on July 1st, 1889, was 42,372.

"THE OLD CURIOSITY SHOP."

It has been supposed by some that "the Old Curiosity Shop," rendered famous by the immortal Dickens, was situated in the neighbourhood of

Portugal Street, Lincoln's Inn Fields; but the idea is entirely conjectural, and indeed it is rendered very improbable that it still exists (even if it ever did exist there), by the fact that Dickens expressly says, in his novel, " The old house had long ago been pulled down, and a fine broad road was in its place."

ANECDOTE OF KNELLER AND RADCLIFFE.

Horace Walpole, in his " Anecdotes of Painting in England," tells a very good story about Sir Godfrey Kneller, the celebrated painter, and Dr. Radcliffe, the eminent physician. In Great Queen Street Kneller lived next door to Radcliffe. Kneller was fond of flowers, and had a fine collection. As there was great intimacy between him and the physician, he permitted the latter to have a door into his garden; but Radcliffe's servants gathering and destroying the flowers, Kneller sent him word he must shut up the door. Radcliffe replied peevishly, " Tell him he may do anything with it but paint it." " And I," answered Sir Godfrey, " can take anything from him but physic."

FREEMASONS' HALL.

The ground upon which the old Freemasons' Hall now stands and the original 'Freemasons' Tavern formerly stood was a plot of ground and premises consisting of two large commodious dwelling-houses and a large garden, in the possession of Philip Carteret Webb, Esq., the real value of which is said to have been £3,205. The Freemasons being in want of such a space upon which to build a hall, arrangements were made in 1774 for the conveyance of the premises, the price paid for the freehold premises being £3,200. Lord Petre, who had succeeded the Duke of Beaufort in the office of Grand Master, the Dukes of Beaufort and Chandos, Earl Ferrers, and Lord Viscount Dudley and Ward were appointed trustees for the Society.

On the 22nd February, 1775, the Hall Committee reported to the Grand Lodge that a plan had been proposed and approved for raising £5,000 to complete the designs of the Society, by granting annuities for lives, with benefit of survivorship; a plan now known under the name of tontine. It was accordingly resolved that there should be one hundred lives, at fifty pounds each; that the whole premises belonging to the Society in Great Queen

Street, with the hall to be built thereon, should be vested in trustees, as a security to subscribers, who should be paid five per cent. for their money advanced, the whole interest amounting to £250 per annum ; that this interest should be divided among the subscribers and the survivors or survivor of them, and upon the death of the last survivor the whole to determine for the benefit of the Society. In less than three months the scheme was completed, and the trustees of the Society conveyed the estate to the trustees of the Tontine.

On the 1st May, 1775, the foundation-stone of the new Hall was laid by the Grand Master, Lord Petre, in solemn form, in the presence of a numerous company of the brethren. The Grand Master, preceded by the Grand Stewards, past and present grand officers, in their regalia, and an excellent band of martial music, went in procession to the ground about noon, when his Lordship, attended by his deputy, wardens, secretary, treasurer, and architect, went down into the trench, and laid the stone with the usual forms. Within the foundation-stone was deposited a plate, upon which was engraved a Latin inscription. An anthem was then sung by brother Du Bellamy, and an oration pronounced by brother James Bottomly. After the ceremony was completed the company returned in procession in coaches to Leathersellers' Hall, where an elegant entertainment was provided on the occasion, and it was at this meeting that the office of Grand Chaplain was first instituted.

The building of the Hall went on so rapidly that it was completed in little more than twelve months. It was opened on May 23rd, 1776, and dedicated, in solemn form, to Masonry, Virtue, and Universal Charity and Benevolence, in the presence of a brilliant assembly of the brethren and great numbers of strangers. A new ode, written and set to music for the occasion, was performed before a number of ladies who honoured the Society with their company on that day. An exordium on Masonry was given by the Grand Secretary, and an excellent oration was given upon the same occasion by the Grand Chaplain, Dr. William Dodd. The oration was printed and published by the sanction of the Society, and dedicated to Lord Petre, Grand Master, and Rowland Holt, Esq., Deputy Grand Master.

The architect was Thomas Sandby, and the ceiling, which is a very fine and elaborate piece of work, was designed by Richard Cox.

In connection with the original Freemasons' Hall there was a coffee-house, called the Freemasons' Coffee-house. That house was rebuilt in the years 1788-9, Messrs. Sandby and Tyler being the architects, and Mr. Hobson being the builder.

In the year 1813 a union was brought about, by the Dukes of Sussex, Kent, and Athole, between the rival Grand Lodges of England, formerly designated " Ancients" and " Moderns," thenceforth known as the United Grand Lodge of England.

In the years 1830-1 a new masonic hall, called the Temple, was built, from the designs of the famous Sir John Soane, but it was demolished in 1867, in order to make way for the present banqueting-hall in Freemasons' Tavern. A sketch of the Temple was published in the *Freemasons' Quarterly Review*, 1838, p. 476.

The present building of Freemasons' Hall, exclusive of the old Hall proper, is little more than twenty years old, the foundation-stone having been laid by Lord Zetland on April 27th, 1864, and the inauguration ceremony taking place on April 14th, 1869.

In the year 1883 a fire partially destroyed the roof and the richly ornamented ceiling of the old Hall. This damage was, however, skilfully repaired, under the direction of Sir Horace Jones, then architect to the Grand Lodge, and the Hall now presents as fine a spectacle as it did during the early part of the present century.

The old Hall, from which the present extensive building takes its name, is a very fine room, 92 feet in length, 43 feet in breadth, and upwards of 60 feet in height. We have mentioned the ceiling, beautifully moulded and richly gilt. The walls are also rich with gold and colour. At the end opposite the entrance-door there is a dais, raised by two steps above the floor of the Hall. Upon the dais are placed the throne of the Grand Master and other seats occupied by Masons of high rank when grand meetings are held. Immediately behind the throne of the Grand Master there is a very beautiful alcove, of a semicircular form, in which is placed a noble statue, in white marble, of the Duke of Sussex, G.M., executed by G. H. Bailey, R.A. The remaining part of the Hall is for the use of the Grand Stewards and the other members of the Grand Lodge. There is a fine organ near the dais, hidden from the Hall by some delicate open metal-work. There are a good many full-length portraits of past Grand Masters hanging around the walls. They are copies of the originals which were too much damaged by the late fire to admit of a satisfactory restoration.

A gallery formerly occupied the sides of the Hall where the dais now is, but it has been removed many years, and no trace now remains of it.

The windows, which are purposely placed very high in the walls, in order to ensure strict privacy during the celebration of the mystic rites of Masonry, do not admit sufficient light to show the room to advantage without the aid of artificial illumination, but they leave large wall-spaces, of which the artist has taken advantage in the exquisite ornamental workmanship by which they and the ceiling are covered.

Numerous private lodges are held in the newer apartments connected with Freemasons' Hall, and situated upon different floors of the building.

GREAT QUEEN STREET CHAPEL.

In the year 1692 steps were taken to ascertain what number of pews would be taken by the gentry of Lincoln's Inn Fields and its vicinity, in case a new chapel should be erected in that neighbourhood.

The following account of Great Queen Street Chapel was given in 1720, in Strype's edition of Stow's "Survey of London:" "There is a Chapel in Great Queen Street in this Parish of St. Giles lately erected by the Means of one William Raguley pretending to be a Minister of the Church of England. Wherein for some Time he preached without Licence or Authority, consecrated the Holy Sacrament, and administered the same. Wherefore in this Chapel the Bishops of London and Peterborough caused two Declarations to be read " (December 22nd, 1706).

Unsuccessful negotiations were made by the Church people, in the year 1706, for the purchase of this chapel, and after a time the place appears to have been pulled down. On the site where this chapel stood the Wesleyan Methodists, in the year 1811, built a commodious place of worship, which is called Great Queen Street Chapel. The architect, Mr. W. Jenkins, was unable at the time to complete his design of an appropriate architectural façade, and the entrance to the chapel was through an ordinary dwelling-house. In the year 1841 the present portico and front were added. The pediment is supported by four Ionic columns, above which is a Venetian window, orna-mented with Corinthian columns and pilasters, and a semicircular moulding enclosing the words "ERECTED A.D. MDCCCLI."

CHAPTER VIII.

LINCOLN'S INN.

HE name of this Inn of Court is derived from Henry de Lacy, Earl of Lincoln, whose town house or inn occupied a considerable portion of the present Inn of Court, which bears both his name and arms. Two Inns of Chancery are attached, viz., Furnival's Inn and Thavies Inn. Lincoln's Inn was probably constituted a regular Inn of Court not long after the death of the Earl of Lincoln, which occurred in 1312. The buildings of the inn, however, are of no greater antiquity than Tudor times. The Gate-house, which is a fine specimen of late red brickwork of a Gothic type, and is now said to be almost the only example of that sort of work to be found in London, was built by Sir Thomas Lovell, and bears the date 1518. Just above the date over the gateway are three shields of arms, each in a square compartment. The first are the arms of Henry de Lacy, Earl of Lincoln ; the central shield bears the royal arms of England ; and the shield on the other side of it bears the arms of the actual builder of the Gatehouse, Sir Thomas Lovell. The original doors of oak, put up in 1564, still remain.

The principal gateway and the two flanking towers on either side stand just as they were originally built, but the windows have been altered to suit the taste of modern improvers. The red brick buildings adjoining this gateway are of a later date than the gateway itself. Peter Cunningham was of opinion that it was to this part, perhaps, that old Fuller alluded when he said " he (Ben Jonson) helped in the building of the new structure of Lincoln's Inn, when, having a trowel in one hand, he had a book in his pocket." The bricks and tiles employed in the building of the Gate-house and Hall were made from clay dug from a piece of ground on the west side of the Inn, and called the Coney-garth, " well stocked with rabbits and game." Hatton says that the building northward from the gateway into Chancery Lane was erected in the year 1636. In the year 1558 an order was passed for a brick wall and gates to be set up on the other side of the buildings, for the better enclosure thereof ; but this work seems not to have been .entirely completed until 1667, when also the chambers on the north side of the quadrangle were built.

The old Hall, the most ancient part of this interesting group of buildings, was rebuilt in 1506, and occupies the site of the original Hall, which was repaired in 1625, in 1652, and also in 1704 and 1706. It has a louvre on the roof, of the date 1522, and an embattled parapet. Its internal dimensions are 71 feet in length, 32 feet in breadth, and about 32 feet in height. It has on each side three large three-light windows, with arched and cusped heads, and a great oriel, transomed, with arched head and cusps. The Hall was lengthened by 10 feet at each end, in 1819, and upon the same occasion the open oak roof was removed, and the present incongruous coved plaster ceiling substituted. In 1853 the Hall was divided into two parts, in order to form two courts—the one for the Lord Chancellor, and the other for the Lords Justices of Appeal, until suitable accommodation for the administration of justice could be provided by the country. In 1874 the partition was removed, and the Hall was fitted up so as to form one spacious court for the Lord Chancellor and Lords Justices, when sitting together or alternately. Hogarth's picture of " Paul before Felix " formerly hung in this Hall, just above the seat of the Lord Chancellor.

In this ancient Hall were held all the revels of the Society, their masks and Christmasings, when the benchers laid aside their dignity, and dancing was enjoined for the students, as conducive " to the making of gentlemen more fit for their books at other times ; " and by an order in the seventh year of James I., " the under-barristers were by decimation put out of commons, for example's sake, because they had not danced on the Candlemas Day preceding, when the judges were present."

VIEW OF LINCOLN'S INN.   1755.

Of Christmas, 1661, Pepys writes, "The King (Charles II.) visited Lincoln's Inn to see the revels there; there being, according to an old custome, a prince and all his nobles, and other matters of sport and charge." Here were present Clarendon, Ormond, and Shaftesbury, at the revels of Hale; Ley, and Denham the poet; and the gloomy Prynne standing by. At these entertainments the Hall cupboard was set out with the Society's ancient plate, which included silver basins and ewers, silver cups and covers, a silver college-pot for festivals, and a large silver punch-bowl with two handles.

In the year 1671 Charles II. made a second visit with his brother the Duke of York, Prince Rupert, and the Duke of Monmouth, who were entertained in the Hall, and admitted members of the Society, and entered their names in the admittance-book, which contains also the signatures of all members, from the reign of Elizabeth to the present time.

Not many years ago it was the custom at Lincoln's Inn for one of the servants, attired in his usual robes, to go to the threshold of the outer door about 12 or 1 o'clock, and exclaim three times, "Venez manger," when neither bread nor salt was upon the table.

In the year 1754 Christopher Tancred, of Whixley, Yorkshire, bequeathed a considerable property, to be vested in trustees for the education of twelve students—four in divinity, at Christ's College, Cambridge; four in physic, at Gonville and Caius College, Cambridge; and four in common law, at Lincoln's Inn. The persons elected must not be less than sixteen years of age, must be natives of Great Britain, of the Church of England, and not capable of obtaining the education directed by the settlement without such assistance. The annual value of each studentship was originally fifty pounds, but is now of about double that amount. This aid is continued for three years after the student has taken the degree of Bachelor of Arts, Bachelor in Physic, or Barrister at law; and to keep in remembrance the liberality of the donor, a Latin oration on the subject of his charities is ordered to be annually delivered by one of the students in each branch, in the halls of the colleges before mentioned and of Lincoln's Inn respectively.

The chief part of the buildings was erected in the time of James I. At No. 13, from 1645 to 1650, lived John Thurloe, Secretary of Oliver Cromwell. In these chambers, it is said, was discussed, early in 1649, by Cromwell and Thurloe, Sir Richard Willis's plot for seizing Charles II.; in the same room sat Thurloe's assistant, young Morland, at his desk, apparently

asleep, and whom Cromwell would have despatched with his sword, had not
Thurloe assured him that Morland had sat up two nights, and was certainly
fast asleep; he, however, divulged the plot to the King, and thus saved
Charles's life.   This narrative was given by Dr. Birch in his life of Thurloe,
but rests upon questionable evidence.

In the reign of William III., long after Thurloe's death, the Thurloe
Papers were accidentally discovered, concealed in a false ceiling in the garrets
belonging to the Secretary's chambers.   They were discovered by a clergyman who had borrowed those chambers during the long vacation of his friend
Mr. Tomlinson, the owner of them.   This clergyman soon after disposed of
the papers to Lord John Somers, then Lord High Chancellor of England,
who caused them to be bound up in sixty-seven folio volumes.   They form
the principal part of Dr. Birch's " Thurloe State Papers."

In the year 1557 chambers were built over the kitchen and entry near
the Hall.   About the year 1607 all the old chambers in the long gallery were
rebuilt, and at about the same date twenty chambers were erected on the north
side of the house.

The Chapel is supposed by some to have been built by William Rede,
Bishop of Chichester from 1369 to 1385, but the documentary evidence goes
to prove that the existing Chapel was not built until the days of James I.,
when the old Chapel had become unfit for use.   It is reputed that Inigo Jones
designed the present building, which was erected in 1623.   The size of the
Chapel is 67 feet in length, 41 feet in breadth, and 44 feet in height.   The
estimated cost was £2,000, and was partly raised by voluntary subscription.
The Chapel was consecrated on Ascension Day, 1623, Dr. Donne preaching
the consecration sermon.   The painted-glass windows were executed by a
Mr. Hall, a glass-painter in Fetter Lane.   Winston says of them, "In point
of colour they are as rich as the richest decorated glass I have ever seen."
The windows on the south side are filled with representations of the Twelve
Apostles, executed by Bernard and Abraham Van Linge, Flemish artists ; on
the north by Moses and the Prophets, St. John the Baptist, and St. Paul.
An inscription in the window records that the St. John the Baptist was
executed at the expense of William Noy, who died in 1634, the famous
Attorney-General of Charles I.

The Chapel is elevated upon a crypt with obtusely pointed arches, and
whatever may have been the original cause of this arrangement, it is pretty

certain that the crypt was used as an ambulatory for the lawyers to walk in. Butler, in his " Hudibras," and Pepys, in his " Diary," allude to the fact. In the year 1822, in digging below the foundations of the Chapel, a sculpture representing the Annunciation was discovered. It was about one foot square, and at the time of its discovery the colours and gilding with which it was decorated were well preserved. It probably formed one of the ornaments of the old Chapel.

The entrance to the Chapel is under an archway, above which are carved the lion of the Earl of Lincoln and the initials of Marmaduke Alington, Esq., Treasurer of the Society in 1737. A turret with cupola, surmounted by a weather-vane, rises at the south-western angle of the Chapel, and contains an ancient bell, bearing this inscription, " Anthony Bond made mee, 1615," with the initials " T. H.," being those of Thomas Hitchcock, who was Treasurer of the Society in that year.

The carved oaken seats inside the Chapel are of very superior execution, and are of the same age as the building in which they are preserved. The altar is raised, and enclosed by balustrades. Two large silver flagons and salvers were presented by Nicholas Franklyn, Esq., in 1700, and two silver-gilt chalices, by Sir James Allan Park, in 1806.

The earliest entries in the Register of Lincoln's Inn relative to the appointment of a Preacher, formerly called a Divinity Reader or Lecturer, occur in the year 1581, when Mr. Charles was chosen for that office.

Among the Preachers at this Chapel there have been some celebrated men—Dr. Donne ; Dr. Usher ; Dr. Tillotson, afterwards Archbishop of Canterbury ; Dr. Warburton, afterwards Bishop of Gloucester ; Dr. Heber, afterwards Bishop of Calcutta ; Dr. Langhorne, the translator of Plutarch's Lives.

In the crypt beneath the Chapel lie buried the following : Alexander Brome, the Cavalier song-writer ; Secretary Thurloe ; William Prynne ; William Melmoth ; John Coxe, a benefactor to the Society ; Sir John Anstruther, Chief Justice of the Court of Judicature in Bengal ; Francis Hargrave.

In 1780 a design was put forward for rebuilding the whole of Lincoln's Inn, and the Stone Building, so called from the material of which it was constructed, was built as part of that design. It was designed in the Corinthian style, by Sir Robert Taylor, and completed by Hardwick in 1845. The working drawings, which are still preserved in the Library of Lincoln's Inn, were made by a young man of the name of Leach, then a clerk in Taylor's office, who afterwards became a student of Lincoln's Inn, and ultimately filled the high and lucrative office in the law of Master of the Rolls.

The New Hall and Library, occupying a site almost identical with that of the Coneygarth, stand on the western side of the garden. The architect was Philip Hardwick, R.A., and the buildings, which are reckoned to be finely situated for architectural effect, were designed in the late Tudor style of about the time of Henry VIII. The foundation-stone was laid on April 20th, 1843, and the materials employed are red bricks, intersected with black bricks in patterns, and stone dressings. The south end has a lofty gable, inscribed, in dark bricks, " P. H." (they being the initials of Philip Hardwick, the architect), and the date 1843. The gable is flanked on each side by a square embattled tower, and beneath are shields, charged with lions and milvines, the badges of the Society ; between the towers is the great window of the Hall, of seven lights, transomed, and the four-central arch filled with beautiful tracery. On the apex of the gable, beneath a canopied pinnacle, is a statue of Queen Victoria, by Thomas, the sculptor. The side buttresses are surmounted by octagonal pinnacles. The roof is leaded, and in its centre is an elegant louvre, surrounded by slender pinnacles bearing vanes. The capping has crotchets and gargoyles, and is surmounted by a vane tastefully gilt.

The Hall is arranged north and south, and the Library east and west, the two buildings being connected by a vestibule, flanked by a Drawing-room and Council-room. The entrance to the Hall is at the south-east tower, by a double flight of steps to the porch, above which are the arms of the Inn. Above is the clock, of novel and beautiful design, with an enriched pedimental canopy in metal-work.

The central building, the entrance to the Library and Great Hall, has end oriels, and an octagonal embattled crown or lantern, filled with painted glass. From the esplanade is the entrance by flights of steps to a porch, the gable bearing the lion of the Earl of Lincoln holding a banner; and at the apex of the great gable of the Library roof is a circular shaft, surmounted by an heraldic animal supporting a staff and banner. The Library has large end oriels of beautiful design, and five bay windows on the north side ; the lights being separated by stone compartments, each boldly sculptured with heraldic achievements of Charles II., James Duke of York, K.G., Queen Victoria, Prince Albert, K.G., and Albert Edward Prince of Wales. The buttresses

dividing the bays are terminated by pillars, surmounted by heraldic animals. At the north-west angle of this front is an octagonal bell-turret. On the western front, towards Lincoln's Inn Fields, the clustered chimneys have a beautiful effect. They are of moulded red brick, resembling those at Eton College and Hampton Court Palace. The bosses, gargoyles, and armorial, grotesque, and foliated ornaments throughout the building are finely sculptured.

Entering by the southern tower, the corridor is arranged on the plan of the college halls of the Universities, and has a buttery-hatch, and stairs leading to the vaulted kitchen, 45 feet square, and 25 feet high, with one of the largest fireplaces in England. The adjoining cellars have storage-room for one hundred pipes of wine.

From the corridor, through a carved oak screen, you enter the Hall, which is 120 feet long, 45 feet wide, and 62 feet high. The upper part of the screen serves as the front to the gallery, between the arches of which, upon pedestals, in canopied niches, are costumed life-size figures of the following eminent members of the Society : Lord Chief Justice Sir Matthew Hale ; Archbishop Tillotson, one of the Preachers of Lincoln's Inn ; Lord Chief Justice Mansfield ; Lord Chancellor Hardwicke ; Bishop Warburton, one of the Preachers of Lincoln's Inn ; and Sir William Grant, Master of the Rolls.

The sides of the Hall are panelled with oak, and the cornice is enriched with gilding and colour. The five large stained-glass windows on either side contain, in the upper lights, the arms, crests, and mottoes of distinguished members of the Society, chronologically arranged, from 1450 to 1843 ; and the lower divisions are diapered with the initials " L. I." and the milvine. Above the windows is a cornice enriched with colour and gilding.

The roof is wholly of oak, and is divided into seven compartments by trusses, each large arch springing from stone corbels, and having two carved pendants (as in Wolsey's Hall at Hampton Court), at the termination of an inner arch that springs from hammer-beams projecting from the walls. These pendants are illuminated blue, and red, and gilt, and they each carry a chandelier to correspond. Between the wall trusses is a machicolated cornice panelled and coloured.

In this Hall is the fine fresco painting by G. F. Watts, known as " The Origin of Legislation." This great work was the gift of Mr. Watts, the artist. It was commenced in 1854, but soon after discontinued through illness, and was not finished until October, 1859.

On the northern wall, above the dais panelling, is the picture of " Paul before Felix," painted in 1750 by Hogarth, and removed from a similar position in the old Hall.

At the opposite end of the Hall is a noble marble statue, by Westmacott, of Lord Erskine, Chancellor in 1806.

On either side of the dais, in the oriel, is a sideboard for the upper or Benchers' table.

The other tables, ranged in gradation, two crosswise and five along the Hall, are for the barristers and students, who dine here every day during term ; the average number is two hundred, and of those who dine on one day or the other during the term, " keeping commons," is about five hundred.

From the dais of the Hall large folding doors open into the vestibule, east of which is the Council-chamber ; and west, the Drawing-room. The stone chimney-pieces are finely sculptured. In the Drawing-room are portraits of Justice Glanville, 1598 ; Sir John Glanville, Speaker of the House of Commons, 1640 ; Sir Matthew Hale, 1671, by M. Wright ; Sir Richard Rainsford, Lord Chief Justice, K.B., 1676, by Gerard Soest ; Lord Chancellor Hardwicke, 1737, after Ramsay ; Lord Chancellor Bathurst, 1771, by Sir M. Dance ; Sir John Skynner, Lord Chief Baron, 1771, by Gainsborough ; Sir William Grant, Master of the Rolls, by Harlow ; Francis Hargreave, Treasurer in 1813, by Sir Joshua Reynolds ; and Sir H. Haddington, Speaker of the House of Commons.

In the Council-chamber is a portrait of Sir John Franklin, of Mavourn, Beds, Knight and Master in Chancery thirty-three years. He died in 1707. There are also several copies from the old masters ; and a " Lady with a Guitar," by William Etty, R.A. The walls of both Council- and Drawing-rooms are also hung with a valuable collection of engraved portraits of legal dignitaries, eminent prelates, etc.

The new Hall was inaugurated on October 30th, 1845, by Queen Victoria and Prince Albert, when Her Majesty held a levée in the Library, and both she and the Prince Consort signed their names in the admittance-book.

The Library is 80 feet long, 40 feet wide, and 44 feet high. It has an open oak roof of much originality. The projecting bookcases form separate apartments for study, and have an iron balcony running round them about midway, and another gallery over them against each wall. The oriel windows display the arms of the Benchers.

One of the earliest benefactors to the Library was Ranulph Cholmeley, Serjeant-at-law, and Recorder of the City of London, who gave several rare volumes of the early year-books, etc.

A valuable collection of MSS., mostly bequeathed to the Society by Sir Matthew Hale, is deposited in two rooms opening from the Library. The books and MSS. exceed 25,000 in number. The collection of law books is said to be the most complete in this country, and there are also among the books at Lincoln's Inn Library many important works on history and antiquities. This is said to be the oldest existing library in London, having been founded as early as 1497. Many of the volumes still retain iron rings, by which they were secured by rods to the shelves.

A collection of pamphlets, chiefly upon theological subjects and poetry, some of them very curious, were given in 1706, by John Brydall, Esq., the author of many legal works. The following donors have at various times presented valuable additions to the Library: John Coxe, Esq. ; William Melmoth, Esq. ; Charles Purton Cooper, Esq. ; Hon. Francis Cecil Abbot. Also a valuable collection of legal MSS. was purchased from Mr. Serjeant Hill, and in 1818 the legal MSS. of John Maynard, Esq., King's Serjeant in the reign of Charles II., were purchased.

Long before this place became an Inn of Court the gardens belonging to it were highly cultivated. The accounts of the bailiff to the Earl of Lincoln (twenty-fourth year of Edward I.) show it to have produced apples, pears, large nuts, and cherries, sufficient for the Earl's table, and to yield by sale in one year £135 in modern currency. The vegetables grown were beans, onions, garlic, leeks ; hemp was grown, the cuttings of the vines much prized ; of pear-trees there were several varieties ; the only flowers named are roses. It appears there was a pond or vivary in the garden, as the bailiff expended eight shillings in the purchase of small fish, frogs, and eels, to feed the pike in it.

In more recent times the "walk under the elms," celebrated by Ben Jonson, was a favourite resort of Isaac Bickerstaff. In the time of Mary I. the walk under the trees in the Coneygarth, or Cottrel-garden, was made ; and in 1663 the said garden was enlarged, and a terrace walk made on the left side. Pepys, writing in his famous "Diary," says, "To Lincoln's Inn, to see the new garden which they are making, which will be very pretty."

ST. GILES-IN-THE-FIELDS.

GRAY'S INN.

Gray's Inn stands upon the site of the ancient manor of Portpoole, or Purpool, an estate which in early times is known to have been the property of one of the Canons of St. Paul's Cathedral. The manor is mentioned in a deed dated the 46th of Henry III., by which Robert de Purtepole, possibly its then owner, gives to the Hospital of St. Giles ten shillings annual rent, issuing from his house in the parish of St. Andrew, Holborn, to find a chaplain to celebrate his anniversary obit in the Hospital Church.

In the following reign, *i.e.*, that of Edward I., it became the property of the Lords Gray of Wilton, who resided here. From the latter circumstance the modern name of the place took its origin.

John, the son of Reginald de Gray, in 1315 obtained a licence from Edward II. to grant thirty acres of land, two acres of meadow, and ten shillings rent, with the appurtenances, part lying in Kentish Town, near London, and part in the parish of St. Andrew, Holborn, without the Bars of the Old Temple, unto the prior and convent of St. Bartholomew, Smithfield, " to furnish a certain chaplain to celebrate Divine service every day in the chapel of Pourtpole for the soul of the said John, and for the souls of his ancestors, and for the souls of all the faithful deceased."

About the latter end of the reign of Henry VII. (1505), Edmund Lord Gray, of Wilton, by indenture of bargain and sale passed to Hugh Denny, Esq., and others, the manor of Portpoole, otherwise called Gray's Inn, for messuages, four gardens, the site of a windmill, eight acres of land, ten shillings rent, and the advowson of the chantry of Portpoole, aforesaid ; which sale was confirmed by release of Henry VIII. Eight years afterwards some of the feoffees made a grant to the prior of Sheen, in Surrey, of the said premises. The prior and convent of Sheen being thus possessed of the property, demised it to the students of the law for the annual rent of £6 13s. 4d.

At the dissolution of the monasteries of course the whole estate fell into the hands of the Crown, to whom it still belongs.

Gray's Inn became an Inn of Court before the year 1370, and there is, among the Harleian MSS. at the British Museum, a table showing the number of gentlemen admitted into the Society in each year from 1521 to 1674, together with a list of the names of such nobility, spiritual and temporal, as have been admitted to the Society, and other information of great value.

The buildings of Gray's Inn during the time of the Tudors appear to have been small and inconvenient, insomuch that even the Ancients of the House were obliged to lodge double, owing to the limited amount of house-room. Among the curious orders of the Society, the following may be mentioned :—

In the 21st of Elizabeth it was ordered that "henceforth no Fellow of this House shall make choice of his bedfellow, but only the Readers ; the admission of all others shall be referred to the discretion of the Treasurers." In the 24th of Elizabeth it was ordered that no Fellow of the House should thenceforth lodge any stranger, being no Fellow of the House, upon penalty of losing his chamber.

In the year 1720 the chief courts of Gray's Inn were Holborn Court, Chapel Court, and Cony Court, but the middle row of old chambers had been taken down, and thus the two last-mentioned courts were laid open together. The Dining-hall was described as large and good, but the Chapel was inconveniently small.

The principal entrance to Gray's Inn was from Gray's Inn Lane when Agas's map of London was drawn, but for the greater convenience of persons who wished to pass into Holborn the present passage-way was obtained, by the purchase of a parcel of ground and the building of a gate in 1593 or soon after.

The Hall is a noble apartment, 70 feet in length, 35 in width, and 47 in height. At its eastern end there is a raised dais, on which is placed the chief table, and on the right is a bay window. At the opposite end, to conceal the entrance vestibule, is an oak screen exceedingly rich in design, consisting of fine semicircular arched headings with carved spandrils, brackets, and tympans, having Ionic columns, overlaid with strapwork ornament between each bay.

Above this order, and the enriched cartouche frieze, is a beautiful open gallery front to the minstrels' loft, which although designed in good keeping, is evidently of later date than the lower portion of the screen. The rail, or capping, is supported by six sculptured terminal figures resting on cantilevers, with carved and fluted pediments between them. There is a tradition that this screen, and also some of the dining-tables, were given to the Society by Queen Elizabeth.

The roof of the Hall is a very fine specimen of open timber work, constructed in what is known as the hammer-beam type.

The chief feature of interest is doubtless the painted glass with which

8

the windows are enriched.   These consist of a large number of coats of arms,
some of which have been in their present position for over three hundred
years.

The royal licence granted to John de Gray in the year 1315 mentions
a chapel in connection with Gray's Inn, and it is probable that the present
Chapel stands upon the site of that building.

The earliest actual mention of the Chapel of Gray's Inn found in the
records of the Society is said to be under the date of the 11th year of Queen
Elizabeth, when it was ordered that a pulpit should be made for the Chapel,
and that various internal structural modifications should be effected.

The Chapel was enlarged in the year 1619, and in 1689 it was ordered
that a model should be prepared for a new Chapel altogether, also that the
Treasurer should obtain a new bell for the Chapel, and cause a new wheel
to be made for it if necessary.   That the latter part of the order was duly
executed is pretty certain from the following inscription, which the bell bears :
" James Bartlet made mee, 1689.   Samuel Buck, Treasurer."

The new Chapel, however, was not undertaken so quickly.   In 1699 it
was repaired and beautified, and the walls were handsomely finished.   It
appears from Dugdale's account that in the latter part of the seventeenth
century there were many arms in stained glass in the windows of the chapel.
Of those arms many have now disappeared, although some still remain in
the eastern window of five lights.

The Library, which now contains about 15,000 volumes, apparently
dates from about the middle of the sixteenth century.   Many accessions of
books were made in the first half of the seventeenth century, and amongst the
donors there were Sir John Finch, Sir John Banks, Sir Richard Hutton, Sir
Edward Moseley, John Godbolt, and Francis and Nathaniel Bacon (nephews
of the famous Lord Bacon).

In the year 1669 about a hundred volumes were missing from the
Library, borrowers having apparently failed to return them.   In the same year
the Library-keeper, Mr. Raworth, was instructed to make an exact catalogue
of the Library.   Another catalogue, still in existence, which was made in 1689
by the Treasurer and two Benchers, shows that the collection at that time
comprised about 320 volumes.

The selection of the books which form the present Library has, of course,
been largely determined by the purpose for which the collection exists—that

of a practical law library—but a reasonable proportion of the books relate to historical subjects and general literature.

Gray's Inn has an historical past which is rich in its association with men remarkable for piety, achievements in law, literature, poetry, and other departments of fame. Among former residents here were Dr. Johnson, Oliver Goldsmith, George Chapman, Samuel Butler, John Cleveland, James Shirley, and Edward Ward. Lord Bacon was a member of Gray's Inn, and occupied chambers there for many years. Sir Philip Sidney, Robert Southey, and Thomas Babington Macaulay, in their respective periods, were closely connected with Gray's Inn; the last-named, between 1829 and 1834, occupied chambers at No. 8, South Square, Gray's Inn.

Close by the entrance leading from Holborn to the classic localities around this retired spot, there was formerly a celebrated coffee-house, known as Gray's Inn Coffee-house, where Thackeray often dined in the company of one or two select friends. His favourite beverage was claret, and he sometimes drank it liberally. His conversation, which was of the finest order, flowed unceasingly, enchaining in deep attention those of his friends who were privileged to dine with him.

RED LION SQUARE.

That this now somewhat neglected spot was at one time a place of fashion and importance appears pretty clear from the account given of it, in the year 1720, in Strype's edition of Stow's "Survey of London." At that time it had graceful buildings on all sides, which were inhabited by gentry and persons of repute. The houses had palisado pales and a freestone pavement before them. The middle of the square was enclosed, and the enclosure was laid out in grass-plots, rows of trees, and gravelled paths.

There were four watch-houses in the square, one at each corner, and an obelisk which was supposed to cover the remains of Oliver Cromwell, Ireton, and Bradshaw, whose bodies had been disinterred from Westminster Abbey. The obelisk bore the following inscription :—

OBTUSUM
OBTUSIORIS INGENII
MONUMENTUM
QUID ME RESPICIS VIATOR
VADE.

In the year 1737 Red Lion Square had become so much neglected, being used as a place in which to deposit all kinds of rubbish, and was so much infested by vagabonds, beggars, and disorderly persons, that it was found necessary to enclose it (the old fence having probably become decayed), and have it paved, watched, and properly adorned.

Among the celebrated persons who have lived in Red Lion Square may be mentioned John Wilkes, the politician, and of the *North Briton;* Lord Robert Raymond, an eminent judge ; Sharon Turner, the historian ; and Jonas Hanway, the eccentric traveller, and the first man to carry an umbrella.

THE FOUNDLING HOSPITAL.

As the circumstances which led to the establishment of this excellent and most useful institution may not perhaps be generally known to all who may read this account, a brief summary of the chief facts in connection therewith may be not altogether unacceptable, by way of preface to what may be said of the building itself and its subsequent history.

The name of Captain Coram is closely connected with the Foundling Hospital in the earlier years of its existence. Thomas Coram, the son of John Coram, the captain of a ship, was born at Lyme Regis in 1667 or 1668.   In process of time Thomas Coram adopted a maritime career, and, like his father, he became captain of a ship. In 1719 his ship was stranded off Cuxhaven, and after that he settled down to business near London.   His residence was at Rotherhithe, and in the journeys, early in the morning and late at night, to and from the City, which his business compelled him to take, he frequently saw infants exposed and deserted in the streets.   His kind heart was touched at the pitiable sight, and he immediately set about inquiring into the causes of so outrageous a departure from humanity and natural affection.

For seventeen years he laboured hard for the establishment of a foundling hospital, and at length a charter was obtained, funds were provided, and the Board of Guardians which had been appointed met for the first time in 1739. The body of Governors and Guardians comprised John Duke of Bedford and 350 other persons, including several Peers, the Master of the Rolls, the Chief Justices and Chief Baron, the Speaker, the Attorney, and Solicitor-General, and Captain Coram.

A house in Hatton Garden was first taken, and in 1741 children were first admitted to its benefits, but only twenty children could be received, and the large number of applications for admission soon proved that the limits of the house must be greatly extended. It was required of all who brought children that they should " fix on each child some particular writing, or other distinguishing mark or token," so that the children might be identified if it were subsequently found necessary to do so. This wise condition removed the danger of a woman being punished for the supposed murder of her child, when she had really placed it in this excellent asylum. The number of applicants was so great that sometimes a hundred women would crowd round the door with children when only a very few of them could possibly be admitted, and a kind of ballot was taken, those who chanced to draw a white ball being admitted subject to the approval of the Board, those who drew a black ball being excluded, and those who drew a red ball being allowed to wait and draw among themselves to fill up any vacancy which might chance to arise where a candidate was found to be ineligible.

The necessity of more extended premises led to the purchase of a magnificent site, fifty-six acres in size, at the top of Lamb's Conduit Street. The foundation was laid in September, 1742, and the western wing of the present hospital was opened in 1745, and the house in Hatton Garden was given up. The other two portions of the edifice soon followed, and in 1747 the Chapel was commenced.

The Governors of the hospital having appealed for assistance in 1756, the House of Commons promised and gave substantial support, and the hospital was thereupon thrown open for the general admission of foundlings. A basket was hung outside of the gates of the hospital, and an advertisement publicly announced that all children under the age of two years, tendered for admission, would be received. On June 2nd, 1756, the first day when this regulation came into force, 117 children were tendered, and received within the hospital walls.

Children were sent up from all parts of the country in baskets and bags, and so little care was taken that many of them perished by the way. One man is said to have made a regular trade of bringing up from Yorkshire two children in each of his panniers, for which he received the sum of eight guineas.

In the first year of this indiscriminate admission 3,296 infants were received ; in the second, 4,085 ; and in the third, 4,229. Of course it was found quite impossible to attend properly to the wants of this enormous number of young and often delicate children.   Only a comparatively small proportion of the children lived to be apprenticed.   To remedy this evil to some extent, it was resolved that some children should be received upon the payment of £100 each ; but of course this unpopular resolution, so out of harmony with the plan and intent of the venerable and kind-hearted founder, was soon abolished.   Since January, 1801, no child has been received into the hospital with any sum of money, large or small.   Children are now admitted solely upon the committee being satisfied that the case is genuine and deserving of consideration.   The chief requirements are that the child be illegitimate (except in the case of the father being a soldier or sailor killed in service), that it be under twelve months old, that the father be not forthcoming, and that the mother shall have borne a previous good character.

In 1745, upon the completion of the western wing of the hospital, Hogarth contemplated the adornment of its walls with works of art, with which view he solicited and obtained the co-operation of some of his pro-fessional brethren.   On November 5th in each year the most prominent of the artists and the Governors of the hospital dined together at the Foundling Hospital.   The effect of these meetings was to bring a large number of valuable paintings together for the beautifying of the walls, and a visit to the Foundling Hospital to see the pictures became the most fashionable morning lounge in the reign of George II.

Hogarth was not only the principal contributor, but the leader of his brethren in all that related to ornamenting the hospital.   One of the richest treasures of art which is comprised in the Foundling collection is Hogarth's celebrated "March to Finchley."   Hogarth disposed of this picture by lottery, and as 167 chances remained unappropriated when the subscription-list was closed, the artist generously gave them to the hospital.   The lucky number is said to have been among that remainder, but another account says that a lady was the possessor of it, and intended to present it to the Foundling Hospital, but that some person having suggested what a door would be open to scandal, were any of her sex to make such a present, it was given to Hogarth, on the express condition that it should be presented in his own name.

Hogarth delivered the picture to the Governors the same evening, and thus the hospital became possessed of a picture for which hundreds of pounds have been offered.

The next work which Hogarth presented was "Moses before Pharaoh's Daughter." It was painted expressly for the hospital, and was designed by the artist to assist in ornamenting the Board-room, where it now hangs. In the year 1740 Hogarth had presented to the hospital a whole-length picture of Captain Coram ; so that there were now in the possession of the Foundling Hospital three of Hogarth's pictures, each of which was an excellent example of the genius of that celebrated artist.

It has been remarked by Charles Lamb, in one of his critical essays, that Hogarth seemed to take particular delight in introducing children into his works. There can be little doubt that he was passionately fond of children. His sympathy with the work of the Foundling Hospital was so great and so practical that he had some of the young children sent down to Chiswick, where he at that time resided, in order that he and his wife might more effectually see after their welfare.

The pictures at the Foundling Hospital are arranged chiefly upon the walls of three of the apartments there ; viz., the Secretary's office, the Board-room, and the Picture-gallery. Some of the chief of them may be enumerated.

PICTURES IN THE SECRETARY'S OFFICE.

"The March to Finchley." *Hogarth.*

Portrait of Handel (in oil colours). *Kneller.*

A view of London from Highgate (in oil colours). *Lambert.* This is reckoned to be one of Lambert's finest works. The foliage is especially good.

A sea-piece representing ships employed in the British Navy (in oil colours). *Brooking.* A very fine example of this artist's work. It was given to the hospital by the painter.

Two oil paintings upon wooden panels, representing portraits of Shakespeare and Ben Jonson. These paintings are known to be of considerable antiquity and they are certainly possessed of some merit. It is to be regretted, however, that nothing whatever is known as to their history, or of the person who gave them. They have been in the possession of the hospital since the beginning of this century, if not longer.

There are some prints, too, in this room, which deserve notice :—

Prints of Hogarth's portrait of himself, and also of Captain Coram.

Mezzotint portraits of George Washington and Benjamin Franklin.

OIL PAINTINGS IN THE BOARD-ROOM.

" Fear not ; for God hath heard the voice of the lad where he is" (Gen. xxi. 17). (Hagar and Ishmael.) *Highmore.* This is one of the artist's most famous pictures.

" Suffer the little children to come unto Me, and forbid them not" (St. Mark x. 14). *Rev. James Wills,* Chaplain to the Society of Artists. This is Wills's principal performance, and was presented to the hospital by the painter.

" And Pharaoh's daughter said unto her, Take this child away, and nurse it for me, and I will give thee thy wages" (Exod. ii. 9). *Hayman.*

" And the child grew, and she brought him unto Pharaoh's daughter, and he became her son. And she called his name Moses " (Exod. ii. 10). *Hogarth.* Presented by the artist.

The four pictures just mentioned are of large size, and occupy the principal parts of the wall, but there is a series of eight circular oil paintings of hospitals, etc., which, although of much smaller proportions, aie works of great merit. The following is a list of them, with the names of the artists : —

> Christ's Hospital. *Samuel Wale, R.A.*
> Greenwich Hospital.   „   „
> St. Thomas's Hospital. „   „
> Bethlem Hospital. *Haytley.*
> Chelsea Hospital.   „
> The Charterhouse. *Thomas Gainsborough, R.A.*
> The Foundling Hospital. *Richard Wilson, R.A.*
> St. George's Hospital.   „   „

Before leaving the Board-room there are one or two other works of art worthy of mention. The handsome marble mantelpiece has a fine basso-relievo, by Rysbrack, representing children engaged in navigation and husbandry, being the employments to which the children of the hospital were supposed to be destined.

The side table, of Grecian marble, is supported by carved figures in wood.

PORTRAIT OF CAPTAIN CORAM. *After the Painting by Hogarth.*

representing children playing with a goat. It was presented by Mr. John Sanderson.

The ornamental ceiling was done by Mr. Wilton, the father of the eminent sculptor.

THE STONE HALL, OR VESTIBULE.

Among the pictures exhibited in the Stone Hall are portraits of Archdeacon Pott, Lord Chief Justice Wilmot, Dr. Heathcote, etc. There is also an oil painting by Casali, representing " The Offering of the Wise Men."

PICTURES IN THE PICTURE-GALLERY.

This gallery contains a large collection of paintings and other valuable works of art and objects of interest. The cartoon of Raphael representing " The Murder of the Innocents," of course, deserves first mention. This very valuable work of art was bequeathed to the Foundling Hospital by Prince Hoare, Esq., in 1835. By the will of that gentleman it was directed that it should be offered first to the Royal Academy of Arts for £2,000 ; or, if declined, to the Directors of the National Gallery for the sum of £4,0co ;. and if that offer was not accepted it was then to be presented to the Foundling Hospital or to a public hall or college. The Royal Academy and the National Gallery both declined the offer, and the picture was accordingly presented to the Foundling Hospital.

This cartoon belonged to a set of ten cartoons executed by Raphael by the order of Pope Leo X. They were afterwards sent to Flanders, to be copied in tapestry, for which purpose the Flemish weavers cut them into strips for their working machinery. When the tapestry was completed and sent to Rome the original cartoons were carelessly thrown into a box and left mingled together. When Rubens was in England he told Charles I. the condition they were in, and the King desired him to procure them. Seven perfect ones were purchased and sent to His Majesty ; the remainder appear to have been scattered in fragments, here and there, in different parts of Europe. When the royal collections were dispersed these cartoons are said to have been bought in for £300 by Cromwell's express orders.

This portion of " The Murder of the Innocents " was sold at Westminster as disputed property, and Prince Hoare's father purchased it for £26. The-artistic merits of this superb composition are beyond all praise, and some of the heads represented in it are considered to be unequalled by any of the great works of art in the world. Seven of Raphael's cartoons are now in the South Kensington Museum.

In this picture-gallery hangs the portrait of Captain Coram by Hogarth, of which the artist wrote, some time after—

"The portrait which I painted with most pleasure, and in which I particularly wished to excel, was that of Captain Coram, for the Foundling Hospital ; and," he adds, in allusion to his detractors as a portrait-painter, "if I am so wretched an artist as my enemies assert, it is somewhat strange that this, which was one of the first I painted the size of life, should stand the test of twenty years' competition, and be generally thought the best portrait in the place, notwithstanding the first painters in the kingdom exerted all their talents to vie with it."

There are also portraits, among other pictures, of the following :—

Duke of Cambridge.	*G. P. Green.*
Earl of Macclesfield.	*Wilson.*
Theodore Jacobsen, Esq.	*Hudson.*
King George the Second.	*Shakleton.*
Dr. Mead.	*Ramsay.*
John Milner, Esq.	*Hudson.*

In some glass show-cases there are exhibited various documents connected with the hospital, autographs of various celebrated personages, the pocket-book of Captain Coram, and the original draught in pen and ink of the arms of the Foundling Hospital. It is thought probable that this was executed by Hogarth.

The connection of Handel with the Foundling Hospital forms one of the most pleasing features in the hospital's history, and the following notice is very properly preserved and exhibited in one of the glass cases :—

"At the Hospital for the Maintenance and Education of exposed and deserted Young Children in Lamb's Conduit Fields, on Tuesday y⁰ first day of May, 1750, at 12 o'clock at Noon, there will be performed, in the Chapel of the said Hospital, a Sacred Oratorio called ' The Messiah,' Composed by George Frederick Handel, Esq.

" The Gentlemen are desired to come without Swords, and the Ladies without Hoops. . . ."

In the same show-case are preserved the MS. scores of " The Messiah " which Handel generously bequeathed to the hospital. " The Messiah " was performed for the first time in London on March 23rd, 1749.

Upon several occasions Handel showed his personal sympathy with the objects of this charitable institution, by conducting musical performances in aid of its funds. In 1749 he gave a performance in aid of the funds for completing the chapel, upon which occasion he gave the " music of the late Fire Works, the anthem on the Peace, selections from the oratorio of Samson, and several pieces composed for the occasion." The tickets were sold for half a guinea each, and the audience numbered above a thousand persons.

When the hospital chapel was completed, Handel presented the Governors with an organ for it, and his amanuensis and assistant, Mr. John Christopher Smith, was appointed the first regular organist.

One of the Governors of the hospital presented the communion plate ; the king's upholsterer gave the velvet for the pulpit ; and many other valuable gifts were presented.

In the year 1750, upon the completion of the hospital chapel, Chevalier Casali presented an altar-piece painted in oil colours, entitled " The Offering of the Wise Men." In 1801, however, the Governors removed that picture, and replaced it by West's masterpiece of harmony and colouring, " Christ Presenting a little Child." The artist, speaking of this work, says—

" The care with which I have passed that picture, I flatter myself, has now placed it in the first class of pictures from my pencil ; at least, I have the satisfaction to find that to be the sentiment of the judges of painting who have seen it."

In order to make the picture as nearly perfect as possible, West almost entirely repainted it, and the Governors, in acknowledgment, and to show their high appreciation of West's talents and generosity, resolved to elect him one of their corporate body. It was West's intention to fill in two panels in the chapel with oil paintings, but unluckily his professional engagements were too numerous to permit him to carry out his excellent intention.

Coram, the venerable founder, died in 1751, and was buried in the catacombs beneath the chapel. Many of the Governors of the hospital have subsequently been buried there.

Among the objects which every one who visits the hospital should see
are the miscellaneous contents of two glass show-cases.   One cannot look
upon.these objects without feelings of deep and pathetic interest.   These cases
are filled with small articles of personal ornament and old and rare coins,
which have been attached by a mother's loving hands to the infants as a token
whereby, if necessary, it might be possible to identify them, after their names
were changed and many other circumstances of their history forgotten.

When the Governors of the Foundling Hospital were negotiating for the
purchase of the site in Lamb's Conduit Fields, the owner of the land, the Earl of
Salisbury, declined to sell them so small a plot as they desired, and they were
therefore forced to buy a large area, fifty-six acres in extent.   Fortunately,
this has turned out a very good investment.   The Governors could hardly
have done a wiser thing, for as the neighbourhood has grown and the value
of land has increased so enormously, the rents from the surplus ground have
proved a very substantial source of income to the hospital.

BLOOMSBURY.

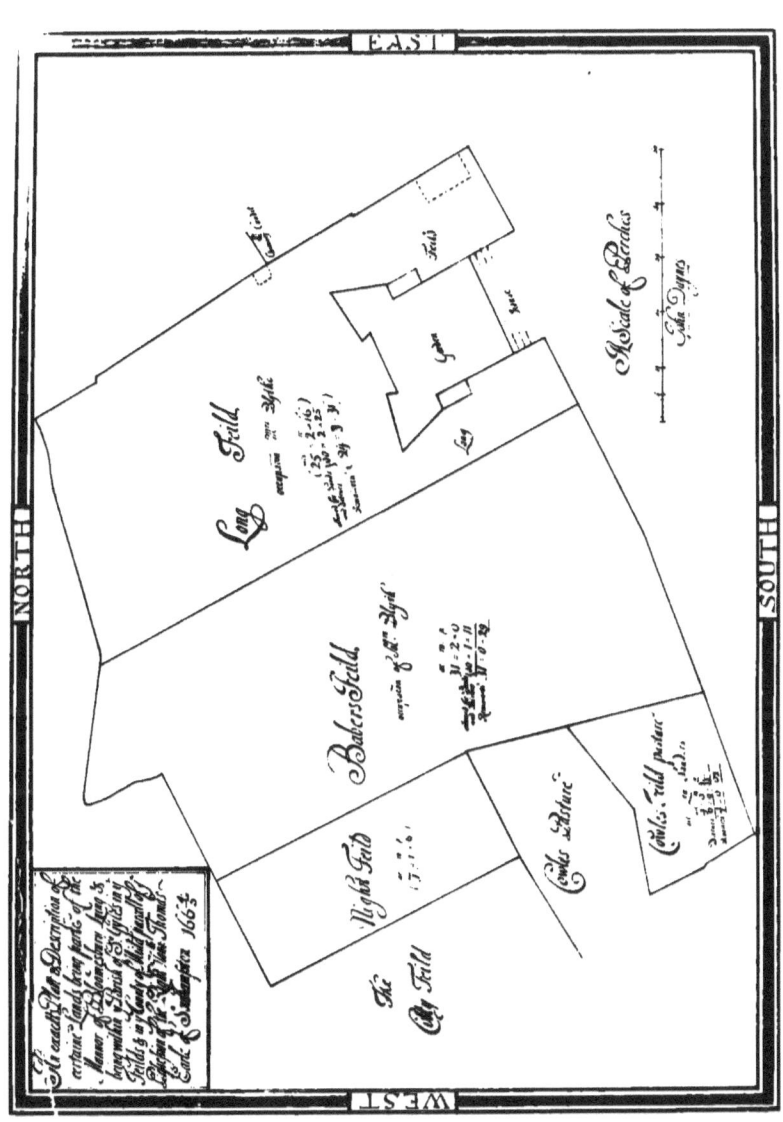

CHAPTER IX.

BLOOMSBURY.

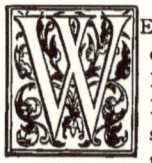E have had occasion already, in treating of the early history of St. Giles's parish, to advert to the origin of the name Bloomsbury. In the reign of Henry III., one William Blemund was the lord of this manor. His name appears as such in several of the deeds appertaining to the hospital at that period, and it generally appeared as " Blemund's Land " (Terr' de Blemund), " Blemund's Fee " (Feod' de Blumund), etc. The name of the place has gradually become modified and changed into Blemundsbury, and finally Bloomsbury.

In early times Bloomsbury was mere fields and open country. In the early part of the reign of Queen Elizabeth Southampton House seems to have been almost the only building of any consequence in that district which now surrounds St. George's Church.

In common with St. Giles's, however, which showed great marks of increase during the early years of the reign of James I., this part of the parish was also considerably augmented by new buildings. By the year 1623 a neighbourhood had begun to accumulate both in the west and east parts of Bloomsbury, when the following places and houses were assessed ; viz., "street side of Bloomsbury," nineteen houses ; "north side of Bloomsbury," eleven houses ; " Bloomsbury, west side," thirty-seven houses ; "east side of Bloomsbury," forty-five houses ; and " Little Alley, in Bloomsbury," twenty-four houses.

Thus, in Bloomsbury, part of St. Giles's parish at that time, there were in 1623, 136 dwelling-houses, large and small.   They were doubtless all built along by the sides of the chief thoroughfares, and much open ground around and beyond Southampton House was left untouched.

The manor of Bloomsbury passed into the possession of the Bedford family at the same time and in the same manner as did that of St. Giles.

Early in the eighteenth century the rapidly increasing population of the parish of St. Giles-in-the-Fields led to the formation of a new parish and the erection of a new church.   In 1710 an official return showed that while the inhabitants of St. Giles's numbered 34,800, there were but one church, three chapels, and one Presbyterian meeting-house for their accommodation. In the year 1705 the Vestry of St. Giles's ordered that persons were to be appointed to go from house to house, to take subscriptions for a new chapel and school-house, to be built on ground near Hart Street, given by Lady Russell.

The creation of a new parish of St. George, by dividing the old parish of St. Giles, was finally effected on January 8th, 1724, when the deed for setting out the new parish of Bloomsbury was enrolled in Chancery.

A piece of land was purchased of Lady Rachel Russell and the Duchess of Bedford.   It was situated between Hart Street on the north side, and Little Russell Street on the south side, and comprised in the front and rear about 106½ feet, by about 165 feet in depth.   This had been called Plough Yard, and was purchased for the sum of £1,000.

The new church was erected before the year 1724, at a cost, it is said, of £9,793.   Nicholas Hawksmoor was the architect who designed the building. He had been a clerk and pupil under Sir Christopher Wren, and had worked under him during the whole of the time of the building of St. Paul's Cathedral, and in the erection of the large number of churches which were built or rebuilt about that time.   Hawksmoor also acted as chief surveyor, after Wren's death, over the works at Westminster Abbey.   With so much tuition, under a teacher of such good taste and eminence, one cannot help marvelling that Hawksmoor should have committed so grave an architectural error as the designing of the ridiculous steeple of St. George's Church, which is awkward, unsightly, and wholly out of character with the body of the church, and in every way an objectionable feature.

The tower has an expression of majestic simplicity, and is adorned by a range of unattached Corinthian pillars, and pediments extend around its

St. GEORGE'S CHURCH, BLOOMSBURY.

four sides, with a kind of double base, ornamented in the lower division with a round aperture on each side, and a curious little projecting arch at each angle. Above this stage commences a series of steps, gradually narrowing, so as to assume a pyramidical appearance. The lowest steps are ornamented at the corners by lions and unicorns guarding the royal arms. At the apex, on a short column, is a statue of George I., in Romanesque costume, which was given by Mr. William Hucks, an opulent brewer of this parish.

Walpole stigmatises this extraordinary steeple "a masterpiece of absurdity," and there is no doubt that subsequent critics in the main support his opinion. Nothing but the novelty and originality of the design saves the steeple from unanimous condemnation.

The bad taste of the implied compliment to the King, and the absurd inconsistencies of the whole idea, were satirically alluded to in the following contemporary epigram :—

"When Henry the Eighth left the Pope in the lurch
The Protestants made him the head of the Church;
But George's good subjects, the Bloomsbury people,
Instead of the Church, made him head of the steeple."

It is but fair to say that, save for the steeple, St. George's Church is a handsome building. Hawksmoor is supposed to have been much influenced by the magnificent church of St. Martin-in-the-Fields when he designed this church at Bloomsbury. The portico is very fine, and is a much-admired feature of the building. It is supposed to have been chiefly copied from that at St. Martin's, but in certain details it shows an improvement upon that portico.

RECTORS OF ST. GEORGE'S, BLOOMSBURY.

	Inducted
Edward Vernon, D.D.	February 23rd, 1731.
Charles Tarrant, D.D.	May 1st, 1761.
Thomas Willis, LL.D.	March 16th, 1791.
John Lonsdale, B.D.	February 8th, 1828.
Thomas Vowler Short, B.D. ...	February 22nd, 1834.
Hon. Henry Montagu Villiers, M.A. ...	July 9th, 1841.
Sir John R. L. E. Bayley, M.A. ...	May 24th, 1856.
Edward Capel Cure, M.A.	July 13th, 1867.
Field Flowers Goe, M.A.	January 20th, 1877
Archibald Boyd-Carpenter, M.A. ...	April 1st, 1887.

9

BLOOMSBURY MARKET.

Bloomsbury Market appears to have been one of the earlier buildings which were erected on this spot. In 1708 its chief business was in flesh and poultry, and in 1720 it is described by Stow as "a long Place with two Market Houses, the one for Flesh and the other for Fish; but of small account, by reason the Market is of so little use and so ill served with provisions; insomuch, that the Inhabitants deal elsewhere." The map of St. Giles's parish which was published with this account shows the building to have occupied a space resembling the three sides of a quadrangle.

In the year 1822 the market was still standing, but·it exhibited little of that bustle and business which distinguished other similar establishments.

SOUTHAMPTON HOUSE.

This mansion, originally the manor-house of Bloomsbury, formerly stood upon the north side of Bloomsbury Square—in fact, where Bedford Place now is. It received its name from its founder, the Earl of Southampton, lord of the manor in the reign of Henry VIII., and retained it until the marriage of the daughter and heiress of the last Lord Southampton with William Lord Russell. This amiable lady addressed several of her letters from the house, mentioning it by the name of "Southampton· House, Southampton Square," and in one case she writes "Russell House, Southampton Square." From the last-mentioned circumstance it is probable that that name was first applied to the house, before it became to be generally known as Bedford House.

Babington's Plot, the object of which was to assassinate Queen Elizabeth, and place Mary Queen of Scots on the throne, was concocted at Southampton House, and at other places in the parish of St. Giles-in-the-Fields. The plot was discovered, and Babington and his accomplices, seven in all, were hanged and quartered in Lincoln's Inn Fields. Mary's presumed share in this conspiracy alarmed Elizabeth, and was the principal cause of her subsequent trial and execution.

In the grounds of this mansion the Parliament erected a fort, consisting of two batteries and a breastwork, for the defence of London.

John Evelyn tells us, in his Diary, that on February 9th, 1665, he dined here, at the house of the Lord Treasurer, the Earl of Southampton, which house, he considered, stood too low, but had some good rooms, a pretty cedar chapel, a naked garden to the north, and good air.

A new mansion was built here, under the direction of the celebrated architect Inigo Jones, and for more than a century it was the town residence of the noble family of Russell.

The following are some particulars as to this. spot which appeared in Stow's "Survey of London" (1720 edition) :—

Southampton Street was very spacious, with good houses, well inhabited and resorted to by gentlemen for lodgings. This street came out of High Holborn, and fronted the square called Southampton Square (now Blooms-bury Square), being a large place railed in; with rows of large buildings on all sides. That on the east side was called Seymour Row ; that on the south, Vernon Street ; that on the west, Allington Row ; and the whole of the north side of the square was occupied by Bedford House, or as it is called in the "Survey," Southampton House. There was a spacious courtyard in front of the house, and a curious garden behind, open to the fields.

Bedford House (for so it seems to have been generally known after it became the residence of the Dukes of Bedford) was demolished in the year 1800. The Duke of Bedford having disposed of the materials of the house for £5,000 or £6,000, a sale of the furniture, pictures, etc., by Mr. Christie, commenced on May 7th, when the most crowded assemblage were gratified with a last view of this fine old house.

The late Duke fitted up the gallery, which was the only room of conse-quence in the house, and placed in it Sir James Thornhill's copies of the cartoons upon which that eminent artist bestowed three years' labour. They were purchased by his Grace, at the sale of Thornhill's collection, for £200, and at the Bedford House sale they were purchased by the Duke of Norfolk for £450. "St. John Preaching in the Wilderness," by Raphael, fetched 95 guineas; "The Archduke Leopold's Gallery," by Teniers, 210 guineas ; a beautiful painting of an Italian villa, by Gainsborough, 90 guineas. Four paintings of a battle, by Cassanovi, which cost his Grace £1,000, were sold for 60 guineas ; a landscape by Cuyp, 200 guineas ; two beautiful bronze figures, Venus di Medici and Antonius, 20 guineas ; Venus *couchant*, from the antique, 20 guineas. Another of the pictures was the duel between Lord Mahon and the Duke of Hamilton.

The week after were sold the double rows of lime-trees in the garden, valued one at £90, the other at £80. They occupied the space upon which Russell Square now stands.

One of the chief artistic treasures of Bedford House was a fine statue of Apollo, which used to ornament the hall. It was not sold, but removed to Woburn Abbey.

Thomas Pennant, writing in 1790, mentions that the chapel of South-ampton House (*i.e.*, of Bedford House) was at that time rented by Mr. Lockyer Davis as a magazine for books. Davis was a well-known printer, publisher, and auctioneer of books, of the eighteenth century. He was bookseller to the Royal Society, printer of the Votes of the House of Commons, Master of the Stationers' Company, and an honorary registrar of the Literary Fund, founded in 1790. He died in 1791.

MONTAGUE HOUSE.

The earliest account of this mansion, which in its prime was reckoned one of the finest residences in or near London, appears to be that contained in Evelyn's "Diary." From an entry under the date of May 11th, 1676, we learn that the "new palace" of Mr. Montague was built by Mr. Hooke, a member of the Royal Society.

In an entry describing a visit to the place on November 5th, 1679, Evelyn mentions that it was most nobly furnished, and had a fine but too much-exposed garden.

On October 10th, 1683, Evelyn went to see Montague House, "a palace lately built by Lord Montague, who had married the most beautifull Countesse of Northumberland. It is a stately and ample palace. Signior Verrio's fresca paintings, especially the funeral pile of Dido, on the stayrecase, the labours of Hercules, fight with the Centaurs, effeminacy with Dejanira, and Apotheosis or reception amongst the gods, on the walls and roofe of the greate roome above, I think exceeds any thing he has yet don, both for designe, colouring, and exuberance of invention, comparable to the greatest of the old masters, or what they so celebrate at Rome. In the rest of the chamber are some excellent paintings of Holbein and other masters. The garden is large, and in good aire, but the fronts of the house not answerable to the inside The Court at entrie, and wings for offices seeme too neere the streete, and that so very narrow and meanely built that the corridore is not in proportion to the

rest, to hide the court from being overlook'd by neighbours, all which might have ben prevented had they plac'd the house further into the ground, of which there was enough to spare. But on the whole it is a fine palace, built after the French pavilion way, by Mr. Hooke, the Curator of the Royal Society."

Robert Hooke was an eminent English mathematician, and a man remarkable for the possession of one of the most inventive minds the world has ever seen. For many years of his life he was closely associated with the Royal Society, and among the buildings which he is said to have designed were Bethlehem Hospital and the College of Physicians.

Signor Verrio, whose skill was so largely employed in the ornamenting of the interior of Montague House, was born in Naples in 1634. He came to England in 1671, on the invitation of Charles II., who proposed to re-establish the tapestry manufacture at Mortlake. When his talents for painting became recognized the King employed him to paint the ceilings of Windsor Castle. James II. also patronized him, and he was employed at Burleigh by Lord Exeter, and afterwards at Chatsworth. He died at Hampton Court, in 1707.

It is very greatly to be regretted that these beautiful works of art have not been fated to remain to our day. In January, 1686, Montague House was burnt to the ground, "than which," says Evelyn, "for painting and furniture there was nothing more glorious in England. This happen'd by the negligence of a servant airing, as they call it, some of the goods by the fire in a moist season ; indeede so wet and mild a winter had scarce been seene in man's memory."

Lady Rachel Russell, who at that time was living in Southampton House, thus describes the lamentable occurrence, in a letter addressed to Dr. Fitzwilliam, and dated January 22nd, 1686 :—

"If you have heard of the dismal accident in this neighbourhood, you will easily believe Tuesday night was not a quiet one with us.

"About one o'clock in the night I heard a great noise in the square, so little ordinary, I called up a servant, and sent her down to hear the occasion ; she brought up a very sad one, that Montague House was on fire ; and it was so indeed ; it burnt with so great violence, the house was consumed by five o'clock.

"The wind blew strong this way, so that we lay under fire a great part of the time, the sparks and flames covering the house and filling the court. My boy awoke and said he was almost suffocated with smoke, but being told the reason, would see it, and so was satisfied without fear ; and took a strange bedfellow very willingly, Lady Devonshire's youngest boy, whom his nurse had brought wrapt up in a blanket. . . . Thus we see what a day brings forth, and how momentary the things are we set our hearts upon."

The house was built up again, after the fire, upon the same plan as before, but the valuable works of art and furniture were utterly destroyed.

It is said that the new building of Montague House was erected under the direction of Pierre Puget, an eminent sculptor, painter, and architect, but there does not appear to be much evidence in support of the assertion.

In 1708 Montague House was described as constituting three sides of a quadrangle, and composed of fine brick and stone rustic-work ; the roof covered with slate, and the front decorated with four figures, representing the four cardinal virtues, viz., Fortitude, Justice, Prudence, and Temperance.

A contemporary critic finds fault with the arrangement by which the main part of the house was hidden behind a brick wall, so that it could only be seen from the inside of the court, which was a large square. At each corner there was a turret, and over the great Ionic arch of entrance a large and handsome cupola. Within the court there was a grand colonnade of chaste and well-proportioned Ionic pillars.

The visitor, who crossing the courtyard entered the building, found himself in a stately hall at the foot of the grand staircase, which was one of the most striking features in the interior architecture, and a representation of which is given in Ackermann's " Microcosm of London." Its walls and ceiling, and the walls and ceilings of all the principal rooms, were adorned with fresco paintings by three French artists—Charles de la Fosse, Jacques Rousseau, and Jean Baptiste Monoyer, executed with admirable skill, and representing flowers and dead game, as well as several of the stories in Ovid's " Metamorphoses." The show-rooms, twelve on the ground floor, and as many on the first floor, were in general stately and well lighted, the front row looking on the courtyard, and the back on the garden. A ground-plan of the whole was published in Dodsley's " London and its Environs," in 1761, and another in Britton and Pugin's " Public Edifices in London," in 1823.

The gardens around the house were laid out in the French manner, conformably with the building, and in them were statues of a gladiator, Venus and Cupid, etc., and several fountains and formal parterres, so common in the last century.

MOUNTAGUE HOUSE
in Great Russell Street

These gardens occupied a large space at the back of Montague House, and about the end of the eighteenth century they were laid out in grass terraces, borders with flower-beds, and with two large grass-plots in the centre, divided by a large gravelled walk, where the gay world resorted in the summer's evening.

The back was open to the country, to the west as far as Lisson Green and Paddington ; to the north to Primrose Hill, Chalk Farm, Hampstead, and Highgate ; and to the east to Battle Bridge, Islington, St. Pancras, etc.

The second wife of the first Duke of Montague was the mad Duchess of Albemarle, widow to Christopher, second Duke of that title. She married her second husband as Emperor of China, which gave occasion to a scene in the play of Cibber's " Sick Lady Cured." She was kept in the ground apartment during his Grace's life, and was served on the knee to the day of her death, which happened in 1734, at Newcastle House, Clerkenwell, at the age of ninety-six.

The ground behind the north-west end of Great Russell Street was occupied by a farm belonging to two old maiden sisters of the name of Capper. They wore riding-habits and men's hats ; one rode an old grey mare, and it was her spiteful delight to ride with a large pair of shears after boys who were flying their kites, purposely to cut their strings ; the other sister's business was to seize the clothes of the lads who trespassed on their premises to bathe. There were only a few straggling houses between Capper's Farm and the King's Head Inn, celebrated by the famous picture of Hogarth's " March to Finchley."

The whole of the ground north from Capper's Farm, at the back of the British Museum, so often mentioned as being frequented by duellists, was in irregular patches, many fields with turnstiles. The pipes of the New River Company were propped up in several parts to the height of six or eight feet, so that persons walked under them to gather watercresses, which grew there in great abundance and perfection, or to visit " the Brothers' Steps," in connection with which there were many local traditions.

Perhaps the tradition which was most generally believed in was to the effect that two brothers were in love with a lady, who would not declare a preference for either, but coolly sat upon a bank to witness the termination of a duel, which proved fatal to both. The bank, it was said, on which she sat, and the footmarks of the brothers when pacing the ground, never produced grass again. These marks were in a field which was the site of Mr. Martin's Chapel. The reason of the grass not growing was to be found, of course, in the frequency with which the spot was visited by curious persons.

Aubrey, in his " Miscellanies," states, " The last summer, on the day of St. John Baptist (1694), I accidentally was walking in the pasture behind Montague House; it was 12 o'clock. I saw there about two or three-and-twenty young women, most of them well habited, on their knees very busie, as if they had been weeding. I could not presently learn what the matter was; at last a young man told me, that they were looking for a coal under the root of a plantain to put under their heads that night, and they should dream who would be their husbands. It was to be found that day and hour."

CHAPTER X.

THE BRITISH MUSEUM.

HIS magnificent establishment, of which the nation has such
good reason to be proud, is, by reason of its extent and
wide sphere of usefulness, and the grandeur of its priceless
collections, by far the most important institution of its kind
in the kingdom, and the most important object for the
student and sight-seer in Bloomsbury.

There is a peculiar appropriateness in the fate which led to the selection
of Bloomsbury as the site for the British Museum, inasmuch as many of its
most valuable contents, and its chief original founder, were for many years
associated with that parish.

Sir Hans Sloane, an eminent physician, naturalist, and benefactor to
learning, was born at Killileagh, co. Down, April 16th, 1660. His father,
Alexander Sloane, was a native of Scotland, but removed to Ireland, and was
collector of the taxes for the county of Down both before and after the Irish
rebellion.

The early years of Hans Sloane, until he was nearly sixteen years of age, were spent in natural history studies, a subject of which he was passionately fond, and to which he devoted great and careful attention. When in his sixteenth year an illness of a serious nature confined him to his room for three years, and necessitated the relinquishment of his favourite studies. Upon the recovery of his health, he studied chemistry and the preliminary branches of physic. He also studied his favourite science of botany at Chelsea Garden, which was then but just established by the Druggists' Company, and at that early period of his life he made the acquaintance of Boyle and Ray.

Four years after, he attended the lectures of Tournefort and Du Verney at Paris, and he is supposed to have taken his degree in medicine at Montpellier or Orange. He returned to England, and on January 21st, 1685, he was elected a Fellow of the Royal Society. In 1687 he entered the College of Physicians, yet so great was his ardour for natural science, that he relinquished these flattering prospects in order to pursue his more congenial studies.

He embarked for Jamaica, as physician to the Duke of Albemarle, in 1687, and made so good use of his short stay there, and at the other places where his vessel called, as to come home laden with a rich harvest of natural history specimens and curiosities. Dr. Sloane returned to England in 1689, and fixing his residence in London, soon became an eminent man. In the year 1694 he was chosen physician to Christ's Hospital. In 1693 he was elected Secretary to the Royal Society, and he revived the publication of the "Philosophical Transactions," which had been interrupted from the year 1687. About the same time he became a member of the College of Physicians, and in 1719 he became its President. In 1701 Dr. Sloane was incorporated Doctor of Physic at Oxford ; in 1708 he was elected a foreign member of the Royal Academy of Sciences at Paris, a distinction of the highest estimation in science, and the greater at that time as the French nation was at war with England, and the Queen's consent was necessary to the acceptance of it.

The commencement of a museum of Dr. Sloane's collections was made at an early date, and numerous gifts from friends rapidly augmented its contents. His residence in Bloomsbury Square was crowded with specimens and curiosities. In the year 1725 the collection comprised 26,200 articles of natural history, exclusive of 200 volumes of preserved plants. He began in February, 1741-2, to remove his library and museum from his house at

Bloomsbury to that at Chelsea, whither he went himself to reside on the 12th May following. It was quite natural that he should object to the dispersal of his magnificent museum after his death, and therefore he bequeathed it to the public on the condition that £20,000 should be paid by Parliament to his family.

It was this circumstance which led immediately to the founding of the British Museum. An Act of Parliament was passed in 1753 (Sir Hans Sloane having died in 1752), providing for the purchase of the collection of Sir Hans Sloane, and of the Harleian Collection of Manuscripts, and for procuring one general repository for their reception, along with the Cottonian Collection, etc.

For this purpose the sum of £300,000 was needed, and recourse was had to a public lottery for raising or helping to raise the money. Above £95,000 was raised in this way, in 1753 and 1754. The £20,000 due to the daughters of Sir Hans Sloane were paid out of it. By the Act of Parliament incorporating the Museum in 1753, forty-seven trustees had been appointed. These gentlemen now proceeded to choose a suitable building for the reception of the collections, and Montague House, Bloomsbury, at that time the property of Lord Halifax, was bought by them for the sum of £10,000, and fitted up for the purpose.

·In treating of Montague House we have already given some particulars of its history up to this point.

Statutes and rules having been framed, and proper officers appointed, the British Museum was opened to the public on January 15th, 1759. Nothing was charged for admission, but only ten persons were admitted at a time, and these were broken up into two companies, and allowed only one hour's space for the examination of each department.

Great fears appear to have been entertained in those early days that harm or robbery would be committed if the general public were admitted. It was suggested that upon those days when a general public holiday occurred a committee of the Trustees should be in attendance, "with at least two justices of the peace and the constables of the division of Bloomsbury; but besides, these civil officers would have to be supported by a guard, such as usually attended at the play-house; and even after all this many accidents must and would happen." It is almost unnecessary to say that these fears proved entirely groundless, and experience has shown that the public are thoroughly able to appreciate the collections which have been provided for their instruction and entertainment.

In order to inspect the British Museum it was necessary to make application in writing for a ticket of admission. The list of such " studious and curious persons " as desired a ticket was submitted every night to the Principal Librarian, or in his absence to another officer of the Museum, who, if he considered the parties admissible, was to "direct the porter to deliver tickets to them according to their said request, on their applying a second time for the said tickets," observing, however, that not more than ten tickets were delivered for each time of admission. As has already been stated, only a limited time, three hours in all, was allowed for the inspection of the Museum, and the party was taken in charge by a different officer for each of the three departments into which the Museum was at that time divided.

The following minute of the Trustees of the British Museum, dated June 21st, 1759, gives some rather amusing information as to an officer's duty in the first year of the Museum's history :—

"The Committee think proper to add that the requiring the attendance of the officers during the whole six hours that the Museum is kept open is not a wanton or useless piece of severity, as the two vacant hours (if it is not thought too great a burden upon the officers) might very usefully be employed by them in better ranging the several collections, especially in the Department of Manuscripts, and preparing Catalogues for publication, which last the Committee think so necessary a work that till it is performed the several collections can be but imperfectly useful to the public."

" In point of fact," says Fagan, in his " Life of Panizzi," " these *Librarians* were *ciceroni*. In 1802, after forty-three years, three attendants were appointed to relieve the Under and Assistant Librarians from the daily duty of showing the Museum, and their salaries were advanced."

But it does not appear, says the Report of 1807, "that the Under or Assistant Librarians received any particular injunctions to execute the several duties proposed for them, nor does it appear by their subsequent conduct that they understood themselves to be under any specific duties of that description." " So that," continues the Report, "the public has been, and is, at an annual expense of above £2,000 a year for the mere purpose of showing the house to strangers, and providing an attendant upon the Reading-room."

In the first " Synopsis," or official guide to the Museum, published in

1808, it is stated that on the first four days of the week 120 persons may be admitted to view the Museum, in eight companies of fifteen each ; but no mention is made of the necessity of their previously obtaining tickets. In the "Synopsis" of 1810 a great advance appears. "According to the present regulation," it is stated, "the Museum is open for public inspection on the Monday, Wednesday, and Friday in every week (the usual vacations excepted), from ten till four o'clock, and all persons of decent appearance who apply between the hours of ten and two are immediately admitted, and may tarry in the apartments or the gallery of antiquities without any limitation of time, except the shutting of the house at four o'clock."

From that period the regulations have been constantly growing more liberal, and the collections have been made as accessible as possible to the general public.

In the year 1850 above a million persons, and in the following year more than two and a half million persons, visited the British Museum. It is very remarkable that with these large numbers of visitors the only conspicuous act of destruction of the Museum property that has occurred was the act of a madman—the breaking of the Portland Vase in 1845.

One very satisfactory feature in the history of the British Museum, from its very first establishment, is the number and value of the accessions to its stores which it has received, in the form of donations. From the commencement, valuable objects and collections of every description, and from every part of the globe, were poured in upon it, until at the beginning of this century it was so over-filled that the antiquities gained by the Egyptian expedition in 1801, and the Townley Marbles, bought in 1805, lay scarcely sheltered from rain in the Museum yards, and a gallery was erected for both collections in 1807. A new gallery was also built to receive the magnificent library of George III., which was given to the nation in 1823. This wing, which may be said to be the first part built of the present British Museum, was ready for the reception of the royal library in 1828. This magnificent apartment, forming the first part of the projected building, is what is generally known as the "King's Library."

Parliament having voted supplies, the work of building the new Museum went on gradually. In the year 1845 old Montague House had entirely disappeared. The new building was finished in 1847. It was designed by Sir Robert Smirke, R.A., and is pronounced by universal verdict not unworthy the noble collection within its walls.

The building (as Sir Robert Smirke designed it) was a hollow square, in the Grecian Ionic order. Its principal front, facing Great Russell Street, presents an imposing columnar façade, 370 feet in length. The residences of the chief officers of the establishment are situated on each side of the Museum.

It was not long before better accommodation was found to be necessary for the Library, which was increasing, both in readers and books, at a rapid rate. The quadrangular plot of ground enclosed by the four sides of the Museum afforded the necessary space for a new building for the Library and a large Reading-room. How well that space has been utilized, and how admirable are all the arrangements of the large circular Reading-room, are well known to the many thousands of students who make use of its advantages from time to time.

Mr. (afterwards Sir) Anthony Panizzi, whose name is very intimately asso-ciated with the British Museum, was keeper of the Department of Printed Books when the proposal was made to build a new Library, and he sketched out a plan for the new building, the centre of which was to be the circular Reading-room, and the four angles and other available spaces of ground round it to be occupied by a building, chiefly of bricks, iron, and glass, specially calculated for the safe storage and easy accessibility of the rich bibliographical treasures which it was destined to receive. Mr. Panizzi's plan was adopted. Parliament voted the first grant of money for the new building in 1854, and the foundations of it were commenced in May, and the first brick laid in September, in the same year. In less than three years the great work was completed, the new Reading-room being entirely finished by the end of April, 1857. The opening ceremony took place on May 2nd, 1857, a grand break-fast being given at the British Museum in honour of the occasion. Amongst other notabilities present were the following : The Archbishop of Canterbury, Earl and Countess of Clarendon, Earl Cawdor, Earl of Aberdeen, the Speaker of the House of Commons, Sir Charles and Lady Eastlake, Lady Cranworth, Baron Marochetti, the Dean of St. Paul's and Mrs. Milman, Professor Owen, Lord Panmure, Lord and Lady John Russell, Sir George and Lady Grey, Earl Spencer, the Duke of Somerset, the Bishop of London and Mrs. Tait. His Royal Highness the Prince Consort would have been present had he not been unavoidably prevented by the death of the Duchess of Gloucester.

Everything considered, perhaps it was the proudest day in the history of the British Museum. The new buildings met with universal approval from the distinguished visitors who inspected them, and who breakfasted in the central Reading-room, using the catalogue-desks as tables.

To Panizzi is due the praise not only of suggesting the idea of the new Reading-room and Library, upon which the architect, Sydney Smirke, R.A., worked out his plans, but also of overseeing the details of the work as the structure progressed towards completion. This successful issue brought compliments and congratulations from all quarters, and it was almost universally admitted that Panizzi had planned the most elegant, convenient, and perfect Reading-room which was possible upon the space at his command.

The Reading-room, which contains ample accommodation for more than three hundred readers, is constructed principally of iron, with brick arches between the main ribs, and is roofed over by a magnificent dome of copper, 106 feet in height, and 140 feet in diameter. The dome is formed into two separate spherical and concentric air-chambers, extending over the whole surface—one between the external covering and brick vaulting, the object being the equalization of temperature during extremes of heat and cold out of doors ; the other chamber, between the brick vaulting and the internal visible surface, being intended to carry off the vitiated air from the Reading-room. This ventilation is effected through apertures in the soffits of the windows, and partly by others at the top of the dome ; the bad air passing through outlets provided around the lantern. In size the dome is second only to the Pantheon of Rome. Two galleries run round the walls on the inside of this room, giving access, including those books within reach from the floor of the room, to 60,000 volumes. There are about twenty-five miles of shelves in the Library, and nearly all this almost incredible space is occupied by books.

The whole of the quadrangle is not occupied by the new Library and Reading-room, there being unavoidably a clear interval of from 27 to 50 feet all round, to give light and air to the surrounding buildings.

This addition to the British Museum provided for the extension of the Library for many years to come, but the archæological and natural history collections had much outgrown the spaces allotted to them in the new buildings, and for the convenience of both, and after much deliberation, it was eventually determined to separate them, and give the collections of natural history specimens a home of their own. They were transferred to the branch

Museum specially built for their reception at Cromwell Road, South Kensington, in the years 1880—1883.

The life-like bust of Panizzi, executed in marble by Marochetti, which stands over the public entrance to the Reading-room, was the result of a movement initiated by Mr. Winter Jones, at that time the Keeper of the Department of Printed Books, for the provision of a suitable and permanent memorial of one whose name must ever be intimately associated with the British Museum.

The internal arrangements of the Reading-room are perhaps as nearly perfect as it is possible for any reading-room to be. In the centre, and raised sufficiently above the floor to command a view of the whole room, sits the Superintendent, and around him are the officials whose business it is to examine the books which readers return after consultation. The next circular desk contains catalogues of maps, manuscripts, and various books of reference. On the outside of this is another ring of desks, which contain the volumes of the Catalogue of Printed Books, a stupendous work, which, until partially reduced by printing, occupied about two thousand volumes. From this point partitions extend in lines from the centre of the room to its circumference, and on both sides of each partition are seats for eight readers. Every seat is amply furnished with pens, ink, blotting-pad, and racks for books. All around the Reading-room, within reach of the readers, there is a magnificent selection of standard books of reference and the works of authors in greatest request. These books, like all the books throughout the British Museum Library, are arranged upon the shelves with reference to their subject, irrespectively of language or date. There is an excellent key-plan to the books in the Reading-room, from which it is easy at a glance to see where any particular book is likely to be found. In addition to that, there is a special catalogue for these books, arranged according to subject as well as according to author.

The reader is at liberty to consult all these volumes at his pleasure, with the very reasonable condition that he replace each volume as soon as he may have finished with it. The books which are reached from the two circular galleries which run all around the room are such as are most often in request. A special catalogue of them, too, has also been prepared. The great advantage of having them within the Reading-room is that they are thus accessible in the winter evenings, long after the general Library is in complete darkness. In order to consult these books in the galleries of the Reading-room, and also in

PORTRAIT OF SIR HANS SLOANE. *After the Painting by Kneller.*

the general Library, it is necessary for the reader to fill up and sign a form, which is then kept as a check against him until he return the book to the central desk when he has done with it.

The floor of the Reading-room is covered with kamptulicon, which deadens all foot-falls, and the tables and book-rests are so covered with leather as almost to prevent the possibility of disturbance; thus perfect silence is maintained, although more than three hundred literary men and women are working together in the same room.

The Reading-room is illuminated by electric light, five brilliant arc-lights being suspended at a convenient height from the dome. The light is produced on the premises, one part of the basement of the building being devoted to the engines which are necessary for its generation.

Early in the year 1890 the public galleries of the British Museum were fitted up with electric light, by which means the various collections are available to the public during the dark evenings of winter.

WHITE WING.

One of the most important of the recent additions to the building of the British Museum is that known as the White Wing, a fine series of rooms, built with the money munificently bequeathed for that purpose by William White, Esq., a barrister, who died on the 13th May, 1823. By his will, dated the 10th December, 1822, he directed that, on the death of his wife and child, his landed property, consisting of an estate named Hildern and Holms, near Botley, in Hampshire, and houses in Cowes, Isle of Wight, and, after payment of legacies, his personal estate, on the death of his wife, should revert to the Trustees of the British Museum.

The claim of the Trustees to the landed property was disputed, and by a decree in the Vice-Chancellor's Court, July, 1826, disallowed, the devise to the Museum being pronounced to be invalid, as within the provisions of the Statute of Mortmain. The net sum of upwards of sixty-five thousand pounds, however, came into the possession of the British Museum in the year 1879, and it came very opportunely, for at that time Government was spending large sums of money on a new building at South Kensington for the Natural History Departments, and was altogether inaccessible to appeals for similar outlay at Bloomsbury, where, notwithstanding the great gain of space obtained by the separation of these collections, there was still urgent need of further accommodation for some of the departments.

The Greek and Roman sculptures wanted space for proper arrangement ; relief was urgently demanded for the crowded state of the Reading-room ; the Department of Manuscripts had no suitable room for readers consulting the select manuscripts used only under special supervision ; and the Department of Prints and Drawings had been waiting many years for space adapted to the growth of the collections and for their exhibition. All these wants were very pressing, and they were met more or less satisfactorily by the help of Mr. White's bequest. A gallery was built in connection with the Department of Greek and Roman Antiquities, for the better display of the remains of the Mausoleum of Halicarnassus ; and an extensive building was erected on the south-eastern side of the Museum, with front to Montague Street, and with wings on each side connecting it with the main building.

Within this new structure a Reading-room for newspapers has been opened, and space has been found for the storage of the London journals and Parliamentary papers. Working rooms, and additional space for its collections, have been provided for the Department of Manuscripts. The Ceramic and Glass Collections have gained a well-lighted gallery ; and the entire Department of Prints and Drawings has obtained convenient accommodation, with a large gallery for the exhibition of its treasures.

The following is a list of the Principal Librarians of the British Museum, with the dates of their tenure of office :—

GOWIN KNIGHT, M.D., 1756—1772.
MATTHEW MATY, M.D., 1772—1776.
CHARLES MORTON, M.D., 1776—1799.
JOSEPH PLANTA, 1799—1827.
SIR HENRY ELLIS, K.H., 1827—1856.
SIR ANTHONY PANIZZI, 1856—1866.
JOHN WINTER JONES, V.P.S.A., 1866—1878.
EDWARD AUGUSTUS BOND, C.B., LL.D., F.S.A., 1878—1888.
EDWARD MAUNDE THOMPSON, D.C.L., LL.D., F.S.A., 1888.

Originally there were only three departments in the British Museum, viz., of Manuscripts, Printed Books, and Natural History, and from them others have been gradually developed.

DEPARTMENT OF PRINTED BOOKS.

This is the largest of the various departments into which the British Museum is divided, with respect both to the space which is occupied by its collections, and also the number of the studious public who avail themselves of its inestimable advantages.

Among the treasures bequeathed by Sir Hans Sloane were 50,000 volumes of printed books. These formed a very good nucleus for a large library, and as time went on many valuable additions were made to them. In 1757 George II. presented the library of printed books which had been collected by the Kings of England since Henry VII., and which included the libraries of Cranmer and Casaubon.

The collection comprised about 10,500 volumes, and was rich in interest from its numerous memorials of the Tudors and the Stuarts.

Before the end of the last century the Library received several presentations, one of which was a remarkable collection of about 30,000 tracts relating to the Civil War, 1641-49, collected by George Thomason, and presented by George III.; other gifts included those of Mr. Salomon da Costa, Dr. Birch, Mr. Speaker Onslow, and Major Edwards; also Hawkins's works on music, Garrick's collection of old English plays, Dr. Bentley's collection of the classics, with his own MS. notes, Musgrave's biographical library, Methuen's books in Italian and Portuguese, and the magnificent library formed by Mr. Cracherode, which consisted of about 4,500 volumes, including sumptuously printed works, and rare editions of the classics.

In 1820 this department was enriched by Sir Joseph Banks's bequest of his natural history library, comprising 16,000 volumes. The next great accession was the splendid library of George III., which was presented to the nation by George IV. in 1823. This gift comprised upwards of 65,000 volumes of printed books, 8,000 pamphlets, a large geographical and topographical collection, and 446 volumes of manuscripts. The "King's Library," as it was thenceforth called, is rich in Caxtons, contains a copy of the Mazarine Bible—the earliest known printed book—and specimens of early, sumptuous, and rare books. Anything like an enumeration of its most noteworthy items is, however, quite impossible. Twenty thousand pamphlets relating to the French Revolution were obtained in the same year.

In 1847 the large and priceless library of the Right Hon. Thomas

Grenville was added by bequest. It contains 20,240 volumes, many of which are the rarest editions of works, the finest specimens of printing, and nearly all in perfect and well-preserved condition.

George II. annexed to the British Museum the important privilege which the royal library acquired in the reign of Queen Anne, of being supplied with a copy of every publication entered at Stationers' Hall.

A mere list of the many libraries and collections of books which, upon their dispersal, have contributed towards the augmentation of the treasures of the British Museum would fill many lines, and would be too lengthy for mention here.

The Department of Printed Books includes the Sub-department of Maps ; the Newspaper Room, situated in the building which has resulted from the White bequest ; the Oriental Room, situated upon another floor in the same part of the building ; and the Chinese and Japanese Room. Among the contents of the last-mentioned room is a very remarkable Chinese encyclopædia.

The bookcases in the library are of novel and simple construction, the uprights or standards being formed of malleable iron galvanized and framed together, having hard wood inserted between the iron to receive the brass pins upon which the shelves rest. The shelves are formed of iron galvanized plates, edged with wainscot and covered with russet hide leather, and having a book-fall attached. They are fitted at each end with galvanized iron leather-covered and wadded pads, placed next the skeleton bookcase framing, to prevent injury to the binding when the books are taken out or replaced.

In all cases, except against the external walls, the bookcases are double, the books being placed with their edges opposite. The whole building is divided into convenient sections by floors of iron grating, which grating contains a sufficient number of apertures to allow of the passage of light from the glass roofs to the basement. Lifts have also been constructed for the easy and expeditious removal of books from and to the various floors.

All the books are arranged upon the shelves according to the subject on which they treat. Thus, all books upon History may be expected to be found near together, without any reference to the place or date of publication. Each bookcase, or press, is numbered, and all the books belonging to it also bear the same number. The volumes are arranged in each press pretty much with reference to size. Thus, all octavos would as a general rule be together. Each shelf in a press is distinguished by a certain letter of the alphabet, the top shelf being *a*, the next *aa* or *b*, and so on. The books, therefore, are marked not only with the number of the press, but also with the shelf letter. In many cases, too, the volumes bear a third mark, each several book being marked 1, 2, 3, etc., according to its position upon the shelf, counting from the left hand. The necessity of accuracy in these marks is of the greatest importance, inasmuch as they form the key by which the particular volume wanted may easily and quickly be found among the many hundreds of thousands of volumes by which it is surrounded.

In consequence of the rapidly increasing accumulation of books upon certain subjects, many of the presses have become quite filled up, and an ingeniously planned press moving upon wheels has been fitted up in many cases, to relieve the undue crowding of books upon the shelves. This hanging press is so made as to fit the existing ironwork of the building, and so light and strong is it that whilst a slight pressure will suffice to move it along the iron bars, its capacity for the storage of books is double that of the old presses; and this economy of space is effected at no serious expense of convenience.

DEPARTMENT OF MANUSCRIPTS.

The history of this department is in some respects similar to that of the Department of Printed Books. It was formed at the outset by the union of three great collections, viz., the Harley, the Sloane, and the Cotton collections. These formed the nucleus of the department, and in the year 1757 the Royal Collection was added to them.

The Sloane Collection was named after Sir Hans Sloane, the eminent physician, naturalist, and benefactor to learning. It formed part of the library which he collected with great pains, and consists of 4,100 volumes, for the most part of paper, and chiefly written in the sixteenth and seventeenth centuries. The greater portion of the manuscripts treat of medicine, alchemy, astrology, etc.; there are, moreover, many important historical papers, journals of voyages and travels, and original correspondence, including that carried on between Dr. Sloane and nearly all the eminent scientific men of his day, in thirty-four folio volumes.

The Cottonian Manuscripts form one of the chief sources from which historians;and writers on Constitutional subjects, topographers, antiquaries, and, in short, all persons interested in the literature or history of past ages, have derived their materials. They were collected by Sir Robert Cotton, a descendant from a very ancient family which, in the reign of Edward III., flourished in the county of Chester. He was born at Denton, near Conington, in Huntingdonshire, on the 22nd January, 1570. He had imbibed a taste for the history and antiquities of his county, and he neglected no opportunity of increasing his collection of chronicles, chartularies, and other original muniments, which, at the late dissolution of the monasteries, had found their way into the hands of private persons. The collection consists chiefly of ancient chronicles, Biblical manuscripts, State papers of the fourteenth, fifteenth, and sixteenth centuries; chartularies; early copies of the Holy Scriptures, and of other works; transcripts of and extracts from records; collections relative to various courts, offices, etc.; and numerous and valuable manuscripts written in the Anglo-Saxon language.

The books are called by the names of the twelve Cæsars, from having, when in Sir Robert Cotton's possession, been deposited in presses over which were placed the busts of those emperors, together with those of Cleopatra and Faustina.

Sir Robert died in May, 1631, his death being hastened by the loss of his library, which had twice been taken possession of by the Government, on the plea of it containing information too dangerous to be disseminated. At his death the library was delivered up to his only son, Sir Thomas Cotton, from whom it descended to his son, Sir John Cotton.

In the year 1700 a statute was passed for the better settling and pre serving of the library kept in the house at Westminster called Cotton House, in the name and family of the Cottons, for the benefit of the public. In 1707 an agreement was made, by virtue of an Act of Parliament, with Sir John Cotton, for the purchase of the inheritance of the house where the library was deposited, for the sum of £4,500. The library was removed to Essex House, in Essex Street, in the Strand, in the year 1712, where it remained until 1730. It was then conveyed to Westminster, and deposited in Ashburnham House, situated in Little Dean's Yard, which was purchased by the Crown for that purpose. In the year 1731 a fire unfortunately occurred, and destroyed and injured many of the manuscripts. Several of them have been since restored. Before the fire occurred there were 958 volumes; 114 volumes were destroyed, and 89 volumes were rendered defective ; so that only 746 entire volumes remained sound and entire. The library was removed into a new building designed for the dormitory of Westminster School, where they remained until the establishment of the British Museum in 1753, when it was deposited there for the use of the public.

The Harley Collection was founded by Robert Harley, Earl of Oxford, who was born on the 5th December, 1661. At his death, in 1724, his son and successor, Edward, the second Earl, followed the noble example set by his father, and devoted a great part of his fortune to the increasing of the collections of books and manuscripts. At his death, in June, 1741, the library became the property of his daughter and heiress, Margaret Cavendish, Duchess of Portland, and on the institution of the British Museum, in 1753, it was purchased of the Duke and Duchess, by the country, for the sum of £10,000. The collection contains 7,639 volumes, exclusive of 14,236 original rolls, charters, deeds, and other legal instruments. Its contents are of great importance and value, but of a too miscellaneous character to allow of a bare enumeration even of the classes of its various treasures. ·

The " Old Royal Library " has been mentioned already, in connection with the Department of Printed Books. It contained, in addition to upwards of ten thousand volumes of printed books, a collection of manuscripts, dating from the reign of Richard III. to that of Charles II., in about 1,950 volumes. In the year 1757 King George II., under an instrument that passed the Great Seal, presented this valuable library of books and manuscripts to the nation. At that time it was deposited in the Old Dormitory at Westminster, to which place it had been removed from Ashburnham House at the time of the fire there in 1731. From thence it was transferred to Montague House, and placed among the other collections.

The Royal Collection is particularly rich in old scholastic divinity, illuminated manuscripts, chronicles, etc.

The Lansdowne Collection was purchased in the year 1807, of William Petty, first Marquis of Lansdowne, for the sum of nearly five thousand pounds. The number of volumes amounts to 1,245, and among the contents of them are the State papers and miscellaneous correspondence of Lord Burleigh ; the correspondence and other papers of Sir Julius Cæsar (*temp.* Queen Elizabeth) ; the collections of Dr. White Kennett, chiefly relating to ecclesiastical history and biography ; letters and State papers from eminent personages, between the reign of Henry VI. and that of George III. ; Petyt's Parliament collections ; selections from the Patent Rolls, in fifteen volumes ; reports of law cases, from the reign of Henry VIII. to that of Charles I., in fifteen volumes, and other legal manuscripts ; collections for topography and heraldry ; and valuable Biblical and classical manuscripts.

The Hargrave Collection is so called after its founder, Francis Hargrave, Esq., who was born about the year 1741. He was an eminent law writer, and so greatly distinguished himself in the *habeas corpus* case of James Somersett, a negro, in 1772, that he was appointed one of the King's Counsel. He was afterwards made Recorder of Liverpool, and died in August, 1821. In 1813, Parliament, in compliance with a proposal from himself, passed a vote for the purchase of his valuable library for the sum of eight thousand pounds.

The manuscripts, about five hundred in number, relate almost exclusively to law. They consist of year-books, reports, readings on various statutes, treatises on the authority and jurisdiction of the several courts of law and equity, collections of cases and opinions, collections respecting the customs and privileges of London and other places, and tracts and dissertations on numerous points and matters of law, with a few historical, political, and miscellaneous papers and letters.

The Burney Collection is named after Rev. Charles Burney, D.D., the son of Dr. Burney, author of the "History of Music." At the death of Rev. Charles Burney, in 1817, his fine library was purchased by the Government for £13,500, a sum that scarcely exceeded one-half of what it had cost. The manuscript collections amounted to about 520 volumes, the most important being copies of classical authors. More than eighty of the number are in the Greek language.

The King's Collection. The magnificent library of printed books collected by King George III., and presented to the nation in the year 1823, by King George IV., was accompanied by a fine collection of manuscripts, amounting to about 440 volumes. When first deposited in the British Museum, in the year 1828, they were suffered to remain in the position which they had occupied when in the royal library, namely, intermixed with the printed collection. Some years afterwards, however, it was deemed advisable that a place should be assigned to them among the collections in the Department of Manuscripts. They were accordingly transferred, in the year 1840, to that department, and received the name of the "King's Collection."

THE BRITISH MUSEUM. 1853.

They are miscellaneous in their contents. They comprise many elegantly written copies of the Latin classics, important historical works, large collections of instructions to ambassadors at various courts, between the years 1525 and 1656, valuable treatises and papers on the harbours and fortifications of England and its dependencies, numerous manuscripts on fortification and military architecture, journals of sieges, etc., and beautiful manuscripts relating to heraldry.

The Egerton Collection takes its name from Francis Henry Egerton, eighth Earl of Bridgewater, who collected and bequeathed to the Trustees of the British Museum sixty-seven volumes of manuscripts and ninety-six charters. By a further bequest, two separate sums of five thousand pounds and seven thousand pounds, invested in the Three per Cent. Consols, were left to them "upon trust ; " the interest of the first-named sum to be laid out "in maintaining, improving, keeping up, augmenting, and extending, and in binding " the said collection of manuscripts ; and that of the second, amounting to £227 0s. 6d. a year, "to be paid over to such person or persons as shall, from time to time, be charged with the care and superintendence of the said collection."

The manuscripts, which chiefly relate to the history and literature of France and Italy, were deposited in the Museum on July 24th, 1829.

In the year 1838 the funds of this collection were greatly augmented, at the decease of the Right Hon. Sir Charles Long, Baron Farnborough, who left the fixed annual sum of £86 3s. 4d., being the interest of £2,872 6s. 10d. in the Three per Cent. Consols, for the purchase of manuscripts, "as an addition to the Bridgewater bequest."

The Egerton Collection is consequently being added to from year to year, as funds allow.

The Arundel Collection was brought together by Thomas Howard, twenty-third Earl of Arundel, Duke of Norfolk. After his death in 1646, his collections were partially dispersed ; his printed books being presented in 1681, by Mr. Henry Howard, to the Royal Society, and his manuscripts being shared between that Society and the College of Arms.

In the year 1831, in consequence of an agreement with the Trustees of the British Museum, the manuscripts which came into the possession of the Royal Society, with the exception of those in Oriental languages, were transferred to the British Museum. The Oriental manuscripts, about fifty in number, and mostly in the Arabic language, were not received until the year 1835. That portion of the collection, exclusive of the Oriental, now deposited in the British Museum amounts to 550 volumes, and is of unusual interest and value in almost every branch of learning. It is singularly rich in the materials for the history of our own country, including many important chartularies and monastic registers, together with ample materials for illustrating the origin and progress of the English language.

The Additional Collection includes those manuscripts, whether purchased by or presented to the Trustees, since the foundation of the British Museum, which have not been deemed of sufficient bulk or importance to form separate collections. Their numbers are, of course, being added to from year to year.

The Stowe Collection of manuscripts was formed by the Marquis of Buckingham at the beginning of the nineteenth century, and derives its name from Stowe, his country seat, where it was kept. The collection amounted to nearly a thousand manuscripts, and included Anglo-Saxon charters, early English historical manuscripts, also a number of manuscripts in the Irish language and relating to Ireland, and other valuable historical and literary papers.

In April, 1849, the collection was offered to the Trustees of the British Museum, but the negotiations for the purchase failed ; and the collection was eventually sold to the late Earl of Ashburnham.

In the year 1883 the Trustees of the British Museum purchased the Stowe manuscripts, apart from Lord Ashburnham's other collections, and this valuable mass of historical material was, by order of the Government, deposited in the British Museum, excepting certain Irish manuscripts, and manuscripts relating to Ireland, which were transferred to the library of the Royal Irish Academy in Dublin.

Large acquisitions to the treasures of the Manuscript Department have been made from time to time by purchase and donation.

DEPARTMENT OF PRINTS AND DRAWINGS.

Among the contents of this department are included the collections of Sir William Hamilton, acquired in 1772 ; Mr. Townley, 1805, 1814 ; Baron Moll, 1815 ; Mr. Payne Knight, 1824 ; Mr. Sheepshanks, purchased in 1836 ; Mr. Harding, purchased in 1842 ; Raphael Morghen's works, purchased in 1843 ; Sir William Gell's drawings, bequeathed by the Honourable Keppel Craven, 1852 ; the political prints of Mr. Edward Hawkins, formerly Keeper of the Antiquities, purchased in 1867 ; the collection of Mr. Felix Slade, bequeathed in 1868 ; and that of Mr. John Henderson, bequeathed in 1878.

A fine series of prints is exhibited to the public in the second northern gallery.

The contents of the department are of the greatest value and interest, many of the prints being in the finest possible state, and many of the original drawings being the work of the old masters, but it is quite impossible to particularize them in this account.

In addition to the various official catalogues, etc., published by order of the Trustees, a valuable "Handbook to the Department of Prints and Drawings in the British Museum" was published in the year 1876, by Mr. Louis Fagan, one of the officers of that department.

DEPARTMENT OF ANTIQUITIES.

This department took its rise from the purchase, in 1772, of the collection formed by Sir William Hamilton, while Ambassador at the Court of Naples, the foundation of which was the collection of fictile vases belonging to the family of Porcinari. It included, in addition, numerous objects in terra-cotta and in glass, very many coins and medals, together with bronzes, sculptures, gems, and miscellaneous antiquities. A sum of £8,400 was specially voted for the purchase of this collection. A large portion of a second collection, of equal extent to the first, was lost by shipwreck.

The foundation of the Egyptian Section of the department was laid by the acquisition, in August, 1802, of the antiquities which came into the possession of the nation upon the occasion of the capitulation of Alexandria.

In the years 1805 and 1814 the department was further enriched by purchases of classical sculpture and other objects collected by Charles Townley, of an ancient family of Lancashire. The collection includes the majority of the finer single statues now in the Museum. The chief of them came from excavations at Hadrian's Villa, near Tivoli ; from the Mattei collection at Rome ; from excavations at the villa of Antoninus Pius at Monte Cagnuolo, near the ancient Lanuvium, and from the Villa Montalto at Rome ; or were acquired by various purchases.

During the collector's life these marbles were preserved in a house adapted for the purpose in Park Street, Westminster. Mr. Townley, who died in the year 1804, by his will bequeathed his collection to his brother, on condition of his expending on a building, for its exhibition, a sum of not less than £4,500 ; or failing his brother's acceptance of the condition, to his uncle, on the same terms ; and if declined by both legatees, it was to go to the British Museum. In the following year, 1805, a grant of £20,000 was obtained from Parliament, to enable the Trustees of the British Museum to make an arrangement with the family for the purchase of the marbles ; and subsequently, in 1814, the bronzes, coins, gems, and drawings of Mr. Townley's Collection, which were not included in the bequest, were acquired for the sum of £8,200.

In the years 1814 and 1815 the department was enriched by the addition of portions of the frieze, metopes, and pedimental sculptures of the Parthenon of Athens, and of the frieze of the Temple of Apollo at Phigalia, in Arcadia.

The Parthenon sculptures—partly the work of Phidias, and the most precious relics of antiquity—with other works of Greek art at its highest points of excellence, had been brought together by the Earl of Elgin, chiefly during his embassy at Constantinople in the years 1799 and 1811 ; and an Act for the purchase of his collection, for £35,000, was passed in July, 1816.

The Lycian Marbles were procured during two expeditions in the years 1842-44, by Sir Charles Fellows, and consisted chiefly of reliefs from an Ionic edifice, and from the so-called Harpy Tomb, at Xanthus ; together with a miscellaneous assortment of sculpture from different places at the south-western angle of Asia Minor.

The sculptures from the Mausoleum of Halicarnassus comprised several bas-reliefs, with combats of Greeks and Amazons, and were procured for the Museum through Sir Stratford Canning, at that time H.M. Ambassador at Constantinople.

The excavations of Sir A. H. Layard, on the site of the ancient Nineveh, between the years 1847 and 1850, resulted in the discovery of many antiquities, which, with others subsequently obtained, were exhibited in a suite of three long, narrow rooms, originally intended for other purposes, exceeding 300 feet in length. A collection of Persepolitan marbles, presented in the year 1825, by Sir Gore Ouseley, were placed for exhibition in the same part of the Museum.

Further sculptures and other antiquities, excavated by Sir C. T. Newton, from the site of the Mausoleum of Halicarnassus, during the years 1856-58, and comprising many additional slabs from the frieze, two colossal statues, together with portions of two colossal horses, and of the quadriga which surmounted the edifice, with columns, etc., were also brought to the British Museum, and placed with other valuable specimens of ancient art.

A curious collection from the site of the Temple of Apollo at Didymi, and from Cnidus, embracing several sitting figures of the earliest Greek art, also a colossal lion in stone, were obtained by Sir C. T. Newton in 1857-58, and deposited in the British Museum.

During the years 1856-59 a large number of mosaic pavements, and nearly one hundred Phœnician inscriptions, were excavated on the site of ancient Carthage by the Rev. Nathan Davis. The pavements are of Roman date, and are now exhibited upon the walls of the north-west staircase. Since then many choice works of Greek sculpture have been added to the Museum ; especially may be mentioned those obtained from excavations at Cyrene in 1861, and by purchase from the Farnese Palace at Rome in 1864. The latest acquisitions of great importance are the remains of extremely interesting sculptured columns and other objects recovered from the buried ruins of the Temple of Ephesus in the years 1863-75, under the direction of Mr. J. T. Wood, and a series of architectural members and pieces of sculpture, with a number of very important Greek inscriptions, excavated by the Society of Dilettanti, on the site of the Temple of Athena Polias at Priene, and presented by them in the year 1870. These successive acquisitions have made the Museum collection of Greek marbles one of the richest in Europe in works of the finest art.

An interesting account is given of a visit paid by Nollekens, the eminent sculptor, to the British Museum : " Soon after I had the honour of being appointed Keeper of the Prints and Drawings in the British Museum," says the author of his excellent biography, Mr. John Thomas Smith, " Mr. Nollekens, accompanied by Mr. Gibson and Mr. Bonomi, the sculptors, came to visit me. Upon my being apprised of my old friend's arrival in the gallery, I went to meet him, in order to see that he had a chair, as he was then very feeble. I remember, when he was seated in the middle of the Elgin Room, he put the following question to the late Mr. Combe, loud enough to be heard by every one present who approached to see him : ' Why did you not bring the Ægina Marbles with you ? they are more clever than the Phygalian Marbles. How could you be so stupid as to miss them ?' Mr. Combe, thinking to divert him from the subject, said, ' I thought you wore hair-powder, sir. I continue to wear hair-powder, and always use the best I can get.' Mr. Nollekens, not hearing him, repeated nearly the same question in a louder voice : 'I say ! why did you let them go ?' Fortunately for Mr. Combe, however, he was sent for, and so escaped a farther interrogation.

"Mr. Nollekens then walked up to No. 64, the fragment of a male figure, and exclaimed, 'There, you see—look at that shoulder and a part of the breast—look at the veins ! The ancients *did* put veins to their gods, though my old friend Gavin Hamilton would have it they never did.'

"When he was again descending to the Townley Gallery he stopped at the first flight of steps, and taking hold of a button of my coat, desired me to go and stand there ; adding, 'Now, you stand where Queen Charlotte sat when she came to see the Museum : she was very tired ; they brought her a chair, and I stood upon the steps below.' .

"As we were passing along the gallery he said, 'Ay, I remember seeing the tears fall down the cheeks of Mr. John Townley when the Parliament said they would buy the marbles. He didn't wish 'em to take 'em, and he said to me, "Mr. Nollekens, if Government don't take my nephew's marbles, I'll send 'em down to Townley Hall, and make a grand show with 'em there." Poor man, I shall never forget how forlorn he looked.' When he arrived at the Terra-cotta Room he exclaimed, looking up, 'How white these things are getting now ! I daresay they put 'em into the wall with wet plaster ; they should have put 'em in with what Mr. Townley used to call bitumen, and then they wouldn't moulder. Well, make my compliments to Mr. Planta ; I've remembered him, and so I have Combe, though he did let the marbles slip through his fingers ; and so I have you, Tom. Well, good-bye ! this Museum will be a fine place very soon.' 'Ay, sir,' observed I ; 'suppose you were to leave us your fine heads of Commodus and Mercury ;' to which he answered, 'Well, perhaps I may : Townley wanted *'em* very much, but I could not get my price ; he sent to me about *'em* just before he died.'"

THE PORTLAND VASE.

A word or two may be said about the destruction of the Portland Vase, one of the most beautiful specimens of Grecian art in existence.

On the 7th February, 1845, Panizzi, at about a quarter to four, when descending the staircase of the Museum, leading from the room where the Portland Vase stood, to the outer door, observed the perpetrator of this singular piece of barbarity in the act of running away; and he used to relate, with the greatest emotion, how delighted he should have been to stop him (as he might have done), had he known the man's dastardly conduct, and to have inflicted on the spot that ' chastisement which the law was powerless to administer. The suddenness and unexpectedness of the deed probably saved the rascal from an immediate attack ; he had seized an ancient brick kept in the room, and deliberately aimed it at the treasure, nor would he, on being questioned at the time, give any account of the motives which had prompted him to commit so wilfully mean and base an act. His name was William Lloyd, and he was a native of Dublin. No time was lost in conveying him to Bow Street, where he was remanded by the sitting magistrate. The utmost punishment the magistrate, Mr. Jardine, was able to inflict—£3, or two months in default—was absurdly inadequate to so signal an offence. The money was, moreover, paid very soon after, by some perverse sympathiser, and the offender was set free.

The vase has been cleverly restored by experts, so that upon a superficial examination it is almost impossible to detect a flaw in it.

The principal part of this beautiful vase is composed of dark blue glass, the subject upon it being in white opaque glass in cameo. It was discovered about the middle of the sixteenth century, in a tomb under the Monte del Grano, near Rome, enclosed within a marble sarcophagus. The tomb is supposed to have been that of the Emperor Alexander Severus and of his mother, Julia. The vase and sarcophagus were deposited in the palace of the Barberini family at Rome, and the vase was purchased, in the year 1770, by Sir William Hamilton, from whose possession it passed into that of the Duchess of Portland, who purchased it for 1,800 guineas. In the year 1810 the Duke of Portland allowed it to be exhibited in the British Museum, and in 1845 occurred the lamentable incident of which we have just given some particulars.

DEPARTMENT OF EGYPTIAN AND ORIENTAL ANTIQUITIES.

The foundation of the extensive and valuable collection of Egyptian antiquities for which the British Museum is famous was laid when the great monuments of Egypt collected by French *savans* during the occupation of that country by the army of Napoleon I. were ceded to England, at the capitulation of Alexandria, in the year 1801.

In the year 1823 the Trustees of the British Museum purchased, by aid of Parliament, Mr. Salt's first collection of Egyptian antiquities (exclusive of the sarcophagus afterwards purchased by Sir John Soane) for two thousand pounds. In 1834 another collection, particularly illustrative of the domestic manners of the ancient inhabitants of Egypt, belonging to Mr. Joseph Sams, was purchased by the Parliament for the British Museum, for the sum of two thousand five hundred pounds. A considerable number of antiquities of the same description were presented to the British Museum in the same year by J. G. Wilkinson, Esq., and in 1835 a still larger accession was obtained by an expenditure of £5,081 16s., at the sale of Mr. Salt's third collection of antiquities, including numerous papyri which have since been unrolled. In that year also Lord Prudhoe presented to the Museum the two fine lions of red granite which he had procured at Jebel Barkal, in Nubia.

From that time to the present day no year has passed without considerable additions being made to the Egyptian and Oriental collections.

The collection of Egyptian mummies which is exhibited in a room on the upper floor of the Museum is remarkably fine.

DEPARTMENT OF BRITISH AND MEDIÆVAL ANTIQUITIES.

A collection of British antiquities was commenced in 1851. It comprises illustrations of the early history of the British Islands, through its various phases of early British, Roman, and Saxon, enriched by the donation from Canon Greenwell of his very valuable collection of early British remains excavated from the burrows of England, and comprising about two hundred British urns, and a large number of relics found with them.

The Mediæval Section has been greatly assisted by the following donations and bequests : Rare pottery, Oriental arms, etc., by Mr. John Henderson, in 1878 ; European and Oriental armour, by Mr. William Burges, A.R.A., in 1881 ; Oriental armour, military weapons, and other objects, by Major General Meyrick, in 1878. Specimens of majolica, Oriental porcelain, and antiquities of all descriptions have from time to time been presented by Mr. A. W. Franks, the Keeper of the department.

The addition of the prehistoric and general collection of Henry Christy, presented by his trustees to the nation in 1865, has raised the collection to a character of great importance.

DEPARTMENT OF COINS AND MEDALS.

This department, from being a small branch of general antiquities, has grown to be a separate department. The first considerable acquisitions were derived from the general collections of Sir Robert Cotton and Sir Hans Sloane. The cabinet of Anglo-Saxon coins of Samuel Tyssen was purchased in the year 1802, for £620; and this was followed, in 1805 and 1814, by the Townley Collection; in 1810 by that of English coins formed by Edward Roberts, of the Exchequer, bought by Parliamentary vote for £4,200; in the following year by the Greek coins of Colonel De Bossett, for £800; in 1824 by the coins and medals in Richard Payne Knight's Collection; in 1833 by the Greek and Roman coins of H. P. Borrell, of Smyrna; for £1,000, in 1836, by the Oriental collection bequeathed by William Marsden; in 1856 by Greek and Roman coins from Sir William Temple's collection; in 1861 by Mr. De Salis's collection of Roman coins of all metals; in 1864 by Mr. Edward Wigan's collection of imperial Roman coins; in 1866 by upwards of four thousand coins, chiefly Roman gold, from the Blacas Collection; in the same year by the Greek coins bequeathed by Mr. James Woodhouse.

In the year 1872 the sum of ten thousand pounds was expended in the purchase of the finest specimens of Greek and Roman coins in the Wigan Collection. In 1877 a very important addition was made to the collection by the donation of the cabinet of coins and medals belonging to the Bank of England, including the Cuff and Haggard medals.

A very fine collection of gems belonging to the Department of Greek and Roman Antiquities is placed on exhibition in a room adjoining this department, popularly known as the "Gold Room," where are exhibited many articles of ornament in pure gold and silver, cameos and intaglios, and with other objects of great pecuniary value, apart from that which is derived from their antiquity and historical associations.

CHAPTER XI.

THE GORDON RIOTERS AT BLOOMSBURY.

HE "Gordon Riots," which arose from a bitter opposition by some people to the Act of Parliament passed in 1778 in favour of Roman Catholics, and which took their name from the leader of the movement, Lord George Gordon, are closely connected with the district around Bloomsbury and St. Giles's, and constitute one of the most important political events in its history during the latter half of the eighteenth century.

The sign adopted by the "No Popery" rioters was that of a blue cockade, which each of them wore in his hat. Having collected in great numbers in St. George's Fields, on May 29th, 1780, it was decided to march with Lord George Gordon to the House of Commons on the following Friday, June 2nd, in order to present their petition. When the day arrived Lord George Gordon, at about 11 o'clock, led the assembled multitude; some crossed the river over London Bridge, others over Blackfriars Bridge, and others over Westminster Bridge. A roll of parchment, containing the names of those who had signed the petition, was borne before them.

Upon their arrival at the Houses of Parliament, the multitude soon became unruly, and molested several of the Peers and members of the Lower House, as they were making their way through the crowds, to take their places in the Houses of Parliament. The Archbishop of York, the Lord President of the Council, Lord Bathurst, and Lord Mansfield were treated with considerable violence. The Bishop of Lichfield had his gown torn, the wheels of the

Bishop of Lincoln's carriage were taken off, and the Duke of Northumberland was robbed of his watch. Many others were very badly treated.

Lord George Gordon, having taken his position in the House of Commons, opened his business by informing them that he had before him a petition signed by nearly 120,000 of His Majesty's Protestant subjects, praying "a repeal of the Act passed the last session in favour of the Roman Catholics," and moved to have the said petition brought up. Upon a division leave was refused, and the House adjourned.

Thereupon the mob dispersed in different divisions from Palace Yard, and some of them went to the Roman Catholic Chapel in Duke Street, Lincoln's Inn Fields, others to that in Warwick Street, Golden Square, both of which they in a great measure demolished.

On Sunday afternoon, June 4th, the rioters attacked the chapels and dwelling-houses of the Roman Catholics in and about Moorfields. They stripped their houses of furniture, and their chapels not only of the ornaments and insignia of religion, but tore up the altars, pulpits, pews, and benches, and made fires of them, leaving nothing but the bare walls. On the following day havoc was wrought upon other chapels and houses, including the houses and shops of Mr. Rainsforth, tallow chandler, of Stanhope Street, Clare Market, and Mr. Maberly, of Little Queen Street, who had given evidence on the examination of those who had been committed. The houses and shops were literally stripped, and their contents committed to the flames. On Tuesday the prison at Newgate and the new prison at Clerkenwell were fired, and the prisoners incarcerated therein were released. A party was sent also to the house of Justice Cox, situated in Great Queen Street, and to the residences of certain Roman Catholics who resided in Devonshire Street, Red Lion Square. These houses were pillaged and burnt. The writings of Sir John Fielding were destroyed, and among many other acts of violence was the total destruction of Lord Mansfield's house and library in Bloomsbury Square.

DESTRUCTION OF LORD MANSFIELD'S HOUSE.

The neighbourhood of Bloomsbury Square was the scene of some disgraceful and serious riots in connection with the Gordon Riots. The Earl of Mansfield at that time occupied a house in Bloomsbury Square, and being very unpopular with the riotous mobs which infested the streets of the metropolis, rumours were heard that violence and spoliation were intended. Indeed, it was at one time openly declared that before morning they would burn down his Lordship's house. The threatenings of the mob being narrated to Sir John Hawkins and another Middlesex magistrate, they proceeded with a detachment of the Guards to Bloomsbury Square. Obtaining an interview with Lord Mansfield, they informed him of his danger, and proposed to station the soldiers in and around his house. To this he objected, insisting that they should be marched off and concealed in a church at some little distance, viz., at St. George's Church, Bloomsbury, where they were accordingly hidden. He feared that the sight of the soldiers might tend to exasperate the mob.

After a pause of half an hour's space, distant yells, and the inevitable noises which accompany the marching together of a large, disorderly body of people, proclaimed that the rumours were not without foundation. In fact, an immense multitude, carrying torches and combustibles, were marching down Holborn and entering Bloomsbury Square.

Lord Mansfield was a man of considerable courage, and even when he saw the mob marching towards his house, in the north-east corner of the square, he refused to fly for safety. But when they began to batter his door he retreated by a back passage with his Countess; and he had hardly effected his escape when the leaders of the mob were seen at the upper windows of the house, tearing down and throwing out furniture, curtains, hangings, pictures, books, papers, and everything they could lay their hands on likely to serve as fuel for the fire which was already blazing below. Many of the mob, having made their way into his Lordship's cellars, suffered from intoxication.

The rioters declared that there was to be no pillage, and that they were acting from principle. One of the incendiaries, to show his disinterestedness, threw into the burning pile a valuable piece of silver plate and a large sum of money in gold, which he swore should not " go in payment of masses." The house was soon blazing; flame was vomited from every window; and as no attempt was or could be made to arrest their progress, long before morning nothing of the stately structure remained but the bare and blackened walls.

A very valuable library of books, many of them containing MS. notes by Pope and Bolingbroke, was destroyed in this fire, and numerous papers of perhaps yet greater value, consisting of letters between himself, his family, and his friends, which he had been preserving for half a century, shared the same unhappy fate. It is thought probable that Lord Mansfield proposed to use

ENCAMPMENT OF TROOPS IN GARDENS OF THE BRITISH MUSEUM AT THE TIME OF THE GORDON RIOTS. 1780.

these letters as materials for Memoirs of his time, and it is also believed that he had amused his leisure by writing, for posthumous publication, several treatises on juridical subjects, and historical essays, filling up the outline of the admirable sketch he had given in his " Letters of Advice to the Duke of Portland." Thus the loss of his valuable collection of books and papers is greatly to be deplored.

The following stanzas were written by the poet Cowper upon this occasion :—

" So, then, the Vandals of our isle,
　Sworn foes to sense and law,
Have burnt to dust a nobler pile
　Than ever Roman saw !

" And Murray sighs o'er Pope and Swift,
　And many a treasure more,
The well-judged purchase and the gift
　That graced his lettered store.

" Their pages mangled, burnt, and torn,
　Their loss was his alone,
But ages yet to come shall mourn
　The burning of his own.

　　·　　·　　·　　·　　·

" When wit and genius meet their doom
　In all-devouring flame,
They tell us of the fate of Rome,
　And bid us fear the same.

" O'er Murray's loss the Muses wept ;
　They felt the rude alarm,
Yet blessed the guardian care that kept
　His sacred head from harm.

" There memory, like the bee that's fed
　From Flora's balmy store,
The quintessence of all he read
　Had treasured up before.

" The lawless herd, with fury blind,
　Have done him cruel wrong :
The flowers are gone ; but still we find
　The honey on his tongue "

Lord Mansfield must have felt the loss of his valuable books and papers as a very heavy blow, but he took no steps to claim reparation from the State, knowing that it was impossible for any reparation to be made of his real loss.

Being a man of great wealth, he declined to throw any part of the pecuniary damage upon shoulders less able to bear it.

At the trial of Lord George Gordon, at the Court of King's Bench, Lord Mansfield had to preside as judge, and it was a high compliment to his impartiality that neither the prisoner, his counsel, nor his friends were at all alarmed at Gordon's fate being placed in the hands of one who had suffered so much from the Gordon Riots.

During these riots an encampment was formed in Hyde Park, and also in the gardens of the British Museum, then called Montague House, for the troops who were stationed in London and its vicinity, to quell the rioters.

JOHN SCOTT, EARL OF ELDON.

Lord Eldon, the celebrated Lord Chancellor, who lived at No. 6, Bedford Square, took a principal share in all the political debates of his time, and by his support of the Corn Bill rendered himself so unpopular that on leaving the House of Lords he was pursued by a mob to his residence, in Bedford Square, from which he escaped by the assistance of a sentinel, over a wall, into the gardens of the British Museum. The populace even went so far as to attach a rope to a lamp-post at his own door, for the purpose, as they threatened, of hanging him.

The rioters broke the windows, tore up the iron railings, and bursting open the outer door, rushed into the hall. There they were checked by a guard of soldiers, called in through a back entry from the British Museum, and a manœuvre intended to represent the military force much greater than it really was having succeeded, they were panic-struck and took to flight. Lord Eldon then gallantly sallying forth, brought in two prisoners, and said to them, " If you don't mind what you are about, lads, you will all come to be hanged." On which one of them said, as their friends were coming to their rescue, " Perhaps so, old chap ; but I think it looks *now* as if you would be hanged *first."* In telling the story the old Peer would add, " And I had my misgivings that he was in the right." However, he got his wife and children safely into the Museum, and the mob were dispersed by a large reinforcement of soldiers.

For three weeks his house was a garrison, and during all that time he could only get to Westminster Hall by going stealthily through the Museum gardens, and diving into all the obscure alleys in which he could find a passage, attended by Townsend, the Bow Street officer, and a rear-guard of policemen.

The story of the appointment of Mr. Jekyll to the post of Master in Chancery, rendered vacant by the death of Mr. Morris on April 13th, 1815, is thus told by Lord Eldon himself:—

"The fact was, that Jekyll was a great favourite with everybody ; he was the descendant of an eminent lawyer, Sir Joseph Jekyll, who had been Master of the Rolls ; everybody wished him to be well provided for, in a proper mode. Nobody wished *that* more than I wished it ; but I hesitated for weeks and months before I made the appointment. His most anxious and most powerful well-wisher was the Prince Regent, who was very much attached to him, and with whom Jekyll had spent many convivial hours. He was a person of great humour and wit, and indulged himself in manifesting his wit and humour to a great extent, and, I believe, without having ever said an ill-natured, provoking, or rude thing of or to any man whilst he was so indulging himself.

"The Prince Regent, after having applied to me repeatedly at Carlton House to appoint Mr. Jekyll the Master, without effect, and having often observed that a man of his sense and abilities would soon be able to learn his business (which might be very true, but the appointment would nevertheless introduce a most inconvenient host of candidates from the Common Law Bar for Chancery offices), at length, in furtherance of his purpose, took the following step : He came alone to my door in Bedford Square. Upon the servants going to the door, the Prince Regent observed that as the Chancellor had the gout, he knew he must be at home, and he therefore desired he might be shown up to the room where the Chancellor was. My servants told the Prince I was much too ill to be seen. He, however, pressed to be admitted, and they, very properly and respectfully, informed him that they had positive orders to show in *no* one. Upon which he suddenly asked them to show him the staircase, which, you know, they could not refuse to do. They attended him to it, and he immediately ascended, and pointed first to one door, then to another, asking, ' Is that your master's room ? '—they answering, ' No '— until he came to the right one ; upon which he opened the door and seated himself by my bed-side.

"Well, I was rather surprised to see his Royal Highness, and inquired his pleasure. He stated that he had come to request that I would appoint Jekyll to the vacant Mastership in Chancery. I respectfully answered that

I deeply regretted his Royal Highness should ask that, for I could not comply. He inquired why I could not, and I told him simply because, in my opinion, Mr. Jekyll was totally unqualified to discharge the duties of that office. He, however, repeated his request, and urged very strongly. I again refused, and for a great length of time he continued to urge, and I continued to refuse, saying Mr. Jekyll was unfit for the office, and I would never agree. His Highness suddenly threw himself back in his chair, exclaiming, ' How I do pity Lady Eldon ! ' ' Good God,' I said, ' what is the matter ? '—' Oh, nothing,' answered the Prince, ' except that she will never see you again, for here I remain until you promise to make Jekyll a Master in Chancery.' Well, I was obliged at length to give in ; I could not help it. Others ought really to be very delicate in blaming appointments made by persons in authority, for there often are very many circumstances totally unknown to the public."

DR. JOHN RADCLIFFE.

Among the many eminent and remarkable men who have lived at Bloomsbury, perhaps Dr. John Radcliffe deserves to rank as one of the most eccentric. Although a man of great skill in medicine, his caprice in his profession appears to have been unbounded, and although possessed of ample means, he was avaricious, even to sponging.

Dr. Radcliffe was born in 1650, at Wakefield, in Yorkshire, and in 1684 he went to London, and settled in Bow Street, Covent Garden. When he became an eminent man in his profession he resided among the aristocratic circle in Bloomsbury Square. His house is that which is now known as No. 5, Bloomsbury Square.

After the Revolution he often professionally attended King William and the great people about the Court. This distinction was due solely to his merits as a medical practitioner, for it does not appear that he ever inclined to be a courtier. In 1694 Queen Mary caught the small-pox and died, and, from Bishop Burnet's account, it appears that the physician's part was universally condemned, and that her death was imputed to the negligence or unskilfulness of Dr. Radcliffe. He was called for ; and it appeared but too evident that his opinion was chiefly considered and most depended on. Other physicians were afterwards called, but not till it was too late.

When Queen Anne was taken with her last illness, Dr. Radcliffe was sent for, but for some reason or other this eccentric man refused to attend Her Majesty. He said he had taken physic, and could not come. A few hours afterwards the Queen died. It was proposed in Parliament, four days afterwards, that Dr. Radcliffe should be sent for, and censured for not attending the Queen. Public opinion ran very high against the Doctor, and he states, in a letter written at Carshalton to his friend Dr. Mead, that he feared that he would be pulled to pieces if he ever went to London again.

Dr. Radcliffe only survived Queen Anne three months. He died August 1st, 1714. He left his books and large sums of money to the University of Oxford, and thus founded the library there which still bears his name.

There is a curious story told which illustrates Dr. Radcliffe's remarkable aversion to paying his just debts. A pavior, after long and fruitless attempts, caught him just getting out of his chariot at his own door, in Bloomsbury Square, and set upon him. "Why, you rascal," said the Doctor, "do you pretend to be paid for such a piece of work ? Why, you have spoiled my pavement, and then covered it over with earth to hide your bad work." "Doctor," said the pavior, "mine is not the only bad work that the earth hides ! " "You dog, you," said the Doctor, "are you a wit ? you must be poor. Come in," and the Doctor paid the bill.

In 1699 King William III., returning from Holland and being indisposed, sent for Radcliffe, and showing him his swollen ankles, while the rest of his body was emaciated and skeleton-like, said, "What think you of these ? " "Why, truly," replied the physician, "I would not have your Majesty's two legs for your three kingdoms," which freedom lost the King's favour, and no intercessions could ever recover it.

Bloomsbury Square is ornamented by a large bronze statue of Charles James Fox, the celebrated statesman. The figure is of colossal dimensions, being cast to a scale of 9 feet in height, and is represented in a sitting posture, habited in consular robes, the ample folds of which give breadth and effect to the whole. The likeness of Fox is considered to be well preserved, and it has been remarked by a critical observer that the head is inclined forward, and is expressive of attention, firmness, and complacency, whilst dignified serenity is depicted upon the countenance.

The work was executed by Westmacott, the famous sculptor, and is reckoned to be one of the finest examples of his style.

The statue is elevated upon a pedestal of granite, surmounting a spacious base formed of four steps or gradations. The pedestal and statue together are about 17 feet in height.

The following brief inscription is inscribed upon the pedestal :—

CHARLES JAMES FOX.

ERECTED
MDCCCXVI.

ISAAC D'ISRAELI.

This distinguished literary character resided at No. 6, Bloomsbury Square, from 1818 to 1829, but he was intimately associated with the neighbourhood of Bloomsbury many years before the former date mentioned, as from an early period he read regularly at the British Museum, where he met Douce, who encouraged him in his literary researches. In the year 1791 he issued anonymously his "Curiosities of Literature ; consisting of Anecdotes, Characters, Sketches, and Observations, Literary, Critical, and Historical." D'Israeli pre-sented the copyright to his publisher, John Murray, of 32, Fleet Street (father of John Murray, of Albemarle Street), but the book had an immediate success, and D'Israeli procured the copyright of the book again, by purchase at a sale, a few years later. A second volume was added in 1793, a third in 1817, two more in 1823, and a sixth and last in 1834. The work was often revised and reissued during the author's lifetime.

On February 10th, 1802, D'Israeli married, and the children of the marriage were baptised at St. Andrew's Church, Holborn, in the year 1817. He was no observer of Jewish customs, although until the year 1813 he pro-fessed membership with that body. The final severance took place in that year, when the elders of the London congregation of the Spanish and Portu-guese Jews elected D'Israeli warden without consulting him. He declined to accept the office, and was fined by the elders the sum of £40. This fine D'Israeli refused to pay, although he offered to continue the ordinary con-tributions. His withdrawal was not formally accepted until the year 1821.

During his residence in Bloomsbury Square, D'Israeli is said to have been a frequent attendant at St. George's Church, Bloomsbury. His chief literary work during that period was his "Commentaries on the Life and Reign of Charles I.," a book which is generally regarded as his most valuable work, and as a mark of recognition and honour, D'Israeli was created D.C.L. at Oxford on July 4th, 1832. Whilst living at Bloomsbury Square he also, in 1820, noticed "Spence's Anecdotes" in the *Quarterly Review*, and sought to vindicate Pope's moral and literary character. There is no doubt that much of the literary assistance which he gave to John Nichols and other literary men whom he numbered among his friends at that time was given while he, as a resident of Bloomsbury, was within easy access of that great storehouse of learning and general information the British Museum Library.

D'Israeli removed from Bloomsbury in 1829, and died at Bradenham House, Buckinghamshire, in 1848.

BENJAMIN DISRAELI, EARL OF BEACONSFIELD

The birthplace of this eminent political and literary character has been the subject of considerable discussion and variety of opinion. As is usually the case when a man rises to a high degree of popularity and fame, many neighbourhoods with which the younger Disraeli was known to have been connected during his youth and early boyhood have striven for the honour of having been his birthplace.

According to various authorities who have written upon the subject, Hackney, Islington, St. Mary Axe, and Bloomsbury Square have each, for various reasons, been mentioned as the place of Benjamin Disraeli's birth. A writer in the "Dictionary of National Biography" affirms that the true address is No. 6, John Street, Bedford Row.

It is at least certain that Benjamin Disraeli was born on December 21st, 1804, and baptised at St. Andrew's, Holborn, on July 31st, 1817, and in the register at that church he is described as "from King's Road, and said to be about twelve years of age." It is known that Isaac d'Israeli occupied at that time the house in King's Road, next to the corner of John Street, now known as No. 22, Theobald's Road.

In the year 1817 or 1818, when Benjamin was about thirteen or fourteen years of age, Isaac d'Israeli removed with his family to No. 6, Bloomsbury Square, and both father and son, and probably the other members of the family, attended the services at St. George's Church, Bloomsbury. The house still stands unaltered, except that the brick front has been newly pointed.

Benjamin Disraeli is said to have attended a dame's school in Colebrook Row, Islington, kept by a Miss Palmer, and afterwards he became a pupil at an academy since called Essex Hall, on Higham Hill, Walthamstow, Essex, six miles from town, where his desk and room were carefully preserved many years later.

When he resided in the neighbourhood of Bloomsbury Square he is said to have played frequently with other neighbouring children in the square. Thus, if Bloomsbury cannot boast of being the birthplace of Disraeli, it has undoubtedly a right to such honour as may be supposed to arise from a close association with that eminent man during the early years of his boyhood.

STATUE OF THE DUKE OF BEDFORD.

On the south side of Russell Square there is a large bronze statue of Francis Duke of Bedford. It is the work of Westmacott, and is much admired by some critics. It is of colossal size, the height being 9 feet, and with the massive Scotch granite pedestal upon which it is placed, measures altogether 27 feet in height. His Grace reposes one arm on a common plough, and the left holds the gifts of Ceres, to mark his agricultural pursuits. The four seasons of the year are personified in the figures of children playing around his feet. There are also, at the sides of the pedestal, some very good bas-reliefs in bronze, representing herds of cattle in recumbent postures, reapers and gleaners, and various other pastoral and agricultural subjects.

The pedestal bears the following inscription :—

FRANCIS
DUKE OF BEDFORD.
ERECTED
MDCCCIX.

The statue is placed in such a position as to face that of Fox in Bloomsbury Square, at the other end of Bedford Place.

SIR THOMAS LAWRENCE.

No. 65, Russell Square, was occupied for twenty-five years by Sir Thomas Lawrence, the third President of the Royal Academy. At this house the greater portion of those pictures which ·have ranked him among the most successful painters of his day were executed, and here he died, on January 7th, 1830. This artist had the distinguished honour of painting the allied sovereigns, their ministers, and other exalted personages assembled at the Congress of Aix-la-Chapelle, in 1818. On the death of Mr. West, in 1820, Sir Thomas Lawrence was, without opposition, elected to succeed him as President of the Royal Academy. Sir Thomas was so singularly handsome in his early youth that Mr. Hoare is reported to have said of him that if he had to choose a head for a picture of Christ he would select Lawrence for that study.

As a painter Sir Thomas Lawrence's charges were rather high. He charged £600 for a full-length portrait; but with all his immense receipts he died poor. This may be partly accounted for by his lavish expenditure upon rare prints and other objects of art. His fine collection of drawings and etchings, valued at £40,000, was offered to the nation for half that sum. They were, however, refused; and to the annoyance of every one who could appreciate the merits of this splendid collection, they were permitted to leave this country, and enrich the collection of the King of Holland.

LITERARY ASSOCIATIONS OF BLOOMSBURY.

The neighbourhood all around Bloomsbury and St. Giles's is rich with the associations of noteworthy characters. Some of the more celebrated and notable characters connected with St. Giles's have already been mentioned in that part of the volume which deals specially with that parish, but many men and women famous for literary or other acquirements have lived and died in Bloomsbury and its vicinity, and a few brief facts about some of them are given here, alphabetically arranged under the name of the place.

BEDFORD PLACE

contains the house in which Richard Cumberland, the dramatic author, died, in 1811. The house in which he died was that of a friend.

BEDFORD SQUARE.

It has been mentioned in another part of this volume that No. 6, Bedford Square, was the residence of Lord Eldon. This celebrated Lord Chancellor resided here from 1809 to 1815, and it was here that the Prince Regent (afterwards George IV.), by his insistence at the Chancellor's sick-bed, wrung from him the appointment to the vacant post of Master in Chancery for his friend Jekyll, the wit.

Adelaide Procter was born at No. 25, in the year 1825.

BLOOMSBURY SQUARE

has had many interesting associations with the great and the good.

Colley Cibber, the poet and dramatist, according to his own statement, "was born in London, on the 6th of November, 1671, in Southampton Street, facing Southampton House."

In the year 1681 the wife of Richard Baxter, the Nonconformist divine, died, in his "most pleasant and convenient house" in Southampton Square, now called Bloomsbury Square.

Sir Richard Steele and his first wife lived in Bloomsbury Square for three years, viz., 1712-15.

In 1749 or 1750 Mark Akenside, through Dyson's generosity, was established as a practising physician in Bloomsbury Square.

Lord Ellenborough, previous to his removal to St. James's Square, occupied a house on the east side of Bloomsbury Square.

No. 77, Bloomsbury Square, is said to have been formerly the town house of the Bishops of Rochester. It has handsome rooms, and is distinguished externally by a balcony on the Montague Street side.

The Earl of Mansfield, Dr. John Radcliffe, Sir Hans Sloane, and the elder and younger D'Israeli have been residents in this square, and a few particulars about them will be found in other parts of this volume.

CHARLOTTE STREET.

Theodore Hook, the celebrated writer and wit, was born at a house in this street, on September 22nd, 1788.

GREAT CORAM STREET.

The name of a man remarkable for the kindliness and generosity of his nature is preserved in the name of this street. It is named after Capt. Coram, the founder of the Foundling Hospital.

In 1837 Thackeray, then newly married, lived in Great Coram Street, near the Foundling Hospital.

GREAT RUSSELL STREET.

Percy Bysshe Shelley is known to have lodged at one time at No. 90, Great Russell Street.

During his occasional visits to London, William Hazlitt lodged with his brother John, who lived at No. 109, Great Russell Street.

QUEEN STREET, BLOOMSBURY.

George Vertue,· the engraver and antiquary, lived in this street. He laboured above forty years in collecting "Anecdotes of Painting in England," which, coming into the possession of Horace Walpole, were published by him in five volumes in 1762.

QUEEN SQUARE.

Charles Churchill, the celebrated poet and satirist, acted as tutor in a girls' school in Queen Square, Bloomsbury, but he was compelled to resign that post on account of his irregularities.

Dr. Charles Burney was a resident in the square, as was also his daughter Frances, afterwards Madame D'Arblay, the gifted authoress of " Evelina ; or, The History of a Young Lady's Introduction to the World." This very popular novel appeared anonymously in the year 1778, and Dr. Johnson, upon looking into it, declared that "there were passages which might do honour to Richardson." He got it almost by heart, and mimicked the characters with roars of laughter. Sir Joshua Reynolds took it up at table, was so absorbed in it that he had to be fed whilst reading, and both he and Burke sat up over it all night.

Among the many other eminent persons who have resided in Queen Square were Alderman Barber, the printer, who died here in 1741 ; Jonathan Richardson, the painter, who died here in 1745; and his son, of the same name, who died here in 1770. Dr. John Campbell, author of the "Lives of the Admirals" and many other works, lived, and on December 28th, 1775, died at his residence in Queen Square.

RUSSELL SQUARE.

Sir Thomas Lawrence, the celebrated painter, lived for about twenty-five years at No. 65, Russell Square. He died at his residence, on January 7th, 1830.

In 1836 Mary Russell Mitford had apartments at No. 56, Russell Square, where she writes—

"Mr. Wordsworth, Mr. Landor, and Mr. White dined here. I like Mr. Wordsworth, of all things. . . . Mr. Landor is a very striking-looking person, and exceedingly clever. Also we had a Mr. Browning, a young poet, and Mr. Proctor, and Mr. Morley, and quantities more of poets ; Stanfield and Lucas were also there."

SOUTHAMPTON ROW.

Thomas Gray, the poet, lodged in Southampton Row in the year 1759, and he was a frequent visitor to the Reading-room at the British Museum.

TAVISTOCK SQUARE.

Charles Dickens lived at Tavistock House, Tavistock Square, in 1851. He there wrote "Bleak House," "Hard Times," "Little Dorrit," and "A Tale of Two Cities."

MRS. GRIGGS.

On January 16th, 1792, there died, at her house, Southampton Row, Bloomsbury, a very remarkable woman, named Mrs. Griggs. Her executors found in her house eighty-six living, and twenty-eight dead cats. A black servant was left £150 per annum, for the maintenance of himself and the large number of surviving cats. This lady was single, and died worth £30,000. She drove out almost every day in her coach, but suffered no male servant to sleep in her house. Her maid-servants being tired of their attendance on such a numerous household, she was induced, at length, to take a black woman into her service on purpose to feed and attend upon her cats.

MODERN BUILDINGS.

Towards the end of the eighteenth, and during the early part of the present century a very large number of substantial and roomy houses were erected in Bloomsbury and its vicinity. In the year 1800 Bedford House was entirely demolished, and the very site upon which it stood was used partly for the formation of a spacious street called Bedford Place. Mr. James Burton, an architect, took a very active part in the building of the neigh-

A VIEW OF QUEEN SQUARE. 1787.

bourhood, having previously begun to erect a number of houses on the Foundling Hospital estate. Nearly 700 houses are said to have been built by or for Mr. Burton within a period of eleven years only, viz., from 1792 to 1803. In addition to these, Mr. Burton built upwards of 250 houses in the neighbourhood, including those in the parish of St. Pancras.

The name of this enterprising and successful architect is still preserved in the name of Burton Crescent.

THE DUKE OF BEDFORD.

Francis Charles Hastings Russell, the present Duke of Bedford, is the eldest son of the late Major-General Lord George William Russell (who was son of the sixth Duke), by Elizabeth Anne, only daughter of the late Hon. J. Theophilus Rawdon, and he was born in London in 1819. He married, in 1844, Lady Elizabeth, eldest daughter of the fifth Earl De la Warr. He succeeded his cousin in 1872. In 1838 he entered the Scots Fusilier Guards, but he retired from the Army in July, 1844. He was appointed Major in the Bedford Militia in 1849, and Lieut.-Colonel in the first battalion of Bedford-shire Rifle Volunteers in 1860. He was a Member of Parliament for Bedford-shire from 1847, until he became a peer in 1872.

The following are his Grace's titles, with the dates of their original creation : Ninth Duke of Bedford, 1694 ; Earl of Bedford, 1550 ; Marquis of Tavistock, 1694 ; Baron Russell of Cheneys, 1539 ; Baron Russell of Thorn-haugh, 1603 ; Baron Howland, 1695 (England) ; K.G., 1880.

The first peer of this family was particularly favoured by Henry the Eighth, and in the reign of Mary filled the office of Lord Privy Seal. He was sent as an ambassador to Spain to conduct Philip to England.

The residences of the present Duke of Bedford are as follows : No. 81, Eaton Square, London, S.W. ; Woburn Abbey, and Oakley, Bedford ; End-sleigh, Tavistock ; Norris Castle, Cowes, Isle of Wight.

Mr. Howard Evans, writing under the name of " Noblesse Oblige " in " Our Old Nobility," says, " Spite of their singular fatalist motto *Che sara, sara* (What will be, will be), the Russells have always been active in politics, and almost invariably on the side of progress. Among all the great houses, not one has rendered to the people such noble services as the Russells, though, by the way, these services have been rendered rather by the cadets than by

12

the heads of the house.   I believe that the Russells bear quite as honourable a name as landlords as they do as politicians, and my own observation of the farms and cottages on their estates confirms that impression."

In another part of this volume we have referred to the manner in which the Bloomsbury estates came into the possession of the Russell family, that is to say, by the marriage of a member of the Russell family with the daughter and heiress of the Earl of Southampton.   In addition to the property at Bloomsbury and Covent Garden, the Duke of Bedford possesses immense properties in Northamptonshire, Bedfordshire, and Devonshire.

CHAPTER XII.

BEDFORD CHAPEL.

HIS chapel was first opened for Divine worship in the year 1771. It was erected by Samuel Meeke, a bricklayer, on a piece of ground demised for the term of 101 years, from Lady Day, 1768, by his Grace the Duke of Bedford. The covenants of the lease expressly stated that the chapel should not be consecrated, and that nothing should be done in it except preaching, reading prayers and psalms in the Common Prayer Book. The clergyman's salary was at the same time fixed at £100 a year; or if two ministers should perform the duty, the one officiating in the morning was to be allowed £60 per annum, and the other doing the afternoon duty £40 per annum. Rev. Dr. John Trusler was the first clergyman appointed, and among those who have subsequently held it was Rev. J. C. M. Bellew. Rev. Stopford A. Brooke is the present minister.

THE PROTESTANT EPISCOPAL CHURCH OF THE SAVOY.

The historical associations of this church are much greater than might be imagined by one who merely judged by a superficial view of the comparatively modern building which now stands in Bloomsbury Street. Some years ago Bloomsbury Street was known as Charlotte Street, and the first stone of the new church was laid near Bedford Chapel, by the Bishop of London, who also consecrated the building in December, 1845. The following are the dimensions: length, 68 feet 6 inches; breadth, 38 feet 7 inches. The church is capable of holding a congregation of from 400 to 500 persons.

A memorial relating to the French Church of the Savoy and the chapels annexed thereunto, drawn up and presented to the Archbishop of Canterbury, February 15th, 1747-8, by Rev. J. J. Majendie, one of the preachers of that church, sets forth that the " French Church of the Savoy hath subsisted under that Denomination fourscore years and upwards, as appears by the Records of the said Church, and that the French took possession of it by Vertue of Letters patent, given by King Charles II. at Whitehall, bearing date March 11th, 1661, in the 13th year of his Reign, soon after his Majesty's happy Restoration to these realms."

The Savoy Church was the fashionable French church of the West End, and was resorted to by many of the nobility, who were attracted by the eloquence of the preachers who usually ministered there; amongst whom were the great names of Durrel, Severin, Abbadie, Saurin, Dubourdieu, Majendie, and Durand.

Charles II.'s grant of permission of the French congregation to meet in the little chapel of the Savoy was accompanied by the stipulation " that they use the Book of Common Prayer and submit to the jurisdiction of the Bishop of London." Monsieur Durel, the translator of the Prayer Book into French, preached the first sermon in the new chapel. He subsequently became Dean of Windsor.

As the French *immigrés* became gradually merged in the English population many of the French churches and chapels ceased to exist, for want of support, and many were absorbed in that of the Savoy, which for various reasons had had successively to migrate to Hog Lane (Crown Street) and Edward Street, and found its ultimate resting-place in the present church, in which building in Bloomsbury Street the congregation and trustees are said to have expended " their last farthing."

The church still enjoys, by direct inheritance, the grant in perpetuity made to it by Charles II. in 1675, and until the death of the late minister, Mr. Bouverie, in 1884, it had uninterruptedly received its share of the sum set apart in 1687 for the French ministers and their churches, from the interest of the general sum collected by briefs throughout the kingdom for the support of the French refugees, their churches, and their ministers.

The amount thus collected has been roughly estimated in round figures at about £200,000. This was paid into the Chamber of London, but was afterwards removed by the Crown, and an order issued to the Paymaster of Pensions to pay £15,000 per annum, of which £12,000 were for the poor people, and £3,000 for the ministers and churches. The administration of these sums was entrusted to the Archbishop of Canterbury, the Lord Chancellor, the Bishop of London, the Lord Chief Justices of the King's Bench and the Common Pleas, and the Lord Mayor of London.

In the year 1726 the amount of the annual payments was considerably reduced, and as has just been mentioned, upon the death of Mr. Bouverie, in April, 1884, the Lords of the Treasury found themselves unable to admit that the French Protestant Church had any legal claim to any further assistance from the public funds, and the payment accordingly ceased.

There is a little school adjoining the church, for fifteen girls of Huguenot lineage, who are housed, clothed, fed, educated, and prepared to earn their livelihood usefully. They are the choir of the church, and sing the psalms and hymns in French very creditably.

An interesting paper upon "The Last of the Huguenot Churches," by William Morris Beaufort, Esq., is printed in the second volume of the " Proceedings of the Huguenot Society of London," pp. 493—518.

BLOOMSBURY CHAPEL.

This chapel, which is capable of holding about 1,500 persons, was opened on December 5th, 1848. The style of architecture employed by Mr. John Gibson, of Westminster, under whose direction it was built, is Lombardic. The front of the chapel shows a central position, flanked by two lofty spires, which project slightly from the main building. The centre is divided into two storeys, of nearly equal height, the lower storey projecting nearly to the level of the towers, and a pediment is formed by the gable. An arched corbel-table runs along this lower storey. Three doorways, moulded and sunk, are in this portion ; above them is a large wheel-window, 18 feet 6 inches in diameter. The two handsome towers are divided into four stages, and capped with spires which ascend to the height of 117 feet from the ground. The lower parts of the towers are used for staircases, and the upper parts assist in the ventilation of the chapel by carrying off the vitiated atmosphere. The building covers a superficial area of upwards of 5,000 feet ; the span of the roof, clear of the walls, is 65 feet ; and the ceiling is 39 feet in height above the floor.   The whole of the building is of white brick, with Caen stone dressings.

Bloomsbury Chapel was erected at a cost of £8,700, exclusive of the site, which is Crown land.   Towards this large sum Sir Samuel Morton Peto contributed a princely share.

The following is a list of the pastors who have successively occupied the pulpit of Bloomsbury Chapel :—

Dr. William Brock, Rev. J. P. Chown, and Rev. J. Baillie.

Many of the leading Nonconformist divines of England and Scotland have preached in the pulpit at various times.

The Midsummer Morning Service is a peculiar and interesting feature at this chapel.   It was first instituted by Dr. Brock on Sunday morning, June 24th, 1849, when a service was held from 7 to 8 o'clock in the morning.   The services, which are still continued, have been very popular, the inside of the building having often been quite filled by the number of persons who came to the service, and sometimes a service has been held outside of the building, for the benefit of those who were unable to obtain admission.

SWISS PROTESTANT CHURCH, ENDELL STREET.

In the year 1855 the Swiss Protestants in London, who for nearly a century had met to worship in Moor Street, St. Giles's, erected, by subscription amongst themselves, a new church in Endell Street.   The church, which is built in an Italian style, contains on the ground floor accommodation for upwards of 260 persons, all of the seats being free.   The length of the church, exclusive of the apse, is 67 feet ; the height and breadth are both 35 feet.   The ceiling, which is semicircular, is ornamented with enriched mouldings, and a guiloche band subdividing it into compartments, terminating on corbels in the walls. The architect was Mr. George Vulliamy.

CHRIST CHURCH, ENDELL STREET.

This elegant building, designed in the Early English style, and executed in Kentish ragstone and Bath stone dressings, was consecrated in the year 1845. Although the ground upon which the building stands is of small dimensions, every inch of room has been made use of in order to give accommodation for 1,000 sittings, in accordance with the stipulations of the Church Commissioners.

Another serious difficulty experienced in building the church was that of obtaining sufficient light. On two sides little or no light could be obtained, as the east end abuts against the workhouse, and the south wall is obstructed by houses. In order to obtain light, the building has been carried up very high, so as to get a lofty clerestory, with a series of unobstructed windows ; and by the aid of a small well-hole or area, taken from the workhouse, some partial light has been obtained for the east window.

The spire of this church was struck and much damaged by lightning on August 17th, 1887. A large portion of the masonry was displaced, and in consequence of the serious damage, the tower was taken down and rebuilt.

ST. GILES'S CHRISTIAN MISSION.

The centre of this Mission may be considered to be the Mission Chapel in Little Wild Street, and in connection with this chapel various religious and charitable agencies have been established, designed chiefly for the comfort and reformation of the lowest classes of society. The St. Giles's Christian Mission was established in the year 1860, and the work amongst discharged prisoners was commenced in 1877.

The chief object of this branch of the Mission is to assist in the reformation of prisoners discharged from all convict prisons. Prisoners are met daily, at 9 a.m., at the gates of Holloway, Pentonville, Millbank, and Wandsworth Gaols, and invited, by a paper slipped into their hands, to come and take breakfast, free of charge, at the Mission-rooms near the prison gates. Those who are thought by the Secretary to be desirous of earning an honest living are assisted, if possible, to obtain employment. Some, at the discretion of the Superintendent or Secretary, are admitted to live in the home, to which they are expected to pay when employment has been found for them. Free suppers to thieves are also occasionally held, admission to which is obtained by special ticket.

A Sunday School, temperance society, and night refuges for destitute women are other phases of the Christian Mission which have been the means of doing a great deal of useful and philanthropic service to the poorest and lowest inhabitants of the Seven Dials and its vicinity.

NATIONAL REFUGES FOR HOMELESS AND DESTITUTE CHILDREN, SHAFTESBURY AVENUE.

This very useful institution was established in the year 1843, and besides the boys' refuge and offices of the Institution at Shaftesbury Avenue which have been erected recently, there are two training-ships for boys, and various homes and refuges for boys and girls in various parts of the country. The object of the Institution is to provide a home and industrial training for homeless and destitute children, who would otherwise be in danger of becoming criminals. Admission to all the homes and ships is by application of persons interested, and subscribers, magistrates, policemen, clergymen, city missionaries, ragged-school teachers, and others, after examination into the circumstances of the applicants by the Committee or Secretary.

The home in Shaftesbury Avenue is for boys who are at work and have no home. They pay for their food and clothing, and one or two shillings a week for lodging and washing, according to what they earn. Mr. W. Williams is the Secretary.

THE PHARMACEUTICAL SOCIETY.

The Pharmaceutical Society of Great Britain, which possesses extensive premises in Bloomsbury Square, was established in April, 1841, and incorporated by royal charter on February 18th, 1843.

In December, 1841, the Council of the Society decided to take a house (No. 17) in Bloomsbury Square, at a rental of £240 per annum, and the first meeting of the Council was held there on January 6th, 1842. Mr. G. W. Smith was appointed as the first resident salaried Secretary, and arrangements were immediately made for the delivery of a series of evening lectures upon Chemistry, Pharmacy, and other subjects of a kindred nature. Courses of systematic instruction in Botany were instituted in the following May, and in other subjects in October.

In the year 1857 the two adjoining houses, viz., 72 and 73, Great Russell Street, were taken by the Society on a lease of ninety years ; and although at that time occupied by tenants, they could be appropriated when necessary. Mr. Jacob Bell, the President of the Society, who died in June,

1859, left the sum of £2,000 to the trustees for the time being of the Pharmaceutical Society of Great Britain, to be expended in establishing or otherwise increasing the efficiency of a school of pharmacy. As a memorial and expression of respect to Mr. Bell, nearly £2,000 was subscribed by the members, associates, and registered apprentices of the Society, for the purpose of founding scholarships, to be called "the Bell Memorial Pharmaceutical Scholarships," which were to be awarded, under suitable regulations, to industrious, well-conducted, and competent registered apprentices and associates of the Pharmaceutical Society. Two scholarships, of the annual value of £30 each, were founded.

In order to carry out the intentions of Mr. Bell, the premises at Bloomsbury Square were enlarged, and a suite of laboratories was erected at the top of the house.

Another scholarship, of the annual value of £20, was founded in honour of Professor Redwood, on his retirement from active duty as Professor in the School of Pharmacy.

A committee in connection with the Bloomsbury Society had been in existence in Edinburgh for several years, but it was not until shortly after the passing of the Pharmacy Act, in 1852, that a separate board of examiners was appointed there.

The Pharmacy Act, 1852, made it necessary that candidates should be examined in Chemistry, Pharmacy, Materia Medica, and Botany, with the practical manipulations of the laboratory and dispensary, also in the methods of ascertaining the strength and purity of drugs, the tests and antidotes for poison, the doses of medicines, and the language of prescriptions. Another Pharmacy Act was passed in 1868, which made it unlawful for any person to sell any poisonous drug unless he were a pharmaceutical chemist.

Efforts were made towards the formation of a library in connection with this Society from the earliest days of its existence. The library now contains about 10,000 volumes and pamphlets, and the fifth edition of a catalogue of its contents, compiled by Mr. J. W. Knapman, the Librarian, was issued in 1888. It has upwards of 600 octavo pages. Each entry of a volume is accompanied by a collation of the volume, and a useful system of contractions is adopted, by means of which a great saving of space is effected. In addition to the library in Bloomsbury Square, the catalogue embraces the library of the North British branch of the Society, at Edinburgh.

The Museum, of which Mr. E. M. Holmes is the Curator, has grown, from a small beginning, to be the most important collection of objects of pharmaceutical and chemical interest in the kingdom.

THE HOSPITAL FOR SICK CHILDREN.

This institution, situated in Great Ormond Street, was established in the year 1852, for a threefold object, viz., (*a*) the medical and surgical treatment of poor children ; (*b*) the attainment and diffusion of knowledge regarding the diseases of children ; (*c*) the training of nurses for children. Before the establishment of this useful institution no hospital exclusively devoted to the treatment and study of children's diseases existed in the United Kingdom ; and it was felt that the medical knowledge of such diseases was particularly defective, while, owing to the want of sufficient opportunity for their study, many thousands of children were dying annually from preventable causes, and from diseases which might have been cured if they had been properly understood.

The honour of setting on foot the first attempt to supply this crying need belongs to Dr. Charles West, who, after long and careful study of children's diseases, originated the scheme for the Hospital for Sick Children.

As the result of the efforts of Dr. West, aided by Dr. Bence Jones and a few other gentlemen, a public meeting was held on March 18th, 1851, and a Committee was formed, with Lord Shaftesbury (then Lord Ashley) as chairman. Besides these names, those of Mr. Beresford Hope, the late Lord Kinnaird, Sir Robert Inglis, Sir James Clark, Mr. F. H. Dickinson, Mr. Edward Futvoye, Mr. Henry E. Bathurst (acting as Honorary Secretary), and others appear on this first Committee of the hospital, all of whom contributed largely by their skill and exertions to the success of the undertaking. The hospital was opened on February 14th, 1852, with only 10 beds ; but this number soon increased to 30, and later to 52 ; and in the year 1868 the two houses, Nos. 48 and 49, Great Ormond Street, were occupied by 75 patients. Still the work grew and expanded, and in 1872 H.R.H. the Princess of Wales laid the foundation-stone of the present building, which was formally opened on November 18th, 1875.

It was not until 1862 that proper attention was turned to the necessity of specially trained nurses, and the records of the nursing department before that date would offer a strange contrast to the standards of the present day. This branch of the work has also flourished, and, from Aberdeen to South Africa, a considerable number of the children's hospitals now in existence were organized, and have been administered, by ladies trained at Great Ormond Street.

From the Thirty-seventh Annual Report (1889) we gather that the number of in-patients treated in the year 1888 was 1,100. The number of beds in the hospital is 127. The Convalescent Home, at Highgate, has 52 beds, and patients who have been treated in the hospital are received there for a period of three weeks. Over 300 children enjoyed that privilege in 1888. Thus the total number of beds is 179.

About 1,000 out-patients are treated weekly at the hospital in Great Ormond Street.

The completion of the hospital will soon be a reality, as the new and final wing of the hospital is commenced, and when finished will contain over 200 beds, thus realizing the hope of the founder, of making it the largest and most complete children's hospital.

THE NATIONAL HOSPITAL FOR THE PARALYZED AND EPILEPTIC.

(ALBANY MEMORIAL.)

The chief facts in the history of this institution, established in 1859, are summarized in the following inscription, which has been placed upon tablets erected in the entrance-hall :—

"This Hospital, the first established in the United Kingdom for the treatment of diseases of the nervous system, was founded in public meeting at the Mansion House, in the City of London, at the instance of Johanna Chandler, Louisa Chandler, and Edward Henry Chandler, assisted by the Right Hon. the Earl of Shaftesbury, K.G., the Lord Archbishop of Canterbury, the Lord Raynham, M.P., and others, and under the presidency of the Right Hon. David Wire, Lord Mayor.

"For twenty-five years its work was carried on in old houses situated upon a portion of this site, and achieved a great reputation.

"In 1880 his Grace the Duke of Westminster, K.G., laid the foundation stone of the first part of a new Hospital, being the portion of this building abutting upon Powis Place.

"In 1881 Her Royal Highness the Princess Christian of Schleswig-Holstein declared that portion open.

"In 1882 His Royal Highness Prince Leopold, Duke of Albany, K.G., publicly announced the intention to erect the main building. This was begun in 1883, and finished in 1885. With the sanction of Her Most Gracious Majesty Queen Victoria, the west block of the new Hospital is dedicated as a memorial to the Prince, who did not live to witness the completion of the undertaking he had inaugurated.

"The ceremony of opening the new Hospital was performed on 4th July, 1885, by His Royal Highness Albert Edward Prince of Wales, K.G., and the Divine blessing having been invoked, the Hospital entered upon its merciful career.

"To John Back, Esq., Richard Harvey, Esq., the Lady Harriet Bentinck, John Harding, Esq., Mrs. Jemima Spence ; His Grace the Duke of Westminster, K.G., Mrs. Batty, Miss Margaret Gibbins, Alfred Burges, Esq., Samuel Morley, Esq., M.P., T. W. Reade, Esq., H. E. Murrell, Esq., Miss Cobb, Miss Harriet Hurst, Thomas Tapling, Esq., J. Platt, Esq., E. Homan, Esq., Miss J. Durning Smith, William Bennett, Esq., and Miss Marian Smith ; together with the other contributors to the building fund whose benefactions enabled this great undertaking to be accomplished, and whose names are entered upon the Hospital Register, the grateful thanks of the Board of Management are recorded here.

"G. C. PORTER, Colonel, *Chairman.*

"H. D. RYDER, *Treasurer.*

"B. BURFORD RAWLINGS, *Secretary and Gen. Director.*"

This hospital provides in all 170 beds, with a spacious department for out-patients. More than any other medical charity, perhaps, it may claim that its work is really national, embracing, as it does, patients from every part of the kingdom. This is accounted for by the circumstance that sufferers from various maladies are, as a class, excluded from admission to general hospitals, whether town or country. The National Hospital for the Paralyzed and Epileptic has been described as a " unique " institution, and supplies the greatest opportunity the world has yet possessed for the study and treatment of the most mysterious maladies which afflict humanity.

THE ALEXANDRA HOSPITAL, QUEEN SQUARE.

This hospital, situated at Nos. 17, 18, and 19, Queen Square, and No. 1, Queen Square Place, was founded in the year 1867, for the reception, maintenance, and surgical treatment of the children of the poor suffering from hip disease, which is very prevalent among the poorer classes.

In the London hospitals it is impossible to receive all applicants for admission. The more urgent and acute cases are taken in, but the more tedious cases are necessarily turned away. Chronic cases, especially of hip disease, except in the few instances in which operation is required, are refused admission, or discharged before permanent cure has been attained. A very large majority of these cases are curable with proper and prolonged treatment. The disease is attended with great suffering, and without proper treatment the subjects of it either die of exhaustion or are crippled for life.

In this hospital such cases only are admitted as present a reasonable prospect of cure, and children who may require or who have undergone excision, who are suffering from spine disease, or who are incurable, are not eligible for admission. Girls are received between the ages of three and twelve years, and boys between three and eleven. A payment of 4s. a week is required. Annual subscribers of 1 guinea or donors of 10 guineas may recommend suitable cases for admission, who will be received, subject to the approval of the Committee, as vacancies occur, without payment for the first three weeks of their stay in the hospital, and afterwards upon payment of 4s. weekly.

The Alexandra Hospital opened with 10 beds in one house, No. 19, Queen Square, and it is gratifying to be able to say that it has since increased the number of its beds to 60. It has also a branch hospital at Bournemouth, which contains 21 beds, and to which the patients, as soon as they are well enough, are sent for the benefit of sea air.

FRENCH HOSPITAL AND DISPENSARY.

This institution is situated at No. 10, Leicester Place, Leicester Square and was established in the year 1867, for the medical and surgical relief of all foreigners speaking the French language. Admission is by a letter of recommendation from a Governor, and out-patients (medical and surgical cases) attend daily (Sundays excepted), but urgent cases are received at any time, and treated freely. The Hon. Secretary is Mr. Ernest Rüffer, 39, Lombard Street, E.C.

New premises, of a commodious and substantial nature, are now in course of erection in Shaftesbury Avenue.

THE ITALIAN HOSPITAL (OSPEDALE ITALIANO).

The Italian Hospital, No. 14, Queen Square, Bloomsbury, was founded in the year 1884, by Mr. G. B. Ortelli, a Chevalier of the Crown of Italy, for the following objects : The maintenance and medical treatment of Italians and Italian-speaking people, irrespective of their religious and political opinions, who may be suffering sickness or bodily infirmity, and also of all persons, without any distinction of nationality or language, who may be suffering from sickness or bodily infirmity ; also the provision of surgical and medical relief to Italians and others not being inmates of the hospital, preference being given to Italians and Italian-speaking people.

The very poor Italians who cluster together in the quarter around Saffron Hill, Eyre Street Hill, and in the rear of Hatton Garden speak but little of our language, and from the impoverished conditions under which they exist, there must be frequent sickness amongst them. Doubtless, hitherto they have been received into the existing hospitals, and treated with that special kindness which the English heart will extend to the sick foreigner; but there must be something peculiarly comforting to him to have the kindly words spoken to him in his mother tongue, and to have about him those who best know his national peculiarities. There must naturally be a greater amount of sympathy between the nurse and the patient if they are of the same nationality.

The house which has been adapted for the purposes of the hospital is one of those old-fashioned dwellings which face Queen Square, Bloomsbury, and it derives all the advantages of being in this open situation, while it is at the same time in close proximity to the Italian quarter. The generous founder gave this freehold house and premises, together with the necessary furniture and fittings, which were valued altogether at £6,000.

The total number of out-patients treated in the year 1888 was 2,483, and the total number of in-patients treated during the same year was 226.

CHAPTER XIII.

THE LONDON HOMŒOPATHIC HOSPITAL.

HE London Homœopathic Hospital, established in the year 1849, by the English Homœopathic Association, is situated in Great Ormond Street, Bloomsbury. It was first established in a very modest way in a small house in Golden Square, the capacity of which would not allow the reception of more than 25 beds. Now the capacity of the hospital is 90 beds, although that full total number of beds is higher than the average occupied, which varies from 60 to 70. A large majority of them come from the poorer residents in the parish, and the district just around the hospital is much indebted to this active charity for valuable and prompt help to its sick poor in the time of need. Within the last ten years the income of the hospital has doubled. Its work has also doubled. In addition to its 750 in-patients each year, its 10,000 out-patients attest its popularity. Its nursing, also, under skilful superintendence, has reached a high standard, and the number of its nurses has increased gradually, in response to the application of the outside public for their services.

Instruction in Materia Medica and Therapeutics is given at 3 o'clock p.m. daily, in the wards and the out-patient department.

The instruction at this hospital is especially intended for—

(1) Medical men who are already qualified, and who desire to obtain a knowledge of Homœopathy in addition to their other acquirements.

(2) Medical students desiring to be instructed in Homœopathic medicine.

In-patients are received every morning before 11 o'clock, and out-patients are attended to every day (Sundays excepted), between 2.30 and 3.30 p.m.; while accidents and urgent cases are received at any hour without letters of recommendation, on application to the house surgeon.

Macaulay resided for some time in No. 50, Great Ormond Street, now forming the east wing of the London Homœopathic Hospital. Here he wrote the Essay on Milton, and some of his earliest literary essays for the *Edinburgh Review.* In August, 1857, Macaulay writes, " I sent the carriage home, and walked to the Museum ; passing through Great Ormond Street, I saw a bill on No. 50. I knocked, was let in, and went over the house with a strange mixture of feelings. It is more than twenty-six years since I was in it. The dining-room and the adjoining room, in which I once slept, are scarcely changed ; the same colouring on the wall, but more dingy. My father's study much the same ; the drawing-rooms too, except the papering ; my bedroom just what it was. My mother's bedroom—I had never been in it since her death. I went away sad."

Within a few weeks of Lord Macaulay's visit, the authorities of the Homœopathic Hospital, who were at that time established in Golden Square, acquired the freehold of Nos. 50-2 in Great Ormond Street. The new hospital was publicly opened on May 12th, 1859 ; in his inaugural address, Lord Ebury mentioned that No. 50 had been, as the second Powis House, the home for twenty years of Philip Lord Chancellor Hardwicke. Nearly all the postal numbers in that street have been changed of late, and no number is given to the hospital. When the Macaulays lived there Lord Thurlow's house was numbered 45 ; it is now the Working Men's College.

THE RUSSELL INSTITUTION.

This institution, in Great Coram Street, was originally built by Mr. Burton, in 1802, for an assembly-room. The building was hardly completed, however, before it was entirely destroyed by fire, in 1803. A second building was immediately erected, and for some time concerts and assemblies were held in it, but in the course of a few years they were discontinued, and in 1808 a literary and scientific institution was established, and still remains. There is in connection with that institution a library of about 18,000 volumes, exclusive of a bound set of the *Times* newspaper complete, from 1808 up to the present date.

The building is a handsome structure, and has a handsome portico entrance, with Grecian Doric columns. It is 122 feet in length, by 55 feet in depth.

Mr. E. W. Brayley the elder, author of many valuable antiquarian and topographical works, was for many years the Librarian and Secretary of the Russell Institution.

MUDIE'S SELECT LIBRARY.

Charles Edward Mudie, the founder of this famous establishment, was born in the year 1818, at Cheyne Walk, Chelsea, where his father kept a little newspaper shop, at which stationery and other articles were retailed, and where books of the fugitive fiction class could be borrowed, at the charge of a penny a volume.

In the year 1840 Mr. Mudie opened a little shop in Upper King Street, Bloomsbury, and carried on a lending library on a very small scale. Indeed, the books which he had bought for his own reading were his original stock. He soon materially improved his business, and in the year 1842 he commenced his system of lending out one exchangeable volume to subscribers, at the rate of one guinea per annum. Mr. Mudie was himself in some instances a publisher, and from his establishment issued the first English edition of James Russell Lowell's " Poems," and George Dawson's first " Orations."

In the year 1852, the library having outgrown the limits of the house in Upper King Street (Southampton Row, as it is now named), Mr. Mudie removed his business to two houses which form part of his present establishment, and gradually, as the business has grown, the neighbouring houses have been absorbed. In 1860 the large handsome hall was opened, and inaugurated by a festive gathering of literary men and publishers. Branch houses were opened in the provincial towns, and the business having grown beyond the limits of individual capital, Mr. Mudie, in the year 1864, found it desirable to form his library into a limited liability company.

The large hall, in the centre of the building, has accommodation for about 16,000 volumes, and in addition to the storage-room in the adjoining galleries, there are very extensive cellars, in which are stored large numbers of remainders.

It is said that when the two last volumes of Macaulay's " History of England " appeared 2,500 copies were at once supplied to Mudie's Library.

13

Of Dr. Livingstone's "Travels in Africa" 3,250 copies were in circulation at the same time, and it is calculated that the book must have been introduced to at least 30,000 readers though the medium of this library.   At the present time Lady Dufferin's "Viceregal Life in India" enjoys a very wide popularity among Mudie's readers, and a very large number of copies are in circulation.

THEATRES.

There seems to be little popular demand for theatrical performances in St. Giles's parish, as repeated attempts to establish a theatre have met with little success.

The histories of the various theatres which have been instituted in this district in modern times are chequered by many changes of alternate failure and feeble success.   St. Martin's Hall, Long Acre, in which Charles Dickens appeared for the first time as a public reader, on April 9th, 1858, was afterwards converted into a theatre, and denominated the Queen's Theatre. Among the actors and actresses who have performed there were Mr. Henry Irving, Mr. and Mrs. Rousby, and Miss Hodgson.

The building was afterwards used as the business premises of a co-operative association, and is now the Gymnasium of the Young Men's Christian Association.

The building in High Holborn which is now known as the Central Hall was originally used as a circus, and afterwards for theatrical purposes under the name of the Holborn Theatre.

The theatre in Great Queen Street which is at present known as the Novelty is a rather recent and not very successful institution.   It has at various times been known also as the Bijou Theatre, the Jodrell Theatre, etc.   It is a conveniently arranged house, with bright and tasteful internal decorations, and it is much to be regretted that so small a share of popular support has been accorded to it.

THE ROYAL MUSIC-HALL, HOLBORN.

This celebrated music-hall was originally a chapel belonging to a Nonconformist body, and known as Gate Street Chapel.   About the year 1840 it was purchased by the Socialist fraternity, and by them it was denominated the

National Hall.   It was used for lectures in support of the principles of the Free-thinkers, and also for concerts, dancing, and kindred entertainments.   In 1857 the building was purchased by Mr. Weston, who rearranged it, and adapted it suitably to the requirements of a music-hall.   Towards the end of the year mentioned it was opened to the public, and a contemporary newspaper account gives the following particulars as to the size and appearance of the newly appointed building : The hall was about 100 feet long, about 40 feet wide, and about 40 feet high, and the ceiling, which was divided into ten compartments, and the front of the gallery were elaborately ornamented with a considerable amount of fanciful design.   The gallery was supported upon iron columns with ornamental spandrils, and the end wall, next the orchestra, was enriched with mirrors and drapery.   Five glass chandeliers were provided for the lighting of the hall.   The building work was carried out under the direction of Messrs. Finch, Hill, and Paraire, the decorations were by Messrs. Homan and Beensen, and the approaches were laid with Bale's patent mosaic quarries, by the Poole Architectural Pottery Company.

About the year 1864 the place was purchased from Mr. Weston by Messrs. Sweasey and Holland, who carried it on until 1881, when Mr. W. T. Purkess purchased it.   It is now the property of a limited liability company. In recent years it has been so much enlarged as to make it twice its original size.

The Holborn Casino was a dancing saloon which in its early days attained considerable popularity among the upper-middle classes of society. In course of time, however, it degenerated, and its site is now occupied by the Holborn Restaurant.

MESSRS. COMBE & CO'S. BREWERY.

The extensive establishment, known as the Woodyard Brewery, dates back to the year 1740, when it was founded by one Thomas Shackle, a dealer in timber, hence the name of the brewery.   Mr. Shackle first commenced brewing on a small scale, and in a few years, by industry and perseverance, he made quite a respectable business.   He was succeeded by Mr. Gyfford, who acquired property, and also increased the brewing business.

At the beginning of this century the Woodyard Brewery came into the hands of Mr. Harvey Christian Combe, who was a man of great intelligence and business capacity. He became Lord Mayor of London in 1800, and represented the City in Parliament for many years.

On June 7th, 1807, Alderman Combe gave a " Royal Brewhouse Dinner." A contemporary newspaper thus refers to the event : " On Friday, Alderman Combe gave his annual dinner of beef-steaks to several of the Royal Family, at his Brewhouse in Castle Street, Long Acre, commonly termed Gyfford's Brewhouse. The Prince of Wales, the Duke and Duchess of York, and the Duke of Cambridge were invited. About half-past six o'clock the Duke and Duchess of York and the Duke of Cambridge arrived. The Alderman, Mrs. Combe, Mr. Combe, and the Misses Combe were in readiness to receive them. They were conducted up-stairs to the stage of the Brewhouse, into a corner on the right side, where a table was laid for their reception, principally composed of the materials that the Brewhouse affords. The table-cloth was only a hop sack nailed to the table ; and it was laid for dinner with wooden trenchers, wooden bowls for the sallads, wooden salt-cellars, with bone spoons and Tunbridge-ware pepper-castors. The only articles of a superior kind were good horn-handle knives, and silver three-pronged forks. The Royal Party were joined by the Earl of Lauderdale, Lord Erskine, Mr. Sheridan, Mr. Stepney, and several others. The company, after viewing the Brewhouse, took their seats upon wooden chairs. To prevent the Royal Party finding any inconvenience from wind, or the heat of the copper fire, which was about ten yards from the table, it was inclosed by a temporary screen, made of hop sacks ; this shut out the light, but three patent lamps were introduced.

" Five capital rumps of beef were provided, and a butcher attended to cut prime steaks ; who afterwards handed them, on a wooden malt shovel, to the stoker of the Brewhouse, who is always cook upon these occasions. The stoker placed them on an iron plate, and turned them with an iron instru-ment made in the shape of a horse-shoe. When he thought the steaks sufficiently done, in the Brewhouse style, he put them into a new malt-shovel, covered with a tin lid, made very hot ; it was taken to the table by a brewer, with a clean white apron on, and placed upon the table. The Alderman and his son helped their distinguished guests to the prime pieces. Porter was the only beverage ; and the clerks, with white aprons, acted as waiters. About a quarter before eight o'clock, the company left the Brewhouse, highly gratified with their beef-steaks, on which the Duchess of York was lavish in her praise, for the Alderman's house in Great Russell Street, Bloomsbury, where they were joined by several other Noblemen and Gentlemen, and sat down to a second course and dessert of every delicacy the season could afford, and the choicest of wines. At a late hour the company departed, highly pleased with their worthy host's hospitality."

During the life of Alderman Combe the brewery was rebuilt, and the business was increased in scope and extent. At his death, in the year 1832, the brewery came into the hands of his son, Mr. Harvey Combe, and Mr. Delafield, who immediately set about further enlarging the works, to keep pace with the rapid growth of the business. In the year 1858 Mr. Combe, who was a bachelor and a great sportsman, died, and was succeeded by his two nephews, Messrs. R. H. and Charles Combe, Mr. Joseph Bonsor, his two sons, and Mr. John Spicer.

The present partners still further improved the property, which now covers upwards of four acres, and rebuilt a portion of the premises in Castle Street.

There are three splendid wells on the premises, sunk and bored down into the chalk to a depth of upwards of 520 feet, producing water most suitable for brewing purposes. The machinery used in the brewery is of an exceptionally good quality, and of the most modern and improved design. System and order prevail throughout the establishment.

An extensive cooperage is connected with Messrs. Combe & Co.'s brewery, and is situated in Broad Street, Bloomsbury, where casks in large numbers are made, repaired, and cleaned.

This is one of the busiest breweries in London, and the coppers are hardly ever idle. Nearly 450 men are employed in the establishment, and the annual output of the brewery now exceeds 500,000 barrels.

HORSESHOE BREWERY.

This noted brewery was purchased by Mr. (afterwards Sir Henry) Meux, in the year 1809, when he retired from the firm in Liquorpond Street, Gray's Inn Lane. In the year 1814, just five years after Mr. Meux had established himself at Tottenham Court Road, the great porter vat, which was the talk of London at the time of its construction, unhappily burst, owing to the insecurity and defective state of some of its hoops, causing great destruction and loss of life to the inhabitants of the adjacent property. Small tenements were flooded to such an extent that the walls subsided, and some of them collapsed entirely ; eight persons were drowned or suffocated with the fumes of the old porter, and many were intoxicated by drinking the liquor as it flowed along the streets. The vat was 22 feet in height, and contained 3,555 barrels. Its place is now occupied by seven smaller vats.

Within the last seventy years there was a garden attached to the old mansion-house on the property, the site of which is now occupied by the buildings belonging to the brewery.

The brewery takes its name from the old Horseshoe Tavern, which stands close beside it, and which is known to have been established as an inn as early as the year 1623. The Horseshoe Brewery stands upon part of the site of the celebrated " Rookery." In the office at the brewery there is an oil painting, showing the buildings belonging to the brewery in the year 1830.

From time to time considerable additions have been made to the buildings which are at present of a very extensive character. The large cellars are used for the storage of ales and stouts in casks ; the ground floor is also to some extent used as a storage-place, and casks are filled up with ale or stout upon that floor ; the floors above are occupied by enormous vats and coppers, and granaries for the storage of malt and hops. A very deep well has been sunk at this brewery, and it is worked by a powerful pumping-engine. Another smaller engine is used, in connection with the wooden yeast-presses, for pressing the liquor from yeast. Extensive stabling premises, containing eighty stalls, are attached to the brewery, from which they are separated by a brick wall. The total output of the brewery has been computed at about 200,000 barrels per annum.

MESSRS. PEARS' BUSINESS OFFICES.

This firm of soap-manufacturers, established in 1789, over a hundred years ago, and now of world-wide renown, occupy as their head-quarters palatial business premises at Nos. 71-75, New Oxford Street, which were erected in 1887, the branch houses being at New York and Melbourne, and factories at Isleworth-on-Thames. The architectural part of the new edifice was carried out under the superintendence and according to the designs of Mr. W. B. Catherwood, the builders being Messrs. Holland and Hannen, of Duke Street, Bloomsbury. The front of the building presents a noble and imposing appearance. It is built in the Italian style, and the main structural features strike the view with a pleasing effect of well-harmonized solidity.

The materials employed in the building are Portland stone and small Dutch red bricks, beautifully laid in five courses to the foot. Each of the massive lower stone piers is based on grey Aberdeen granite. The tint is varied where Aberdeen granite is elsewhere employed. For instance, the pillars of the portico, a fine feature of the building, are pink, as are some of the supports and details in the superstructure. The handsome entrance is a walnut lobby, with double doors folding back on either side, decorated with carved panels of bronze and ebony. The entrance-hall is a very striking and beautiful feature of the premises. It has with great skill been made to resemble the atrium of an ancient Roman house. Its walls and ceiling have been painted with various ornamental subjects, Pompeian in general character, by Mr. C. E. Birch, and its floor and certain other portions are covered with beautifully arranged mosaic work. Upon the left-hand side, on entering the hall, is a sunken bath, placed with reference to the Pompeian character of the atrium—that is to say, so little removed from the centre as to come within the site where the impluvium would be if, instead of being a covered chamber, the hall or vestibule were the inner court of an ancient Pompeian house. A fountain sends up a thin column of pure water from the bath, which has been paved with a lustrous aquatinted mosaic by Messrs. Rust & Co., under the direction and from the designs of Mr. Birch. This mosaic imparts to the water a pure translucent blue colour.

At the farther end of the bath is a very handsome hemicycle, a coved niche, likewise lined with mosaic, and occupied by a remarkably fine piece of sculpture in white marble, by Von Weber, representing Venus and Cupid. A replica of Thorwaldssen's Venus, holding the apple awarded by Paris, which used formerly to occupy this hemicycle, has been removed to another part of the hall.

There is a third Venus in this hall, namely that by Miglioretti, and near the window looking upon New Oxford Street is a very fine example of the sculptor's art. It is known as the "The Bather," and was executed by Lawes. Two handsome pillars in the middle of the hall, and several pilasters around its walls, are constructed of grand antique Cipollino marble. Fiore di Pesca marble, now very rare, is employed for the staircase leading to the next storey, and for the bases of the columns just mentioned.

The stone used for the carved face of the hemicycle, for the balustrading of the staircase, and for the doorways is Italian onyx, which has an ivory-tinted ground, and pink veins, deepening to purple. All the marble-work in this room was carved, in accordance with the drawings of Mr. Birch, by Mr. James Houghton, of Great Portland Street. The bronze-work for the hanging lamps, tripod-stands, doorways, and marble-topped open-work pedestals is remarkably good, and great praise is due to Mr. W. Shrivell, who in executing the designs of Mr. Birch has succeeded so well in representing the antique bronzes which have been found among the remains of ancient Roman houses.

A room upon the left-hand side on entering the hall has been beautifully fitted up for the reception and exhibition of some of the works of art which Messrs. Pears possess. Near the window looking upon the street is exhibited the clever piece of statuary by G. Focardi, known as " You Dirty Boy ! " also the companion composition, by the same sculptor, known as " The Nice Clean Boy," and the pictures entitled " The Black Nurse " and " An Out-patient," the latter of which was painted from an actual incident, by J. Y. Carrington.

There is, at the back of the hall, a ware-room, partitioned off by a screen of glazed mahogany. Only a comparatively small stock is kept here, for small deliveries in London, the main part of the export and wholesale deliveries of the manufactures of this eminent firm being made at the large factories of Messrs. Pears at Isleworth.

Upon ascending the handsome staircase which leads from the hall to the first floor, the counting-house, or office, is reached. This is an apartment of large capacity, resembling that of a bank or insurance-office, and it is arranged for the accommodation of forty-two clerks, besides the heads of departments, who have their desks in open compartments at the several angles of the room. Type-writers are extensively employed for correspondence work. There is a good system of electric and pneumatic intercommunication in use in this room, by means of which each chief can convey messages to the others easily and expeditiously.

The waiting-room, which is upon the same floor as the office, has been converted into a picture-gallery, by the collection of beautiful pictures which are there exhibited. Amongst the paintings in this room are the following :—

> " This is the way we wash our clothes." *Hazlaar.*
> " Bubbles." *Millais.*

For this charming picture, the drawing and colouring of which are unusually fine and delicate, Messrs. Pears paid £2,200. The same enterprising firm expended nearly £20,000 in producing the first editions of the coloured print of it.

" The Bath." *Maynard Brown.*
" View of Messrs. Pears & Co.'s Factory, Isleworth."
" Man Shaving." *Bellei.*
" Les Bulles de Savon." *E. Frère.*
" Monkey Washing Cat." *Trood.*
" Reflection." *Peiot.*
" Monkey Shaving Dog." *Trood.*

The upper floors of these premises are chiefly occupied with a very large stock of cards, show-bills, posters, etc., which are ready to be sent out as advertisements of Pears' Soap. One room is entirely devoted to the storage of the electrotype blocks which are used in printing. The larger posters are kept in immense numbers in the basement of the building.

Electric light is used for the illumination of the various rooms, and is generated on the premises, an engine in the basement being expressly employed for that purpose. The various floors are conveniently connected by a lift, which is worked by electric force, and is said to be the only one of the kind at present in use in London.

HOLLOWAY'S.

At No. 78, New Oxford Street, there is a business house which deserves notice in any book which treats of the modern history of Bloomsbury and its locality. We refer to the establishment of Mr. Thomas Holloway, whose pills and ointment have attained world-wide fame.

In a sketch which Mr. Holloway drew up in the year 1877 it appears that October 15th, 1837, was the first day that his advertisements appeared in any newspaper. He says, " My pills and ointment for a considerable time obtained little or no favour. I used to go down to the docks to see captains of ships and passengers sailing to all parts of the world, collecting from them such information as was necessary.

" It was my rule from the commencement to spend judiciously all the money I could spare in publicity, which went on increasing, and in the year

1842 I expended £5,000 in advertising. Time rolled on, and from the hitherto unthought-of yearly outlay of £5,000 I increased it to £10,000 in the year 1845. At the time of the Great Exhibition in London, in 1851, my expenditure was £20,000 ; in the year 1855 it had risen to £30,000 ; and in 1877 it had reached £40,000, in advertising my medicines, in every available manner, throughout the globe. For the proper application of their use I have had ample directions translated into nearly every known tongue—such as Chinese, Turkish, American, Arabic, Sanskrit, and most of the vernaculars of India, and all the languages spoken on the European continent. Among my correspondents I number kings and princes, together with other distinguished persons."

Mr. Holloway commenced his successful business in the Strand, upon part of the site now occupied by the new Courts of Justice, and it was not until about the year 1865 that he removed to Bloomsbury.

Mr. Holloway has munificently established, at Egham, a college for women of the middle and upper middle classes. It accommodates 250 students, with two private rooms for each. The estimated cost of the building and its furniture was about £250,000, and £100,000 was spent in its endowment. The same generous public benefactor has also erected, at a cost of £200,000, a sanatorium for the cure of mental disorders. It is endowed with the sum of £50,000.

BLOOMSBURY AND INNS OF COURT VOLUNTEERS.

This Volunteer corps was formed in June, 1797, and consisted of six companies, besides the attached corps. They received their colours on June 2nd, 1798, from the hands of Lady Loughborough. They had a committee of sixteen members, chosen out of the whole corps by ballot.

The dress was as follows : *round hats* and feathers, white ; *breast-plate,* plain oval ; *cartouch-box,* a star ; *buttons,* plain on full dress, on undress B.I.C.A., in cypher ; *gaiters,* whole ; *motto* on colours, " Nolumus mutari."

In the year 1799 an elaborate book was published upon the Volunteers of London and its environs, entitled " Loyal Volunteers," and the numerous plates with which it was illustrated were drawn by Rowlandson. From that valuable work it appears that the following were the names of the officers of the Bloomsbury and Inns of Court Volunteers in the year 1799 :—

Lieutenant-Colonel, Samuel Compton Cox.

Major, William Watson.

Captains, James Trebeck, John Mitford, Arthur Palmer, James Trower, William Bouth, John Forster, Thomas Plumer.

Lieutenants, F. W. Sanobrs, G. Branwell, G. Brown, Edward King, Sir F. Eden, Bart., S. N. Meredith, John Richardson.

Ensigns, Thomas Mills, Henry Richmond, Hon. Charles Agar, John Kirby, J. H. Newbolt, J. Bernard Bosanquet, James York.

Adjutant, William Harrison.

Surgeon, R. R. Pennington.

Sergeant-Major—Charles Puller.

Secretary—Thomas Lane.

Clerk—Joshua Stafford.

The history of this corps does not extend over many years, as it was disbanded, with the various other Volunteer corps throughout the kingdom, soon after the conclusion of the Treaty of Amiens.

In the year 1859 a circular letter from the Secretary for War to the lord-lieutenants of counties in Great Britain authorized the formation of Volunteer corps, and an association of Volunteers was formed in Bloomsbury in that year, and was known as the "G.G.B.," *i.e.*, the St. George's and St. Giles's Bloomsbury, Volunteers. The association was subsequently known as the "37th Middlesex Rifle Volunteers," and is now known as the "19th Middlesex Rifle Volunteers" (XIX. Middx. R.V.).

In connection with the Bloomsbury Rifles a humorous annual publication was issued at Wimbledon Camp, and was called "the 'G.G.B.' Magazine." The first number, in small quarto form, appeared in the year 1867; the second, in octavo size, in 1868; and the third, also in octavo size, in 1870. The publication ceased with the third number, on account of insufficient support.

THE ROYAL TOXOPHILITE SOCIETY.

In the year 1514 the citizens of London practised archery in the fields round about Islington, Hoxton, and Shoreditch. Henry VIII. was particularly fond of archery, and in 1537 commissioned Sir Christopher Morris, Master of the Ordnance, to revive the amusement, which at that time was rather drooping, by establishing a society of archers, which was called "the Fraternitye or Guylde of St. George," upon which the King conferred many privileges. They were constituted "Overseers of the Scyence of Artyllery, that ys to wyt, for Long-bowes, Cross-bowes, and Hand-gunes."

The Archers of St. George used to assemble in Lolesworth or Spital-fields, and the name of their place of exercise at this spot was Teaselcroft, so called from the thistles with which it abounded.

The Honourable Artillery Company had its origin about the year 1585, when London being wearied with continual musters, a number of its gallant citizens who had served abroad with credit voluntarily exercised themselves, and trained others to the ready use and practice of war. The ground they used was at the north-east extremity of the City, near Bishopsgate, the same which had before been occupied by the above-mentioned Fraternity of Artillery. Fort Street, Artillery Street and Lane adjoin Spital Square, and by their names identify the spot. Within two years there were nearly 300 merchants and others sufficiently skilled to train common soldiers, and in 1588, in connection with the preparations for repelling the Spanish Armada, some of them had commissions in the camp at Tilbury. The association soon afterwards fell into decay, yet as the Company has never since its first creation been altogether extinct, it is at present the oldest representative of the English standing Army. From the Company's Register, the only book they saved in the Civil Wars, it appears that the association was revived in 1611, by warrant from the Privy Council, and the number of the Volunteers soon amounted to 6,000.

Three years after this they made a general muster, when, according to a contemporary authority, the men were better armed than disciplined. In 1622 they erected an armoury, towards which the Chamber of London gave £300. It was furnished with 500 sets of arms of extraordinary beauty, which were all lost in the Civil Wars. Their captain during a part of those troublous times was a Mr. Manby, who detained for his own purposes the arms, plate, money, books, and other goods of the Company, and the Protector was in vain solicited to enforce their restoration. In 1640 they quitted their old field of discipline, and entered upon the plot of ground which they now occupy in Bunhill Fields, leased to them by the City. This ground is described as a parcel of ground consisting of gardens, orchards, etc., situated on the north side of Chiswell Street, and called by the name of Bunhill Fields, which was in the year 1498 converted into a spacious field for the use of the London archers, which is now known by the name of the Artillery Ground.

For many years they kept up an Archery Division, archery being the art cultivated by the Company in their earliest days, when the bow and arrow were used in warfare. In process of time this division was abolished, but archery was still kept alive in the neighbourhood of London, by the Finsbury Archers. Even this remnant of the ancient art of archery had almost died out when the few survivors joined Sir Ashton Lever in the inauguration of the Toxophilite Society, in 1781.

Some years later the members of the Artillery Company appear to have resumed the bow, as they occupied two pairs of targets at the grand meeting of Archery societies on Blackheath, in 1792, and the Toxophilite Society, in its earlier years, mostly held their principal meetings in the Company's ground. But the Finsbury Archers have never reappeared, and the Archers' Division of the Honourable Artillery Company has also become merged into the Royal Toxophilite Society.

Sir Ashton Lever, Knight, who founded the Royal Toxophilite Society on April 3rd, 1781, was son of Sir D'Arcy Lever, of Allington, near Manchester. He finished his education at Corpus Christi College, Oxford, and on leaving the University went to reside with his mother, and afterwards settled at his family seat, Allington, which he rendered famous by forming there the best aviary in the kingdom. He next paid great attention to the study of all branches of natural history, which taste is said to have had its origin from the circumstance of his having shot a white sparrow. He is said to have become possessed of one of the finest museums in the world, in the procuring of which he spared no expense, and he purchased specimens from the most distant regions. This collection was removed to London about the year 1775, and opened to the public in Leicester House, Leicester Square. Unfortunately, the exhibition does not appear to have been a very successful enterprise, as from the want of public patronage Sir Ashton Lever was obliged to dispose of his museum by lottery, and it fell to the lot of a Mr. Parkinson, who built rooms on the Surrey side of the Thames, near Blackfriars Bridge, for its reception, and did everything in his power to render it interesting to the public, but he was obliged to dispose of it by auction in 1806, when the whole of it was dispersed. Between the years 1792 and 1796 a handsome quarto volume was published, entitled "Museum Leverianum ; containing Select Specimens from the Museum of the late Sir Ashton Lever, Kt., with Descriptions in Latin and English. By George Shaw, M.D., F.R.S." This volume, which was published by James Parkinson, the proprietor of the collection at that time, was richly illustrated with full-page coloured engravings, some of which are very fine, but there does not appear to be much method in their arrangement. According to the report of Mr. John Church before the House of Commons, which is quoted in the beginning of the volume, this beautiful collection of specimens was by careful computation estimated to be of the value of upwards of £53,000. Dr. George Shaw, who was the author of numerous works upon natural history, and a lecturer upon the same subject, delivered several lectures upon the Leverian Museum, both before and after that collection was removed from Leicester House, which never failed to attract a numerous and scientific audience.

Sir Ashton Lever died in 1788, of an apoplectic attack, while sitting on the bench with the other magistrates at Manchester.

About the year 1776 Mr. Waring, father of the well-known bowyer of Caroline Street, Bedford Square, being then resident with Sir Ashton Lever at Leicester House, and having by continued application to business contracted an affection of the chest which the doctors could not relieve, resolved to try the effect of archery. He commenced, and continued the practice regularly, and ascribed his cure, which was perfect, solely to the use of the bow. Sir Ashton Lever, seeing the good effect of archery, followed Mr. Waring's example, and was joined by a few friends, who formed themselves into the Toxophilite Society. The practice of archery took place on the lawn at the back of Leicester House. Prince George of Wales (afterwards George IV.), who was fond of archery, shot with the members of this Society, at Leicester House, and on his becoming patron of the Society, in 1787, it assumed the title of " Royal," by which it has ever since been distinguished. William IV., the Prince Consort, and the Prince of Wales have been patrons subsequently.

Among the plate belonging to this Society are the large silver shield given to the Archers' Company by Queen Catherine of Braganza, consort of Charles II., and silver arrows of the same and earlier periods.

In 1791 the Society rented from the Duke of Bedford grounds lying on the east side of Gower Street, where the houses on the west side of Torrington Square now stand ; and also rented rooms and cellars in what was at that period called Charlotte Street, but now 34, Bloomsbury Street (not many doors from New Oxford Street). At the back of this house there still stands a long range of lofty workshops, looking northwards into Streatham Street. The ground-floor and cellars of this building were occupied by the Society, and the suppers were held there, the dinners being in the pavilion in the Gower Street grounds. The grounds near Bedford Square were rented from the Duke of Bedford, at £80 per annum, and £50 was annually paid for the rooms and cellars in Charlotte Street.

In 1805, the Archery Grounds being required for buildings, the Society's property remained in charge of Mr. Waring, in Charlotte Street, Bedford Square, until 1821, when Mr. Waring rented a piece of ground about four acres in extent, at £7 per acre, situated at Bayswater, on the estate of the Bishop of London. Its exact position was opposite the point of separation between Hyde Park and the Kensington Gardens, lying on the east side of Westbourne Street, and extending from the Oxford Road northwards to the Grand Junction Road at Sussex Gardens.

In the year 1834 the Society obtained possession of a most eligible piece of ground, of about six acres in extent, from the Department of Woods and Forests. This is situated in the Regent's Park, adjoining the Royal Botanical Society's Gardens, and upon it was erected a building known as the Archers' Hall. On account of the plantations, the ground is seldom seen from the road. There is a gravelled path enclosing the whole area, which, excepting the greensward reserved for the targets, is tastefully laid out with clumps of trees and flowering shrubs, and beds with a profusion of flowers.

In an old list of the names of members of the Toxophilite Society, printed in 1792, several of the members, including the treasurer, Mr. Thomas Waring, are mentioned as residing at Bloomsbury and in its vicinity.

" The laws of the Toxophilite Society," instituted in the year 1781, and revised and altered in the year 1791, set forth that the number of members of the Society are limited to two hundred ; " that the Members of the Society shall meet every Tuesday and Friday, from the Fifteenth of April to the Fifteenth of October yearly, at Five o'Clock in the Afternoon, upon the Toxophilite Ground, Bedford Square, for the Purpose of shooting, of transacting the Business of the Society, and afterwards of supping together ; which Meetings shall be called The Summer Meetings ; and on the Third Tuesday in the Month of February, yearly, at Three o'Clock, for the Purpose of transacting the Business of the Society, and afterwards of dining together, (at such House as the Majority of the Members present at the last Summer Meeting shall agree upon,) which Meeting shall be called The Annual Winter Meeting ;

and also on such Target Days as are hereinafter appointed. That there shall not be any Business transacted upon any Target Day except the particular Business relating to the Target, nor at any Summer Meeting before Eight o'Clock, or after Supper ; nor at the Winter Meeting after Dinner ; nor unless there shall be present, at such Summer or Winter Meeting, Nine Members or more."

The admission of members was by ballot, two black balls excluding the candidate. A sum of three guineas entrance-fee was charged, in addition to the annual subscription of three guineas. The prescribed uniform of the Society was as follows : " A Green Cloth Coat and White Waistcoat and Breeches of Cloth, or Kerseymere, with Gilt Arrow Buttons, White Stockings, and Black Hussar Half Boots ; a Black Round Hat, with the Prince of Wales's Button, a double Gold Loop, and One Black Cock Feather ; " shooting accoutrements, " A Black Leather Brace, a Buff coloured Leather Belt, with a Pouch and a Green Tassel.".

Mr. Thomas Waring, who in 1814 wrote " A Treatise on Archery ; or, The Art of Shooting with the Long Bow " (" sold only by the Author, at his Archery, Caroline Street, Bedford Square "), mentions, in a set of model laws for the government of archery societies, that one of the articles of the Toxophilite Society was " that if any Member marry, he shall treat the rest with a Marriage Feast."

The same writer, at the end of his book, gives a list of thirty-three toxophilite societies which had been or were in existence within a few years of the compilation of the list.

" HOLBORN DROLLERY."

In the year 1673 a curious little collection of poems and songs was published, under the following title : " Holborn Drollery ; or, The Beautiful Chloret surprized in the Sheets : All the Love Songs and Poems with which she hath been Treated this Long-Vacation being Publish'd. To which is Annexed, Flora's Cabinet Unlocked. London : Printed for *Robert Robinson,* and are to be sold at his Shop neer *Grays-Inne-*Gate in *Holborn,* 1673," 12mo.

Exclusive of the title-page, there are six leaves of prefatory prose matter, containing a witty address " To the Ladies of Quality frequenting Grayes-Inne-Walks," wherein the author says, " I was resolv'd . . . to lay the scene

BEATING THE BOUNDS

of mine (drolleries) in *Holborn*, and thence Lead you into the *Walks*, where you must expect it delighting in its native Air, where the Sun-shine of your Beauties may make those Shades vie Splendour with the *Pal-mal* or a *Piazzo*, and gain that ancient Lustre to our darkened Orb, where formerly not one single Venus shone alone, but a *Constellation* of *Beauties*, making each Walk a *Galaxy*." In the prefatory pages there is also an address " To the Gentlemen," signed " Your kinde Chloret." Then follow ninety-six pages of verses compiled from a variety of sources, but many of the pieces are said to be mere imitations of Carew and other early writers.

There is a copy of this curious little volume in the British Museum Library, wherein a former possessor has inscribed the lines, " Robert Bemman, his book, god give him grace there in to look not to look."

Mr. W. Carew Hazlitt, in his " Bibliographical Collections," mentions the following prose tract : " The Holbourn Hector, Or The Character of a Prophane Debauched Gentleman. London, Printed for C. N., and are to be sold in the Highway to Tybourn, 1675." 4to, 4 leaves.

Amongst the Thomason Tracts, in the British Museum, there is one curious quarto pamphlet of four leaves, entitled " The Sisters of the Scabards Holiday : or, A Dialogue between two reverent and very vertuous Matrons, Mrs. *Bloomesbury*, and Mrs. *Long-Acre*, her neare Neighbour. Wherein is Discoursed how terrible, and costly the *Civill Law* was to their Profession ; and how they congratulate the welcome Alteration. Printed 164 " [1]. There is a roughly executed woodcut on the title-page, representing five of the " very vertuous Matrons." It is to be regretted that the contents of the tract are rather too broad for quotation.

BOUNDARIES.

Roughly speaking, the shape of the united parishes of St. Giles-in-the-Fields and St. George, Bloomsbury, is that of a parallelogram, the sides of which face nearly the four cardinal points of the compass, and there are also projections at the north-east and south-east angles. Beginning with the west end of New Oxford Street, the boundary of the parish of St. Giles is nearly as follows : Charing Cross Road, West Street, Castle Street, Kemble Street, Sardinia Street, Lincoln's Inn Fields (including the square enclosure), then northward to High Holborn through Great Turnstile, then westward, *viâ* High

Holborn and Broad Street, then by an imaginary straight line northwards, to the north end of Torrington Square, thence to the west as far as Tottenham Court Road, and so back to the west end of New Oxford Street. Two sides of the parish of St. George, Bloomsbury, abut on St. Giles's parish, and have already been described. The eastern boundary is a line a little to the east of Southampton Row as far as the west end of Guildford Street, then by a line running north-east to the north side of Brunswick Square, then northward to a point near the east end of Compton Street, and from thence by a direct line to the north side of Torrington Square, where it meets the boundary of St. Giles's parish.

The united parishes contain 245 acres.

INDEX.

INDEX.

www.ingramcontent.com/pod-product-compliance
Lightning Source LLC
Chambersburg PA
CBHW030631030726
47497CB00006B/1734